NORTHROP

AN AERONAUTICAL HISTORY

NORTHROP

AN AERONAUTICAL HISTORY

A COMMEMORATIVE BOOK EDITION
OF AIRPLANE DESIGNS AND CONCEPTS

(With a Special Prologue Dedicated to Founder John K. Northrop)

Authored By FRED ANDERSON
Member, American Aviation Historical Society

WIPF & STOCK · Eugene, Oregon

Resource Publications
A division of Wipf and Stock Publishers
199 W 8th Ave, Suite 3
Eugene, OR 97401

Northrop
An Aeronautical History
By Anderson, Fred
Copyright©1976 Northrop Corporation

Publication date 6/15/2016
Previously published by Northrop Corporation, 1976

1939   N-3PB

1976   F-18

FOREWORD

This book relates the story of Northrop aeronautical products from the year 1939 to the current Bicentennial year 1976. The early aircraft designs — always fresh, always challenging — set a standard for a company tradition of engineering excellence and high performance.

The roots of the Northrop company lie in the early days of aviation and, not surprisingly, in the beginnings of several other major aircraft companies. The Northrop story is in part the story of the design genius of John K. Northrop. It is also the story of a closely-knit group of aeronautical romantics who followed Northrop when he founded this last company to bear his name.

In more recent years, Northrop has broadened its reputation to include a new kind of commitment to high performance under the leadership of Thomas V. Jones. He summarized it this way as far back as 1954, "Technology's traditional objective — maximum possible performance — must be converted to a more sophisticated goal, namely, performance adequate for the accomplishment of a mission objective at the lowest possible cost."

This book concerns itself with the results of that new commitment to performance, as well as with the earlier achievements of the founding company, Northrop Aircraft, Inc.

Allowing for a few exceptions, all the products depicted are airplanes, and the coverage includes every experimental or production model built since 1939.

A word or two about the mechanics of the book. For ease of reading, the book is divided into a prologue dedicated to John K. Northrop and five chapters arbitrarily determined by the historical significance of the era or the aeronautical achievement of the period. Each chapter is introduced by a description of the environment in which the company found itself, together with a summary account of the aeronautical products which evolved in that era. Following the introduction, each aircraft is discussed and pictorially displayed, with respect to both technical and historical content. The placement of a particular aircraft within a particular chapter is fixed by the date of its first flight in the case of a prototype or production version, or the date of its specification in the case of a design model only. In every instance, a three-view drawing of the aircraft, along with specifications and performance data, are offered for the technically-minded reader.

Finally, a comment on the stylistic approach. Place names and organizational names are retained in their usage and employment of the period under discussion. For example, Muroc Dry Lake appears in the Pre-Pearl Harbor chapter but is written as Muroc Army Air Base in later accounts and finally changed to Edwards Air Force Base in more recent times. Similarly, the initial Army Air Corps changes to Army Air Forces (AAF), then to United States Air Force (USAF) in all considerations after 1947.

Fred Anderson
Historian

ACKNOWLEDGMENTS

The author wishes to acknowledge the direction and enthusiastic support of Welko E. Gasich, Corporate Vice President and Aircraft Division General Manager, and Jack Mannion, Aircraft Division Vice President Public Affairs. They gave the author a free hand within the boundaries of his charter, and he decided which events would be included in the book as well as how they would be presented.

Thanks are due to the many Northrop veterans who contributed anecdotes and details which helped to fill in the many gaps and holes in the early history. Special acknowledgment is due to founder John K. Northrop and colleagues Roy L. Wolford and Paul J. Spikula. They gave generously of their time for interviews and supplied photographs and documentation from their private collections to supplement the company archives.

Also deserving of special mention are the several experts in the Graphics department of the Aircraft Division for their creative recommendations and contributions to the design of the book. To H.W. (Bill) Jones and his Library staff I am indebted for the task of producing an index and helping in document search.

These acknowledgments would not be complete if I did not give particular thanks to my editor Dr. Ira E. Chart, a co-worker and a former Air Force Historian, who provided invaluable assistance. Finally, I must mention the members and officers of the American Aviation Historical Society who lent their unqualified support to the project.

F.A.

CONTENTS

JOHN KNUDSEN NORTHROP began his aeronautical apprenticeship in 1916 as a draftsman engineer for the Loughead brothers who were building a twin-engine flying boat at Santa Barbara, California. He rejoined the Loughead (later Lockheed) organization after World War I, designing the S-1 (see below), a small sport biplane with foldaway wings.

⟶ FLY ⟵

THE LOUGHEAD SPORT BIPLANE

MODEL S-1 was designed by John K. Northrop while a member of Loughead Aircraft Manufacturing Co. The above announcement (1920) was part of an advertisement citing the machine's excellence: "... a speed of 52 miles per hour in horizontal flight with a motor speed of 1500 revolutions per minute ... possible to fly at the low speed of 30 miles per hour with absolute safety."

PROLOGUE

"THE BEGINNING"

JOHN K. NORTHROP — PIONEER AIRCRAFT DESIGNER AND AVIATION INDUSTRY LEADER

The historical record places the birth of the present-day Northrop Corporation in a leased Hawthorne, California, hotel room in August 1939. (Northrop Aircraft, Inc. was officially incorporated in March 1939.) But in another, very real sense, the company had taken root nearly three decades before in the small coastal town of Santa Barbara.

It was 1911, a mere eight years after the Wright brothers' famous first flight, when chance brought a sixteen-year-old boy by the name of John Knudsen Northrop to a grassy plot in Santa Barbara. He was one of a handful of spectators who witnessed a French aviator assemble a pusher biplane, then proceed to fly it briefly around town, and finally land it in front of the old Potter Hotel. That single experience was spark enough to launch a distinguished career in aviation. It was to come a few years later when young Northrop obtained a position with Loughead (later Lockheed) Aircraft in Santa Barbara as a mechanical draftsman-engineer. And it was to come only after he had finished his high school education in Santa Barbara and acquired some maturity as a garage mechanic, architectural draftsman, and builder.

At Loughead, John Northrop, better known throughout his career as "Jack," revealed some of the pioneering genius he was to demonstrate throughout his lifetime. In 1916 he designed the wings for what was then to be one of the world's largest flying boats, the F-1. His career at Loughead was interrupted when the U.S. entered the Great War and he was drafted by the Army. After basic training at Camp Lewis, Washington, Northrop was assigned to the Signal Corps, which in those days was the jurisdictional arm for Army aviation. After nine months, he was furloughed back to Loughead because he was needed to direct the engineering effort involved in a new contract to build two Curtiss HS-2L flying boats.

Following completion of the Curtiss airplanes in 1919, Northrop designed the S-1, a small personal plane with an innovative monocoque fuselage. It also had folding wings for easy storage in the owner's garage. The S-1 was originally intended as a $2,500 sport plane for pilots returning from military service. But the idea was ahead of its time. Surplus military airplanes began flooding the market for less than $400, and the Loughead company finally collapsed in 1920.

1

With the new-airplane business in the doldrums, Jack Northrop returned to work for his father in the building trades. Three years were to pass before he would be able to resume his chosen vocation, that of designing airplanes. In 1923, he was employed by Douglas Aircraft in Santa Monica. Douglas had won a contract to build the famous Army Air Service "Round-the-World" Cruisers, and Northrop's first engineering challenge was to design the Cruiser fuel tanks. After regular working hours at Douglas, he studied on his own the concept for a high-efficiency all-wing airplane and designed an airplane that was to become known as the Lockheed Vega. In 1927, Northrop joined Allan Lockheed (phonetically changed from Loughead) and two other associates, to form the Lockheed Aircraft Company in Hollywood, California.

Jack Northrop's place in aviation history was firmly established as the designer of Lockheed's first airplane, the remarkable Vega of 1927. This was the most advanced airplane of its time, both structurally and aerodynamically, and a breaker of records. Flown on historic flights by Amelia Earhart, Art Goebel, Wiley Post, and pilots of the Hubert Wilkins Arctic and Antarctic Expeditions, the Vega became world-famous. Later, Northrop designed the fast Air Express, a parasol-wing version of the Vega. This was another record breaker in the hands of Frank Hawks and Roscoe Turner during the early Thirties.

Dissatisfied with the status quo and wanting to experiment with radically new designs, Northrop joined with Ken Jay in 1928 to form the tiny Avion Corporation in Burbank, California. Here he did pioneering development work on the unique all-metal, multicellular, "stressed-skin" construction, which was to become the standard for future aircraft. He also renewed his revolutionary all-wing studies which culminated in the fabrication of the very first of the Northrop Flying Wings. Its initial flight took place in 1929 at the Burbank Airport.

Later, William E. Boeing, founder of Boeing Aircraft and Transport Corporation, showed a decided interest in Northrop's new all-metal Alpha airplane and in the inventiveness of Jack Northrop himself. Intrigued by the combination of fresh financial backing and modern facilities, the youthful Californian accepted Boeing's overtures. The decision in 1929 turned the Avion Corporation into the Northrop Aircraft Corporation, a division of the giant United Aircraft and Transport Corporation, which also included Boeing.

THE VEGA, Jack Northrop's remarkable new design of 1927. Many speed and endurance records were established by such top-drawer flyers of the day as Wiley Post, Amelia Earhart, Sir Hubert Wilkins, Frank Hawks, and Roscoe Turner. This airplane pioneered the monocoque molded plywood construction so widely used on later "plastic" airplanes. It originally was powered by a Wright "Whirlwind" engine; later installations included Pratt & Whitney "Wasps" and "Hornets."

AIR EXPRESS. Parasol-wing version of the Vega was designed for improved pilot visibility (above). The original Vega was also equipped with Edo floats for water operations (below).

JACK NORTHROP (left foreground above) examines Vega blueprint with Lockheed management, circa 1927. Counterclockwise from Northrop: Kenneth Jay, Allan Lockheed, Ben Hunter (shareholders' attorney), Gerard Vultee (kneeling inside Vega monocoque fuselage), Tony Stadlman. Northrop and Edward Bellande (below) discuss flight plan of the original Flying Wing built in 1928 by Northrop's newly formed Avion Corporation.

EARLY A PUSHER (above), LATER A TRACTOR (below), the first Flying Wing made aviation history at Muroc Dry Lake in the 1929-1930 period. Designed with two cockpits, offset from centerline engine, the airplane was usually flown from the left cockpit, while the starboard opening was faired over. The landing gear was a reversed-tricycle undercarriage.

MULTICELLULAR WING STRUCTURE, a Jack Northrop innovation at the Avion Corporation in Burbank, 1928. His all-metal Alpha was built here and featured this construction, as did the famous "flying wing" faintly visible in the left background (above). Publicity stunt demonstrated strength of the multicellular structure (left). Details of Alpha wing cross-section (below).

In his new Burbank factory, Northrop produced the Alpha high-performance transports for TWA, the Department of Commerce, and the Army Air Corps. These sleek, low-wing machines featured Jack Northrop's new all-aluminum, stressed-skin structure. The Alpha was soon followed by the Beta, a small sport plane with similar design characteristics.

Once again, as the Great Depression settled over the country, aircraft sales went "from boom to bust." As an economy measure, United management decided that Northrop Aircraft should be consolidated with Stearman Aircraft (another division of United) in Kansas.

Not wanting to move his plant to Kansas, Northrop broke with United in 1932 and formed a new Northrop Corporation, in partnership with Douglas Aircraft, in El Segundo, California. (Douglas Aircraft held 51 percent of the stock.)

Shortly thereafter, the new all-metal Gamma was developed. It was purchased by the Army Air Corps; commercial models went to leading pilots of the day for record-breaking flights. During the early Thirties, it was flown by TWA to carry mail and cargo.

One Gamma achieved fame as the "Experimental Overweather Laboratory" owing to its pioneering sub-stratosphere flights which extended from 1936 through 1940. Later Northrop designs from the El Segundo plant included a long series of military aircraft for the U.S. and foreign countries. Derivatives of these designs played key roles during World War II.

In 1938, the Northrop Corporation became known as the El Segundo division of Douglas Aircraft. But Jack Northrop was not satisfied with mere production design. He decided to start fresh once again, so that he could concentrate on experimental design. It was obvious by now that he would never be content unless he was expressing his creativity in his own company.

Thus it was that in August 1939, Northrop Aircraft, Inc. became a reality in Hawthorne, California. Jack Northrop was named president and head of engineering and research. From a beginning of six personnel in a small California community, the company was to grow to one of the 200 largest industrial organizations in the United States.

FIRST FLYING WING was not actually an all-wing airplane. Design did not have all the factors of stability necessary for the elimination of the tail, accounting for the two outrigger-type booms which carried the required tail control surfaces. The two-man crew and engine were housed in the wing itself. The Flying Wing had a span of 30 feet 6 inches, and a 90-hp Menasco, four-cylinder air-cooled engine. It made numerous flights in 1929 and 1930.

BELLANDE, JAY, NORTHROP pose in front of the tractor version of the original Flying Wing. W.K. Jay and Northrop formed the Avion Corporation in 1928 in Burbank, California, affording Northrop the first opportunity to bring to reality a "radical design" idea conceived in 1923. Edward Bellande later joined Northrop as Sales Pilot and Director when Northrop Aircraft, Inc. was chartered in 1939.

ALPHA (1930) was the first all-metal, stressed-skin monoplane embodying modern multicellular wing structure and ushering in the era of modern low-wing monoplanes. The Alpha was a seven-place transport, powered by a Pratt & Whitney "Wasp" engine, and was sold in quantity to TWA as a passenger and mail plane, to the U.S. Army as a transport.

BETA (1931) was the first airplane of 300 hp to exceed a speed of 200 mph. It was the forerunner of all-metal sport planes. Its low-wing design and streamlining were considerably advanced for the early Thirties. The first Beta was a two-place model. Later it was revised and made into a single seater.

GAMMA (1933) was the first "overweather flying laboratory" ever built and was used to pioneer stratosphere flying. The Gamma, able to take off in storms that kept regular transports grounded, flew the coast-to-coast mail route in 11-1/2 hours. Gammas sold to China were the first attack bombers used against the Japanese. The first Gamma, flown by Frank Hawks, pioneered the full-span, split-trailing-edge flaps with "park-bench" ailerons. Others to fly the Gamma were Lincoln Ellsworth on his Antarctic expedition, Jacqueline Cochran, the U.S. Army, and TWA. These high performance airplanes were powered by Wright "Cyclone" or Pratt & Whitney "Hornet" engines.

DELTA (1935) was the nine-place, passenger-carrying version of the Gamma. Notice that the pilot's cockpit was moved from the rear of the fuselage to a position forward of the cabin. The diameter of the cabin was increased from 45 inches to 58 inches to accommodate passengers. It had a service ceiling of 23,500 feet and a cruising speed of 178 mph.

EXPERIMENTAL XFT-1 (1934) was the first low-wing, all-metal 300-mph class fighter. It was designed and built for the U.S. Navy.

THE NORTHROP 3-A (1935) was a fast, high-performing single-seat military pursuit plane built for the U.S. Army. Similar in many ways to the XFT-1, designed and built by Northrop for the Navy, the 3-A was also of all-metal semimonocoque construction. It differed from the XFT-1 principally in the canopy arrangement and in the retractable landing gear. The split-trailing-edge flap improved its landing characteristics. Basic configuration of this series of planes was carried forward into the design of many military aircraft used in World War II.

DIVE BOMBER BT-1 (1936) was a two-place Navy airplane with Northrop split-trailing-edge dive flaps to aid the pilot in dive bombing technique. This model was followed by the BT-2, a larger version, which became the prototype of the Douglas SBD Dauntless.

A-17A (1937) ATTACK AIRCRAFT was an improved version of the A-17 with 15 mph more speed than its prototype. This was due in the main to the addition of a retractable landing gear. Both the A-17 and A-17A were purchased in substantial quantities prior to World War II.

ORIGINAL ALPHA, the first airplane design to carry the Northrop name, was restored in 1976 by TWA at its Kansas City facility (above) for display in the Smithsonian Institution's National Air and Space Museum (below). This was the initial production transport sold first to the Department of Commerce, ownership subsequently passing to Ford Motor Company, to National Air Transport of Chicago, and finally to Transcontinental and Western Air (early name for TWA) in late 1931. Clearly visible in the top photograph is the multicellular wing structure developed by Jack Northrop in 1928. (Photos courtesy TWA)

Until his retirement in 1952, a virtual spate of exciting aeronautical designs was created under Jack Northrop's direction. The aviation buff needs only to recall that remarkable series of World War II experimental Flying Wing airplanes, ranging from one-man diminutive gliders to pilotless "buzz bombs," all culminating in the multi-ton bombers of the postwar period. The different models were driven by rear-mounted propellers, jets, and rockets; some were free-flight. Two of the flying wings had prone-pilot cockpits, and another was an all-magnesium, all-welded fighter.

Also noteworthy among Jack Northrop's aeronautical achievements were the world's fastest military seaplane; the first intercontinental, inertial-guided, stellar-controlled missile; and the sophisticated laminar-flow-control airplane. Nor will the aviation buff overlook the "Black Widow" night fighter, the trimotor "Raider," and the spectacular rocket-launching, twin-jet "Scorpion."

Along the way Northrop found time to contribute to the development of prosthetic devices for the handicapped, a more efficient method for extracting iodine from seaweed, a popular new type of sea anchor for boats, the Studebaker automobile "Hillholder" device, and the giant Turbodyne turboprop engine for aircraft.

Except for the oldtimers, not many people in the aircraft industry realize that Jack Northrop's leadership extended beyond technological breakthroughs. Under his guidance, Northrop Aircraft lived up to its hallmark as "a good place to work," with one of the best employee relations policies in the industry. Jack Northrop made himself available to his fellow "Norcrafters." His office door was always open. He was also an enthusiastic supporter of community activities, especially the Boy Scout movement.

Working for Northrop Aircraft meant enjoying excellent pay and fringe benefits. It also meant generous vacations, including the week-long Christmas holiday, an innovation in the aircraft industry. And most importantly, it meant a management philosophy that looked upon employees not as simple cogs in an industrial machine, but as creative individual human beings with ambition, intelligence, and dignity. These policies have continued.

Jack Northrop took part in a historical drama of the skies — and he touched many lives.

1

PRE-PEARL HARBOR

"A NEW NORTHROP"

The highly complex business nature of present-day Northrop Corporation may be due, in some measure, to the calendar date of its birth. When Jack Northrop left the El Segundo division of Douglas Aircraft in 1938, he did so for the very same reason he started the venture six years earlier. He wanted to channel the company's and his own energies into aeronautical research and development. But the Douglas partnership had been drifting more and more toward production primarily because of the popularity of Northrop's designs. And so, when he resigned in 1938, his intention was to form a new company staffed with the most talented and dedicated engineers he could muster. It would be small enough, yet free enough, to develop advanced designs without the encumbrance and inertia associated with large organizations.

But history and chance seemed to combine in shaping the future of the new enterprise. The year was 1939, a time when the world political situation both in Europe and the Far East was both explosive and tense. While Jack Northrop was in the process of closing negotiations, his long-time friend and colleague Edward Bellande — test pilot and TWA Flight Captain — met with La Motte T. Cohu, a Trans World Airlines official who

happened to be in California on business. Cohu was quick to see the emerging war clouds and to assess the real role of the United States as the arsenal of the Allied nations. He suggested a shift in Northrop's approach — the new company to manufacture aircraft as well as research and develop them. Agreement was not long in coming. Northrop Aircraft, Inc. was incorporated with John K. Northrop named as President and Chief Engineer. La Motte Cohu became General Manager and Chairman of the Board. Eddie Bellande also served on that first Board of Directors.

This closely knit team of aeronautical enthusiasts in a young and growing industry came to be known as "The Northrop Group." Their talents and experience complemented one another. Northrop himself was an established and respected design engineer. Cohu's background was primarily management. During the Twenties, he had converted his early Navy pilot experience in World War I into the aviation fields of finance, management, and industrial relations. He had organized Interstate Airlines, now a part of Eastern Airlines. He also had served as President of American Airlines and American Aircraft and Engine Company, which eventually transitioned into Fairchild Industries.

HISTORIC HOTEL HAWTHORNE. This was where the company started in the summer of 1939. Twenty years later, on the occasion of receiving their 20-year service pins, the first employees returned for a group picture. From left, Tom Chittenden, Tom Quayle, Dick Nolan, Walt Gage, Bob Catlin, Paul Bonham, John Pfarr, Carl Raker, Roy Lindstrom, and Mel Brown.

Another driving force in those beginning years was Gage H. Irving. He was named Vice President and Assistant General Manager of the new company, and also served on the Board of Directors. His area of expertise was production. A graduate of Harvard in 1927, Irving began his aviation career, like most of his colleagues as a pilot, flying for Jack Northrop's El Segundo Division of Douglas Aircraft during the Thirties. But he soon turned his interest to internal plant operations, advancing through the ranks from aircraft inspector to Factory Superintendent to Assistant General Manager.

During the early summer of 1939, Northrop, Cohu and Irving attended conference after conference, formulating business plans. Moye Stephens, one of the men responsible for bringing the three together and on the Board as Secretary of the Company as well as Flight Chief, scouted the countryside for a factory location that could be purchased or leased on reasonable terms.

A 72-acre site in Hawthorne, California, was shortly obtained on lease, with option to buy, as the company's new home. A 122,000-square-foot plant came off the drawing board. In that same time span, the city of Hawthorne began development of a mile-long, 700-foot-wide airport, christening it Northrop Field. While the plant was under construction, Northrop and his business associates were housed in the nearby Hotel Hawthorne in August 1939. Veterans of those days recall the establishment as a former local "house of pleasure" painted a shameless yellow. It was humorously known as the neighborhood "yellow peril."

The engineering staff which had grown from a handful of six to 109 employees in just a few months moved into the spacious new plant in February 1940. While Northrop and his colleagues, headed by Walt Cerny and Tom Quayle, were busily engaged with innovative designs, La Motte Cohu was exploring avenues for prospective business. As Cohu had predicted, the most promising prospects lay overseas. Another possibility was subcontracting to the large U.S. aircraft manufacturers.

PRESIDENT JOHN K. NORTHROP turned the first shovelful of dirt at the site of the new Northrop Aircraft, Inc. plant at Hawthorne, California, on September 30, 1939. Left to right: Sheriff Biscailuz, of Los Angeles County; Mayor Fred Hauser, of Hawthorne; Mr. Northrop; and Mayor Fletcher Bowron, of Los Angeles.

The first break came from Reuben Fleet, President of Consolidated Aircraft, based in San Diego, California. He knew Jack Northrop's reputation and was satisfied that Northrop could build airplanes. Consolidated gave him a subcontract in early 1940 to build Navy PBY-5 tail sections, quickly followed by additional subcontracts for engine cowlings and seat installations. Less than one month later, three of Cohu's friends, including the famous Arctic explorer Bernt Balchen, who had flown Northrop-designed planes in earlier exploits, referred the Norwegian Buying Commission to the fledgling company. The result was a contract for the design and production of 24 seaplane patrol bombers, later designated N-3PB's.

Expansion continued as new business was acquired. Great Britain awarded Northrop a production contract for Vultee-designed Vengeance dive bombers; Boeing Aircraft Company, a subcontract for B-17E "Flying Fortress" engine nacelles and cowlings; and the Navy, a contract for development of the Turbodyne engine. At the same time, the first true all-wing N-1M Flying Wing was started as a company-funded project.

Even at this early stage, Northrop was willing to back his research ideas with allied hardware and test equipment. The first Annual Report to the stockholders states, "In order to insure complete equipment for the testing of our new designs your Company has constructed a modern, large-size wind tunnel. This tunnel will be used not only by your Company's engineers, but will be available for lease to other companies which do not have these facilities and are forced to rely upon the overcrowded tunnels of our West Coast Universities and Colleges."

Expansion also meant training of personnel. Toward the close of 1940, company management opened a school for the training of aircraft mechanics; it was the forerunner of the Northrop Aeronautical Institute (later Northrop University).

Unfilled orders for that first business year (1 August 1939 to 1 October 1940) amounted to slightly over $20,000,000. One can only judge that performance by some comparable yardstick. The Los Angeles Chamber of Commerce had reported that the total backlog of orders for the four major Los Angeles County aircraft manufacturers, as of January 1, 1939, was $70,000,000, or an average of $17,500,000 per company. The referenced firms were Douglas, North American, Lockheed, and Vultee.

AERIAL VIEW of the plant in September 1940.

Here is a view, looking west, of the new Northrop Aircraft, Inc., plant. Most of the pictures taken of the new plant have been taken looking east. This portion of the building is occupied by the general offices on the ground floor and the engineering and design departments on the second floor.

MAIN PLANT photo and caption reprinted from the first issue of the employee magazine, "The Aircrafter," March 1940.

AERIAL VIEW of the plant in September 1941. (Note addition to main building on east side.)

FIRST ENGINEERING DEPARTMENT employees, starting work August 1939: (Left to right) Walt Cerny, Francis Johnson, Ray Gaskell, and Tom Quayle.

AMONG FIRST CORPORATE OFFICERS were (left to right) James N. Wright, Member of Board; Henry Wallace Cohu, Member of Board; Theodore C. Coleman, Secretary; B.P. Lester, Member of Board; Roland Lord O'Brian, Member of Board; La Motte Cohu, Chairman of Board and General Manager.

FOLLOWING FLIGHT TEST at Lake Elsinore, California, the "Northrops," as the N-3PB's were dubbed by the Norwegians, were ferried up the West Coast to Canada where a training base had been established by RNoAF personnel.

BOEING AIRCRAFT COMPANY awarded Northrop, in November 1940, a subcontract for the manufacture of nacelles and cowlings for the B-17E "Flying Fortress." In the following year, Boeing placed an additional order covering the newer, improved B-17F version.

2760-031 NORTHROP
B-17E READY FOR SHIPMENT.

VULTEE "VENGEANCE" (V-72), built to British specifications as an answer to the famed German "Stuka" dive bomber. Full production of the Vultee-designed aircraft was underway in early 1942. Northrop also produced the A-31 and A-35 versions for the U.S. Army Air Forces.

19

ONE OF FIRST CONTRACTUAL ASSIGNMENTS was the "Zap wing" with full-span flaps. Interested in investigating control of landing approach angles and speeds and increasing wing lift for takeoff, the Navy bailed an OS2U-1 airplane to the company in 1940. Northrop designed a new wing with new ailerons and full-span "Zap" flaps. The flaps were extended from the wing and amounted to more than 25 percent of the wing area. Specification called for a landing speed of 55 miles per hour. Tests proved successful. Later, the "Zap" flaps were included in the XP-61 Black Widow prototype but ultimately were replaced because of manufacturing tolerance problems. The "Zap" wing-equipped OS2U-1 (above and below) is shown operating out of unpaved Northrop Field in May 1941.

N-3PB PATROL BOMBER

Designed originally in 1939 for Norwegian offshore patrol duty, the special-purpose N-3PB was to become the first production airplane of the newly formed Northrop Aircraft, Inc. The patrol bomber was a three-place, single-engine, cantilever low-wing monoplane. Two Edo floats were attached by full cantilever pedestals to the left and right wings. First flight-tested by test pilot Vance Breese on November 1, 1940, at Lake Elsinore, California, the N-3PB was soon identified as the world's fastest military sea plane. Maximum speed at military rating was 257 mph.

Twenty-four N-3PB's were ordered by the Norwegian Government on March 12, 1940. In the span of eight months, the design, engineering, and production tooling were completed, and the first airplane rolled off the assembly line.

Shortly after contract award, Norway was invaded by the Germans, necessitating aircraft delivery to the Royal Norwegian Naval Air Force operating as a unit of the British RAF outside of Norway. The Norwegian 330th (N-3PB) Squadron was assigned to three Icelandic sites during World War II, for submarine patrol and convoy escort duty in the North Atlantic. The three flights operated without hangars and from unimproved beach sites on the north, east, and south coasts of Iceland. During 19 months of sea patrol duty, the

"WORLD'S FASTEST" Military Seaplane, the N-3PB with a three-man crew was rated at 257 miles per hour at 16,400 feet. It was also one of the most heavily armed: four 50-caliber machine guns, two 30-caliber flexible machine guns, and a bomb or torpedo load of 2,000 pounds.

N-3PB PATROL BOMBER on duty in Iceland.

Norwegian ground crews performed all maintenance out-of-doors under the harshest of environmental conditions.

Despite these hardships, the N-3PB's established an enviable record in their operational missions of submarine patrol, convoy escort, photo-reconnaissance, air-to-air combat, transport and ambulance duty. The first aerial combat took place over Iceland on May 3, 1942 when a three-man crew successfully drove off a German bomber. The N-3PB was also instrumental in the destruction of German interdiction and reconnaissance aircraft, ships, and submarines. One patrol bomber assisted in the capture of a German submarine, and two others reportedly participated in the sinking of the German battleship "Bismark."

Nine of the ten N-3PB's lost during the 1941-42 Icelandic campaign were damaged beyond repair during water landings under extremely severe arctic weather conditions. A number of the remaining N-3PB's sustained aerial damage, but not a single one was known to have succumbed to enemy fire. The last N-3PB in the Norwegian aircraft inventory was destroyed in 1965 by the collapse of a snow-laden hangar roof at Kjevik Air Force Base.

The N-3PB had a bomb load capacity of 2,000 pounds, and was equipped with six machine guns. Four 50-caliber guns were mounted in the wing leading edge, and two 30-caliber flexible-mount guns in the fuselage — one in the aft upper cockpit and the other in a trap-door in the aft lower section. Bomb load ranged from individual 30-pound to 1,000-pound types, or a single 2,000-pound torpedo.

The fuselage was semimonocoque (a shell-like structure) of 24ST aluminum alloy, incorporating a stressed skin covering. The structure was fabricated in two sections, divided along the horizontal centerline, the lower half built integrally with the center wing section. Formed bulkheads supported longitudinal stringers of extruded aluminum alloy, and the entire framework was covered by aluminum sheet having a stiffening member at each seam. The front end of the fuselage terminated with a stainless steel firewall.

Accommodations were provided for the crew in tandem — the pilot in front, the gunner-observer next in line, and the gunner-radio operator-bombardier stationed in the lower rear.

The wing was of full cantilever design with a stressed skin covering and composed of five separate sections: the center section, two outer panels, and two removable tips. The NACA 2400 series airfoil was used, and the flaps were of split-trailing-edge type.

Power was supplied by a Wright Cyclone GR-1820-G200 series engine rated at 1,200 hp at 2,500 rpm. The engine mount was of welded chrome molybdenum steel tubing attached to the fuselage by four nickel-steel bolts, and rubber bushings were installed between engine and mount for vibration isolation. The engine cowling was of the NACA type; the forward section immediately adjacent to the exhaust collector ring was constructed of steel. The aft section was formed of aluminum. The Wright Cyclone drove a three-bladed, constant-speed Hamilton Standard propeller.

N-3PB UNDER GUARD at an Icelandic operational site in early 1942. First aerial combat occurred May 3, 1942, when an RNoAF-piloted patrol bomber successfully engaged a German bomber. The patrol bomber above is shown on its wheeled "beaching gear."

LAUNCHING AND REFUELING an N-3PB of the Norwegian 330th Squadron off the rugged coast of Iceland during WWII "Battle of the Atlantic." The light bombers were normally assigned to convoy escort duty, submarine patrol, and reconnaissance.

ONE OF TWO 30-CALIBER flexible-mount machine guns in the N-3PB. This one was in the aft upper cockpit; the other was operated by a second gunner through a trapdoor in the aft lower section. The man below also served as a radio operator and bombardier; he had lateral vision through a small window on the side of the fuselage.

ASSEMBLY LINE, "1940 Style." N-3PB is given final touches before shipment to Lake Elsinore for flight test. Plant 1 had opened its doors in February, and by November – a mere eight months after receipt of contract – the first N-3PB rolled off the assembly line.

LAKE ELSINORE, California, was the scene of all initial flight tests of the N-3PB. Eight planes were ultimately christened in Elsinore's waters during the four-month period of late 1940 through early 1941. Fifteen Norwegian pilots were trained under supervision of Northrop crews.

ICE REMOVAL was daily preflight chore by N-3PB Norwegian crews in the harsh year-round Icelandic climate.

OUTDOOR MAINTENANCE was routine in Iceland, where the Norwegian 330th Squadron was based for submarine patrol and convoy escort duty in the North Atlantic.

N-3PB

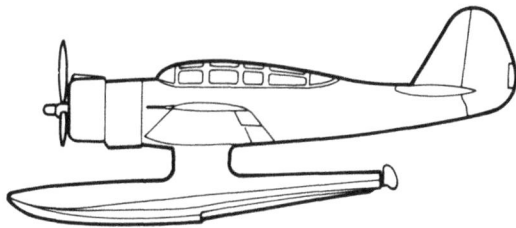

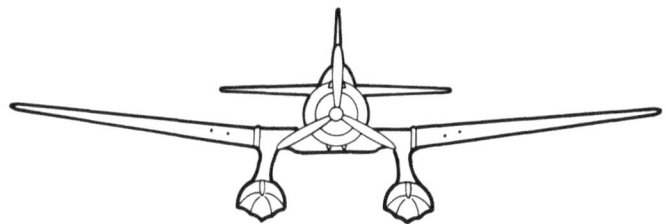

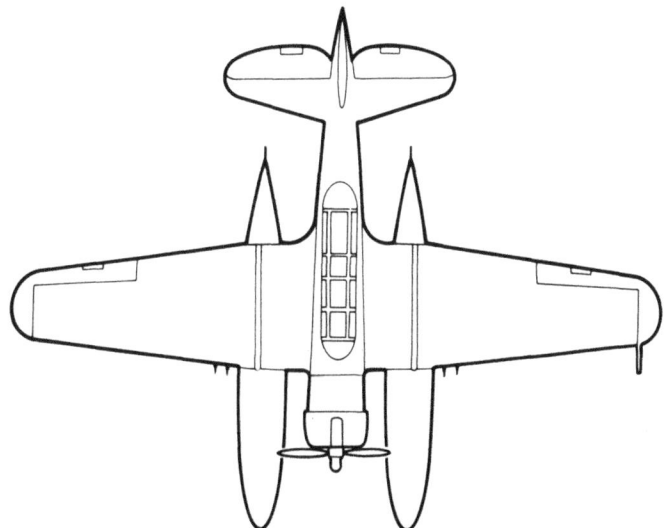

SPECIFICATIONS

WING SPAN ....48 FT., 11 IN.

OVERALL LENGTH ....38 FT.

OVERALL HEIGHT ....12 FT.

WING AREA ....376.8 SQ. FT.

TAKEOFF WEIGHT ....10,600 LB

SPEED-MAXIMUM ....257 MPH

SPEED-CRUISING ....215 MPH

RANGE ....1,400 MILES

SERVICE CEILING ....28,400 FT.

POWER — WRIGHT CYCLONE, AIR COOLED, RADIAL, 1,200 HP

ARMAMENT — (4) 50-CAL GUNS
          (2) 30-CAL GUNS
          (1) 2,000-LB TORPEDO, OR EQUIVALENT
          WEIGHT OF BOMBS

N-1M JEEP FLYING WING

As early as 1923, Jack Northrop had become convinced that conventional airplane design evolution had reached its limit. He believed that it was time for the next logical step to significantly greater performance — an all-wing airplane without drag-producing fuselage or tail. By 1929, this original concept had evolved into an actual flying machine. This Northrop-designed and -developed product of the Avion Corporation, registered X-216H, was a two-seat, single-engine, aluminum alloy "flying wing." It fell just short of being a pure flying wing because it had small tail surfaces supported on twin booms, although pilot and engine were buried within the airfoil. However, the X-216H did point the way to the N-1M of 1940, which must be considered the world's first successful all-wing airplane; the pilot, the two engines, and the landing gear were all enclosed within the airfoil. The popular term "Flying Wing" was coined for the X-216H in 1929 and has referred to all Northrop-designed "all-wing" aircraft since that time.

With the establishment of his new company in

Hawthorne, California, Jack Northrop felt the time was right for the design and construction of a true flying wing configuration. The PBY subcontract and the N-3PB Norwegian prime contract were of sufficient magnitude to underwrite a Flying Wing "mockup" as a company-funded project. In addition, the latest aerodynamic state-of-the-art data, as well as the extensive wind tunnel program of a variety of flying wings, all lent support to the undertaking. But several far-reaching factors were involved in the ultimate design. Not the least was the development of the buried engine installations with their inherent problems of mounting, cooling, and propeller drive on long extension shafts. The concurrent development of new NACA airfoils of low drag and improved stability also had profound influence on the all-wing design, as did the new spoilers, flaps, and other aerodynamic devices.

At an early stage in development, the problems of design were discussed with Dr. Theodore von Karman, Director of the Daniel Guggenheim School of Aeronau-

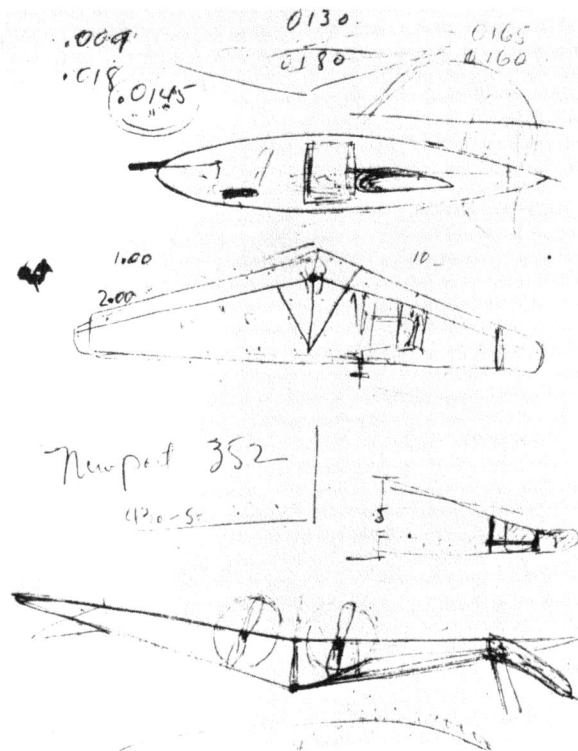

BIRTH OF THE FLYING WING was recorded by Jack Northrop on quick sketches like these during late 1939 meetings with his design team of Ray Gaskell, Walt Cerny, Thomas Quayle, and Francis Johnson.

MOYE STEPHENS AND JACK NORTHROP, Secretary of the Company and President of Northrop Aircraft, Inc., respectively, pose for photo of N-1M. Stephens, John Myers, and other pilots flew the N-1M in over 200 flights in the latter part of the 1941 test program.

DROOPED WING TIPS and two-bladed propellers characterized the early configuration of the N-1M shown being tested at the Muroc Army Air Base, California. It flew for the first time in mid-summer of 1940. Later the plane was modified with straight wingtips without any sacrifice in stability.

STABLE AND EASY TO CONTROL, the straight-wing N-1M is shown here on a flight over Northrop Field, Hawthorne, California.

tics at the California Institute of Technology, and his assistant, Dr. William R. Sears. Later in the project, Dr. von Karman was employed as Aerodynamic Consultant, and Dr. Sears, as Chief Aerodynamicist. Walt Cerny, Assistant Chief of Design, supervised the N-1M program.

The N-1M was configured as a "flying mockup" built up from wood and welded steel tubing so that changes could easily be made during its development. One of the major design problems was how to obtain directional stability without having drag-producing fins or vertical surfaces protruding from the wing surface. The story is told that the answer partially came when Mr. and Mrs. Northrop paid a visit to the home of Moye Stephens, then the company's secretary. Inclement weather cancelled a planned hike, leaving Stephens and Northrop free "to experiment" with folded paper airplanes. Their models were initially folded in the schoolboy's conventional pattern, but later — inevitably — they took on the shape of the Flying Wing. Tips of the wings were alternately bent up and down, and with each change the planes were "test flown." Northrop and Stephens were pleased to find that a downward bend of about 35 degrees gave the best performance.

Wind tunnel tests later confirmed the desired stability of N-1M models with drooped tips. The feature was incorporated in the full-scale airplane. Other novel features included drag-producing devices at the ends of the drooped tips for directional control, and the Northrop-originated "elevons" which combined the functions of the conventional elevator and ailerons into a single set of trailing-edge controls. Also, the wing panels could be

ground-adjusted to vary the sweep and dihedral.

The completed N-1M was trucked to Baker Dry Lake where test pilot Vance Breese conducted ground runs in July 1940. This early Flying Wing prototype was powered by two four-cylinder, air-cooled Lycoming engines rated at 65 hp each, driving two-bladed pusher propellers on extension shafts. The first flight came about as the result of a mishap on July 3, 1940. While taxiing at relatively high speed, the N-1M struck a rough spot in the dry lake bed. Bouncing eight to ten feet in the air, the plane went into controlled flight for several hundred yards before touching down again. It was apparent that with its low drag, the N-1M needed significantly less power to become airborne than that required by conventional airplanes.

Breese reported from the very beginning that the Flying Wing design gave impressive advances in performance. When placed in gentle glide, the N-1M would accelerate at a much faster rate than conventional fuselage-wing-empennage airplanes because of its extremely low aerodynamic drag.

As Breese conducted additional flights, the designers found that straight wingtips could be substituted for the drooped ones, without any significant loss of stability. All subsequent flights were made with straight tips, and Breese reported the handling qualities as virtually identical with those of conventional airplanes, except for the improved acceleration in dives and glides.

With the exception of engine cooling problems, no serious difficulties were experienced during the entire flight test program. Mounted in the pusher configuration and buried completely within the wing, the two small Lycoming engines suffered from inadequate airflow and quickly overheated during taxiing, takeoff, and climb. This hampered the test program until the Lycomings were replaced with six-cylinder, 120-hp Franklin engines with improved baffles, and three-bladed propellers. An immediate improvement in flight performance resulted.

After Vance Breese had flown a number of flights to prove the adequacy of stability and control, Moye Stephens took over the test program. By the end of 1941, Stephens had made over 200 data-collecting flights in the all-yellow N-1M nicknamed "Jeep."

In early 1945, Jack Northrop presented the N-1M to the Army Air Forces for historical display. The Jeep was shipped to Wright Field, Dayton, Ohio. It is currently kept in the National Air and Space Museum storage facility at Silver Hill, Maryland.

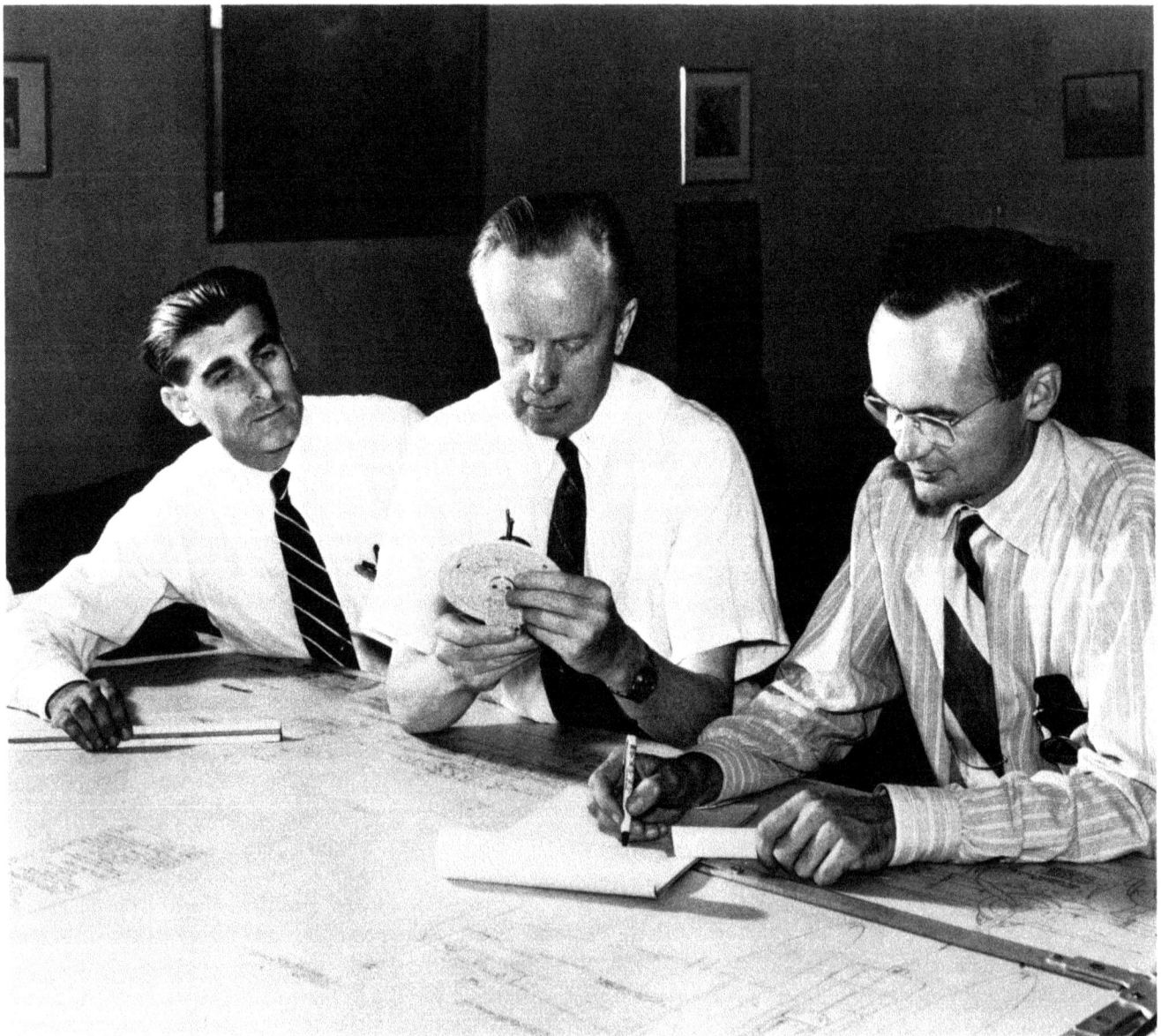

PREMIER DESIGN TEAM (from left) of Cerny, Northrop, and Sears. Dr. William Sears was originally a consultant, later joined the company in 1942 as Chief of Aerodynamics, was influential in the "flying wing" series. Cerny was with Northrop from the beginning; he supervised the N-1M program.

WEIGHT AND BALANCE test of N-1M at the main Hawthorne plant in early 1940 (above). Initial flights were conducted with a pair of two-bladed pusher propellers; later the "flying wing," with the large Franklin engines, was driven by three-bladed propellers; the final version had straightened wingtips (below).

N-1M dwarfed by engineering, flight and ground crew members at Muroc Dry Lake. (Left to right) Walt Cerny, Moye Stephens, Bill Sears, Tom Ruble, Harold Pedersen, Ed Lesnick, Earl Paton, and Ralph Winiger.

65-HP LYCOMING ENGINES experienced overheating in early tests of the N-1M. They were replaced by 120-hp Franklin engines and an improved cooling system. New three-bladed propellers were also installed, as shown.

SPLIT-FLAP RUDDERS at the wingtips of the N-1M were developed for yaw control.

N-1M

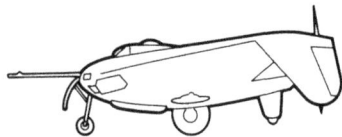

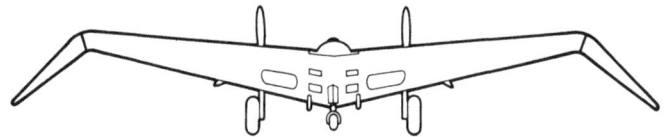

SPECIFICATIONS

WING SPAN . . . . .38 FT.

OVERALL LENGTH . . . . .17 FT.

OVERALL HEIGHT . . . . .6 FT.

WING AREA . . . . .300 SQ. FT.

TAKEOFF WEIGHT . . . . .3,900 LB

SPEED-MAXIMUM . . . . .200 MPH

SPEED-CRUISING . . . . .160 MPH

RANGE . . . . .300 MILES

SERVICE CEILING . . . . .15,000 FT.

POWER — (2) LYCOMING 0-145, 4-CYL, AIR COOLED,
OPPOSED (ORIGINAL), 65 HP
(2) FRANKLIN, 6-CYL, AIR COOLED, OPPOSED
(FINAL), 120 HP

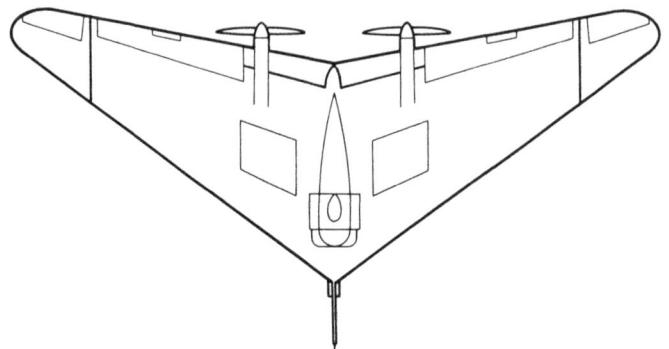

V-72 VULTEE VENGEANCE

With Britain facing an enemy-occupied Europe in 1940, the RAF need for military aircraft become urgent. One of the aircraft types ordered from United States manufacturers was the Vultee V-72, a single-engine dive bomber. This aircraft, named the Vengeance by the British, was designed by Vultee Aircraft, Inc. (later Consolidated Vultee), Downey, California. It was designed to British specifications and requirements which were established after the British had analyzed the most effective German methods and machines.

To satisfy accelerated delivery schedules, two production lines were set up, one at a Vultee factory in Nashville, Tennessee, and the other at Northrop in Hawthorne, California.

In September 1940, Northrop received an order from the British Purchasing Commission for approximately $17,000,000 for the manufacture of V-72 dive bombers. Northrop paid Vultee a royalty for the use of the design and the accompanying engineering data. In June 1941, an additional order worth approximately $16,000,000 was received from the United States Army for 200 Vengeance aircraft under the designation A-31.

Later when the United States entered World War II, a number of the Vengeance aircraft intended for the RAF were repossessed. These aircraft were consequently known to the United States Army as V-72's rather than A-31's.

The first Northrop-produced Vengeance was test flown from Northrop Field on November 30, 1941. In all, 400 Vengeance dive bombers were actually delivered from the Hawthorne plant during the period September 1941 through November 1943.

The Vengeance was a large, all-metal, two-place airplane. The Northrop-produced models were powered by a single Wright Cyclone R-2600-13 air-cooled radial engine driving a three-bladed propeller.

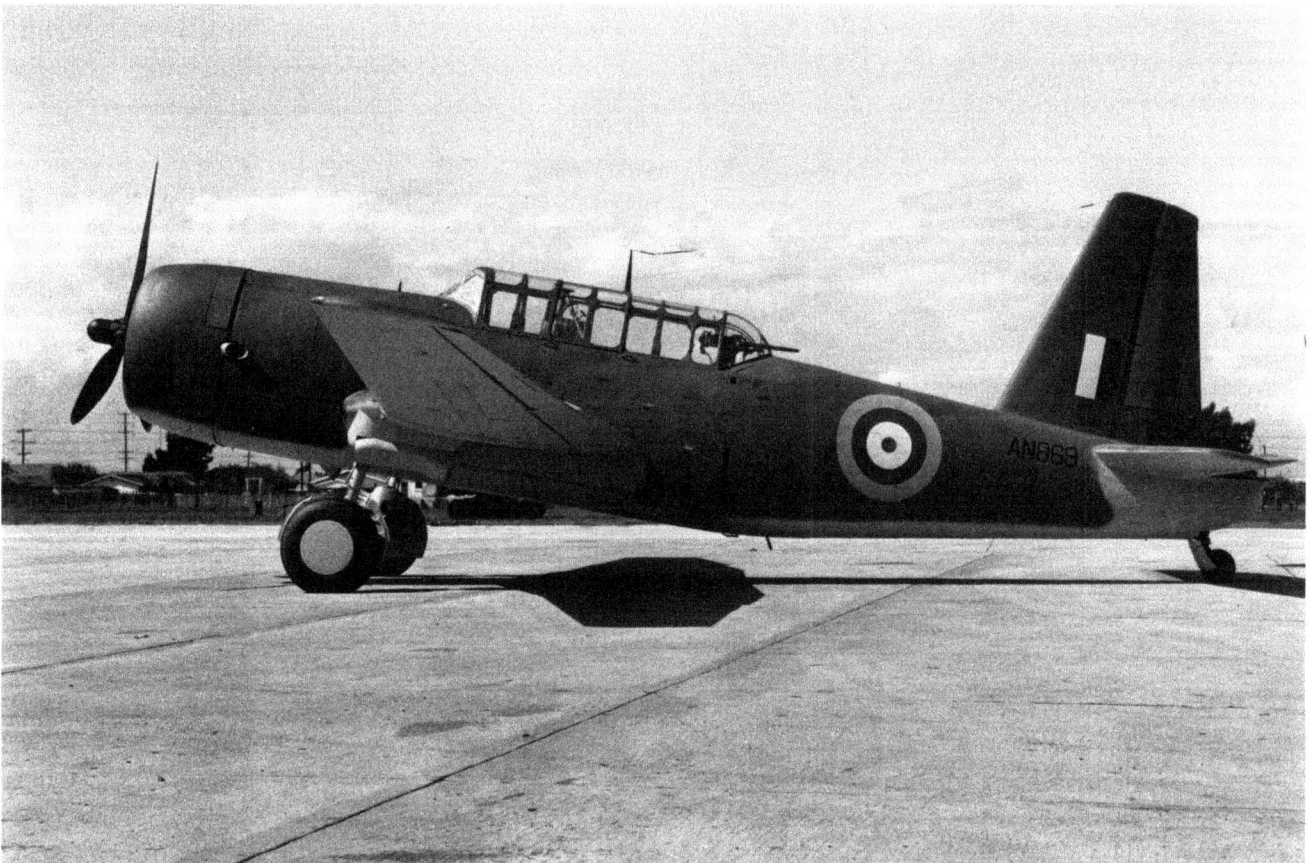

TWO-MAN BRITISH V-72. Pilot operated four wing-mounted, forward-firing 50-caliber guns and bomb release. Rear gunner controlled twin-swivel 50-caliber guns.

V-72 IN FINAL ASSEMBLY. Between 1941 and 1943 Northrop produced 400 dive bombers for the Royal Air Force and the United States Army. Large tail section in background represented subcontract work Northrop was doing for Consolidated Vultee on the Navy PBY-5.

WARTIME EFFORT. "Vengeances" in background, P-61 "Black Widow" in foreground. Banners tell the story. Northrop was building the V-72 for the RAF (designated A-31 for the USA) under license to Consolidated Vultee. The company also held a subcontract from Boeing for B-17E engine nacelles and cowlings.

ARMY AIR FORCES A-31. Those aircraft intended for the RAF, but repossessed when the United States entered WWII, still retained the designation V-72.

ANGULAR WINGS were eight feet longer than fuselage. Split-wing-mounted speed brakes permitted vertical dive from 22,000 feet.

V-72

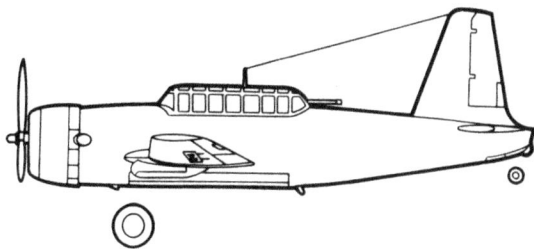

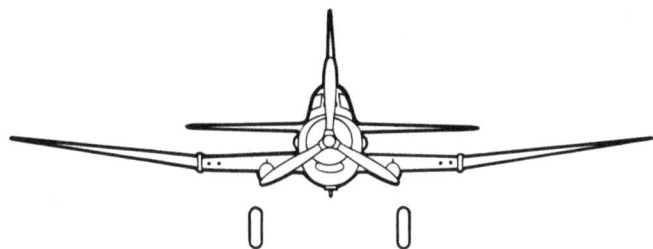

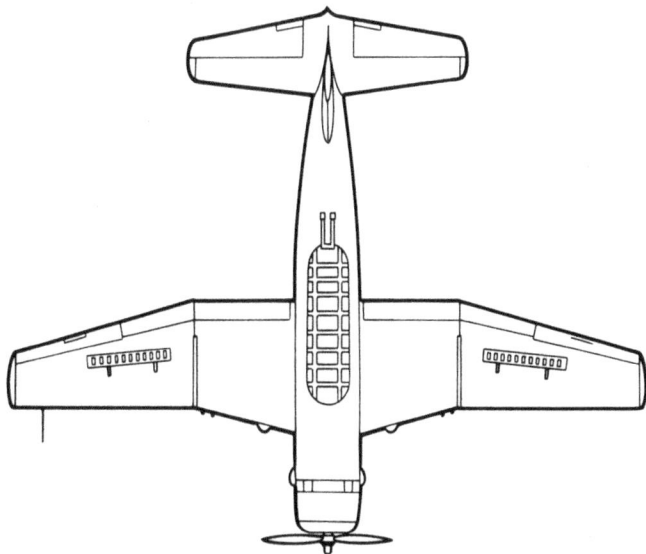

SPECIFICATIONS

WING SPAN	48 FT.
OVERALL LENGTH	39 FT., 9 IN.
OVERALL HEIGHT	15 FT., 4 IN.
WING AREA	332 SQ. FT.
TAKEOFF WEIGHT	16,400 LB
SPEED-MAXIMUM	279 MPH (13,500 FT)
SPEED-CRUISING	230 MPH
RANGE	2,300 MILES
SERVICE CEILING	22,300 FT.
POWER — (1) WRIGHT CYCLONE, R-2600-13, AIR COOLED, RADIAL, 1,700 HP	
ARMAMENT — (6) 50-CAL GUNS, 2,000-LB BOMBS	

33

THE TURBODYNE ENGINE

For what had started out in 1939 as a relatively low-profile, low-budget conceptual research project, the Turbodyne engine 11 years later was on the verge of revolutionizing aircraft propulsion. A news announcement, dated May 31, 1950, asserted:

> The Turbodyne engine, Air Force XT-37, the most powerful aircraft power plant in the world, has successfully completed the official 50-hour endurance proving program and is now fully qualified for preliminary flight tests . . . set a record by delivering 7,500 horsepower continuously . . . 'with a propeller built to absorb 10,000 horsepower, we can go ahead and deliver it.'

But a series of unforeseen events, coupled with the rapid advancement of jet propulsion, was to bring to an end an otherwise challenging enterprise in the company's history.

Vladimir Pavlecka, a 38-year-old Czech, was chief of research on the original company staff. He had conceived the Turbodyne (a Northrop-registered trade name) and interested Jack Northrop in the possibilities of gas turbine power plants for aircraft. In fact, Pavlecka had joined the company because he believed it the best potential sponsor of turbine research.

The state-of-the-art for practical gas turbines was in its infancy. Meager published data existed. The "Northrop Group" was obliged to start virtually from scratch. Following preliminary company-funded studies in 1939, Northrop himself was able to elicit

NORTHROP-DEVELOPED TURBODYNE, a gas turbine engine capable of delivering 10,000 horsepower, was intended to drive huge counter-rotating propellers on the B-35 Flying Wing. Supported by the Air Force, it was designated the XT-37. The power plant was also considered for the Boeing B-52 bomber. But the shift of the B-52 design in 1949 from turboprop to turbojet, and the discontinuance of the B-35 program brought an end to the project.

Navy interest for continued contractual investigation. Early work centered around cycle studies into the relative merits of axial flow versus radial flow, both for compressor and turbine. In view of the paucity of experience with turbine compressors, the Navy Bureau of Aeronautics cautiously decided to concentrate on the compressor portion only. In the same time span, the Army Air Corps also showed an interest in the Turbodyne concept, and a joint Army-Navy contract was awarded to Northrop for $483,600 to design a complete compressor-turbine engine, but confining the fabrication, development, and testing to the compressor.

The new power plant design, which included an 18-stage axial-flow compressor, was designated the Turbodyne "Alpha 1500," and the agreed-upon performance was 2,400 hp at 18,000 feet at 375 mph.

Aerodynamic design procedures were applied throughout the compressor. Far from "hit or miss," the work proceeded from exploratory design to wind-tunnel testing of scale models both at Northrop and at the California Institute of Technology under the guidance of Dr. Theodore von Karman. It was early in this development phase that certain philosophical differences arose between Pavlecka and von Karman. The

EXTENSIVE INSTRUMENTATION to test temperatures of the turbine portion of the Turbodyne engine.

INSTALLED IN TEST CELL at Hawthorne, the Turbodyne was coupled to an existing compressor and combustion system ready for 50-hour flight qualification test run.

EIGHTEEN-FOOT PROPELLER, dual rotation, manufactured by the Aeroproducts Division of General Motors, was driven by the XT-37 engine shown on test stand. Proposed for the huge B-35 Flying Wing, the propeller installation would be at the end of a drive shaft twice as long as the engine itself.

breach could not be closed, and Pavlecka resigned in late 1942. He was replaced by his assistant, Arthur Phelan, a 43-year-old British engineer who formerly headed the engine research division of Chrysler Motors.

In the same time period, the Northrop group was benefiting from the consulting services of Group Captain Whittle from Great Britain — the man credited with the invention of one of the first successful internal combustion aircraft gas turbines. Frank Whittle reviewed Northrop's design concept and made valuable recommendations.

The problem now was how to find a test unit that was capable of driving the compressor at full sea-level power demand. The power needed to test a separate compressor at sea-level static conditions would have to be in the range of 7,000 hp.

Faced with this delemma, Northrop approached Government contracting officers with the proposition that the only way to test the Turbodyne compressor would be as a component of a complete engine. The logic was not wasted. On July 1, 1943, the company was awarded a new contract for $1,505,854 to cover the cost of building two Turbodyne engines, one a ground test

ART PHELAN, pointing to highly geared propeller hub for a group of visitors, headed Turbodyne project from 1943 to 1950. (Turbodyne photos courtesy of Mr. Phelan)

XT 37 NA-1
MODEL L-3
TTC-2093

XT-37 MODEL (covers removed). Air intake at left, then compressor installation and blading combustion chambers in center, and turbine engine on right.

model and the other a complete aircraft turbine with starter and reduction gear driving an aircraft propeller.

By then the research project was taxing the facilities of the small Northrop design group to the limit. Since the company could spare neither time nor space from the war production effort, a new arrangement was sought — and found in the Joshua Hendy Iron Works of Sunnyvale, California. Widely experienced in the construction of steam turbines, Hendy joined Northrop to form Northrop-Hendy, Inc. Each company owned 50 percent of the stock.

Working under the pressure of war-induced schedules, the Northrop-Hendy technicians completed the Turbodyne engines early the following year. Although valuable data were obtained during test runs, engine failures occurred in the 10,000 rpm range, and the Navy bowed out of the project. The Army Air Corps assumed sole monitorship of the project, and test work continued on the remaining units of the original "Alpha 1500" Turbodyne.

Simultaneously Northrop-Hendy was under contract to the Army Materiel Command (AMC) to design and develop a substantially more powerful engine for use in large bombers and cargo aircraft. The basic requirements called for 4,000 hp at 35,000 feet at 500 mph. Designated the XT-37, this engine had the potential of

GAS TURBINE POWER was proposed by Northrop to the Navy in 1949. Advantages in marine application: ability to deliver full power within a few minutes from a cold engine, simplified maintenance by virtue of engine compactness, and light weight. Overall Turbodyne advantage: ability to use several different types of fuel, including gasoline, kerosene, and diesel oil.

powering the B-52 bomber which at the time was still on the drawing board as a turboprop-powered airplane.

One of the principal advantages of the Turbodyne was its ability to use several different kinds of fuel, including diesel oil, kerosene, and gasoline. Other attractive features were its potentially long trouble-free life, and its high power-to-weight ratio. Little wonder that it proved attractive to industries other than aircraft manufacturers. Officials of Union Pacific were the first to consider application of the Turbodyne as locomotive power. It could be a replacement for the Diesel engines used in UP's "Streamliner" locomotives. Diesel fuel costs were low, but maintenance costs high. The Turbodyne with only slightly higher fuel costs but with the promise of trouble-free operation seemed a logical substitution. Immediately following company negotiations, Union Pacific provided Northrop with a Diesel-Electric locomotive chassis for experimentation. The intention was to install a specially designed Turbodyne engine. The bright yellow and red "Streamliner" was a long-familiar sight, parked on a siding at the Hawthorne main plant. But projected high development costs ultimately resulted in termination of the project.

By late 1947, three XT-37 engines had been completed. Testing on one had progressed to the point where 5,150 hp had been demonstrated at the relatively low turbine temperature of 1,350° Fahrenheit. Six months later this same engine has turned out 8,000 horsepower. Subsequent to these tests, one unit was put through a preflight qualification test program which ultimately demonstrated full design performance of 10,000 shaft horsepower. The success of the program was so encouraging that in mid-1948 AMC issued a teletype "letter of intent" amounting to $12,000,000 for continuation of the test program plus the construction of four flight-type engines.

In the following year, a contract was negotiated to modify an existing Northrop YB-35 Flying Wing bomber for installation of the Turbodyne XT-37 engine. This flying test bed, designated EB-35B, was to be powered by six J-35 turbojet engines, with the Turbodyne mounted slightly to the left of the aircraft centerline in the original proposal. The finalized design incorporated two Turbodynes, one on each side of the centerline, in addition to the six turbojets. (See discussion in Chapter 3, B-35, B-49 Flying Wing Bombers.) The Turbodyne was to drive a large counter-rotating pusher propeller manufactured by General Motors Aeroproducts Division.

Perhaps more importantly, the XT-37 engine had been established as alternate engine to the Wright T-35 on the Boeing B-52. With the B-52 planned as a high-production turboprop-powered airplane, the Turbodyne's future seemed assured as it had already developed substantially more power than the Wright engine. But when the Air Force abruptly changed the B-52 design from turboprop to turbojet, both the Northrop and Wright engines were suddenly eliminated from the competition.

The final blow came on October 28, 1949, when the Air Force ordered all work discontinued on the EB-35B. This ended the prospects for any Turbodyne flight test program.

Personnel of the Turbodyne Corporation, the organization which succeeded the Northrop-Hendy partnership in 1949, desperately tried to save the Turbodyne program. The Navy was approached with a proposal for using the engine as a standby power plant for installation in destroyers in the event of battle damage to the main power source. Howard Hughes was approached with the proposal to install Turbodynes in his huge flying boat, the "Hercules."

None of these efforts was productive. With little prospect for future financial support, the Turbodyne Corporation was disbanded. At the direction of the Secretary of the Air Force, in 1950, Northrop turned over the patents, name, and technical data to the General Electric Company, Gas Turbine Division, Schenectady, New York. Features of the Turbodyne have been reported to have been incorporated in General Electric's later gas turbine designs.

XT-37 Turbodyne
INSTALLED IN EB-35B FLYING WING
(See Flying Wing Section, Chapter 3)

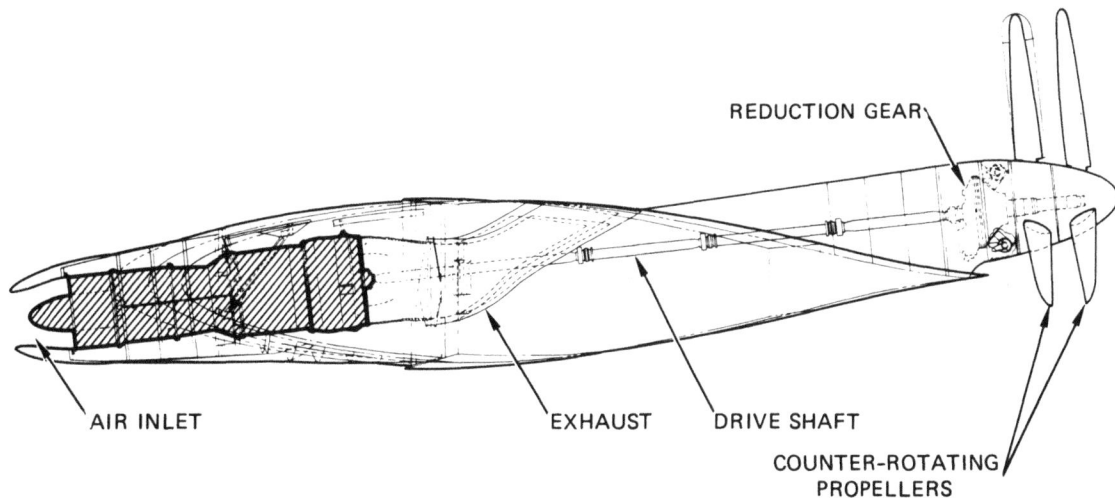

REDUCTION GEAR

AIR INLET EXHAUST DRIVE SHAFT

COUNTER-ROTATING PROPELLERS

ENGINE SPECIFICATIONS

COMPRESSOR

BLADE TIP DIAMETER 31 IN.

14 STAGES, AXIAL FLOW

MASS FLOW 102 LB/SEC. @ SEA LEVEL

EFFICIENCY 87%, DEMONSTRATED

PRESSURE RATIO 7.5:1

TURBINE

BLADE TIP DIAMETER 35.3 IN.

2 STAGES 50/50 REACTION

PERFORMANCE 10,400 HP @ SEA LEVEL, ON DRIVE SHAFT

EFFICIENCY 85%

COMBUSTION EFFICIENCY 95%

SPECIFIC FUEL CONSUMPTION 0.58 LB/HP/HR @ 10,000 HP

TURBINE INLET TEMPERATURE 1,500°F

2

U.S. AT WAR

"EMERGENCE AND GROWTH"

The bombing of Pearl Harbor on December 7, 1941, brought an abrupt end to any complacency that may have characterized official Washington in the two years preceding the United States' entry into World War II. The fence-sitters and vacillators were quickly galvanized into action. By January 1942, President Roosevelt had called for the production of 60,000 airplanes in that year alone, and 125,000 in the following year. These admittedly ambitious numbers, however, did reflect the steep upward trend of actual aircraft output — from 3,000 in 1940 to 19,000 in 1941, and 96,000 by 1944.

Northrop was both typical and atypical of the United States aircraft industry at that time. It shared in the rapid industrial growth, which initially was due as much to Europe's desperate need for military aircraft as to the preparedness of the United States government. But Northrop was a neophyte among some well grounded manufacturers whose reputations had been long established. It found itself in the middle of precipitous growth with only modest capitalization. In a period of only twenty-four months, its work force had risen from

110 employees to 4,700, and plant capacity from 122,000 square feet to 550,000. At the time of Pearl Harbor, business backlog stood at an undreamed of $85,000,000. A year later it saw itself listed among the first (top) 100 United States companies in volume of war contracts received from the government. It ranked 73rd in the list of largest government contractors and 13th among aircraft manufacturers.

Northrop's early war production centered around the Vultee-designed Vengeance dive bomber, peak production being reached in 1942. In the same time span the company was continuing subcontract production of Boeing's B-17E/F Flying Fortress nacelles and cowlings, and Consolidated's PBY-5 Catalina Flying Boat empennages, cowlings, and seats. This policy of maintaining a "bread and butter" production base, grounded on subcontract work, was a hallmark of Board Chairman Cohu's management philosophy.

Few employees realized that the company's most important product was under development as early as 1941. The XP-61 was almost completely "under

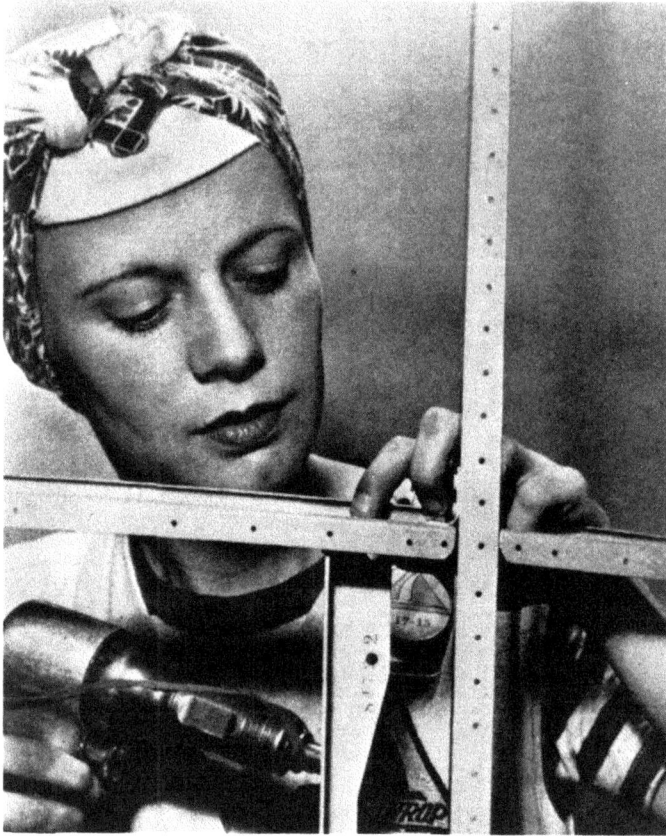

WOMEN constituted a large percentage of the U.S. production force during World War II. Thirty-five out of every 100 Northrop employees were women. The company established many special services (counselling, child care, housing, transportation, rationing) on their behalf.

WARTIME NORTHROP

SIGHTLESS WORKERS' program was established in June 1944. Their record for safety, attendance, and output was above plant average. Their rate of turnover was the lowest of any employee group.

PLANT LABOR FORCE in late 1944 was fairly well seasoned. More than 1,600 employees had been with the company for three years or more – remarkable from the standpoint that Northrop itself was only five years old.

VETERANS were wanted at Northrop. A special department helped assist the transition from hospital patient to war-worker. The company launched a vocational therapy program at the Army's Birmingham General Hospital in Van Nuys, California. The convalescent earned standard aircraft wages while building parts for the P-61 Black Widow. He could hire in at the Hawthorne plant when he was released from the hospital.

wraps'' until the production version was unveiled. The company's Second Annual Report called it an "experimental contract" for the design and development of a "highly specialized type of fighting airplane." By September, the Army was willing to gamble $26,000,000 in contracts, and the end was not in sight.

Army Air Corps observers had been paying particular attention to the outcome of the air war over England. They noted a pressing requirement for a real night fighter to counter enemy bomber strikes. Up to that time, converted British fighters had been used against the Germans with less than satisfactory results. Actually a majority of these radar-equipped fighters were lost in night takeoffs and landings rather than in combat. Engaging in an industry competition, Jack Northrop came up with a unique design — a twin-boom, twin-engine, heavily armed, radar guided fighter.

The company won the award in January 1941. But how Jack Northrop sealed the contract is a lesson in direct decision-making uncomplicated by time-delaying red tape. Later, reminiscing about the event, he said: "There were only three individuals directly involved in the contract negotiations. One was an Air Corps officer who was a project engineer at Wright Field, one was an Air Corps civilian employee, and I was the third. . .The Air Corps officer and I agreed on the basic design. Then we called in the civilian contract specialist to write the contract. Of course we didn't do all the thinking on the project. . .But the major decisions that implemented the project were made by only three of us in face-to-face meetings.''

The production version of the P-61 Black Widow night fighter came on-stream midway in the war. It proved a very successful and, for its time, an extremely complex weapon system.

During the war, Northrop employment had peaked at about 10,000 personnel and by V-J Day (August 14, 1945), plant facilities had grown to over 1.3 million square feet.

Small relative to other aircraft manufacturers, Northrop produced a total of 1,098 airplanes by the end of the war. But it had earned the reputation for excellence as a designer and builder of experimental aircraft. In relative size and numbers, North American Aviation — by comparison — reached a peak of 93,000 personnel and produced 41,188 airplanes!

P-61 BLACK WIDOW, silhouetted in a South Pacific sunset. This particular craft, sharing the tarmac with a P-47, was attached to the 7th AAF and was based in the Mariana Islands.

TRUCK-LOADED P-61 in protective cocoon, or "shrouded widow's weeds," is transported to Long Beach, California (above) for transfer to sea-going vessel (below) and ultimate delivery to bases in the European Theater of Operations (ETO) and the South Pacific.

ROACH DRY LAKE, NEVADA, served as an alternate test site to Muroc Dry Lake, particularly during the winter months of 1944 when rain-swollen floods negated the use of the California base. (Above) XP-56, one of the experimental series of Flying Wings, is shown undergoing maintenance in the hangar. (Below) N-9M, another of the Flying Wings, being readied for flight outside.

At the conclusion of the war, excluding the purely experimental types, Northrop's total war production amounted to: 674 P-61 Black Widows; 24 N-3PB's; 400 V-72/A-31 dive bombers; 1,309 sets of tail surfaces and cowls for Catalina PBY-5's; 44,832 cowls and 25,068 nacelles for the B-17's.

Concurrent with the large-scale airplane production during the war, a series of experimental aircraft were designed, built, and tested to meet military requirements for special and sometimes radical weapon systems. Carrying on the Jack Northrop tradition of the Flying Wing was the N-9M Flying Scale Model, the true forerunner of the full-scale XB-35 bomber which was simultaneously under contract. Four of these 60-foot, flying scale models were constructed. They were to provide considerable flight research data for the XB-35 since they were aerodynamic equivalents of the huge Flying Wing bomber. They also served as pilot trainers for the future Flying Wings.

A few of the lesser known projects included the XP-56 all-magnesium, pusher-propeller, tailless fighter, and a number of small Flying Wings. Two of these so-called small "wings" were of the "flying bomb" category. They had the unofficial names of Flying Bat and Buzz Bomb (an advanced pulse-jet). Other classified Flying Wing projects were America's first military rocket plane, the Rocket Wing; and the first prone-pilot jet interceptor ("Flying Ram"). The war ended before any of these revolutionary machines could be considered for quantity production. Altogether the company designed and flew 12 different kinds of Flying Wings by the end of the war.

One rewarding activity which started during the war under a nonprofit program was Northrop's work in the field of prosthetics development. The company had established a small fabricating and subassembly operation in the Birmingham General Army Hospital, Van Nuys, California, for convalescent veterans to earn standard aircraft wages while building vital parts for P-61 fighters. In light of its activities with handicapped veterans, Jack Northrop became interested in the development of superior artificial limbs. Ultimately, using aircraft technologies and materials, company specialists were able to perfect a vastly improved control mechanism which proved a boon to war amputees and the general public alike.

TWO N-9M's (tip of third visible at right) alongside the XB-35 Flying Wing Bomber in one of the large flight hangars at Muroc. This photograph was taken in August 1946, two months after the historic first flight of No. 1 XB-35 from Hawthorne to Muroc. The N-9M's were designed as true 60-foot flying scale models of the larger ship.

N-9M FLYING SCALE MODEL

The all-wing principle was firmly established by the series of successful N-1M flights in 1940-41. The development of a large Flying Wing bomber-type aircraft was now the next logical step. In September 1941, following a visit to California by Assistant Secretary of War Robert Lovett and Major General Oliver P. Echols, preliminary designs for a Flying Wing bomber (XB-35) were submitted to Army Air Force engineers at Wright Field. Close study and evaluation satisfied them to the extent that a contract for this heavy, long-range bomber in the 1945-50 time frame, was awarded to the company.

As Northrop engineers were about to go into detail design phase of the huge XB-35, the decision was reached to build four 60-foot scale models to provide flight research data. They were designated the N-9M series. Except for the power plants and propellers, the N-9M's were the aerodynamic equivalents of the bomber. They were true 60-foot scale models, slightly more than one-third the size of the XB-35 in every comparable dimension.

The first N-9M flight took place on December 27, 1942, at Northrop Field. Test pilot John Myers was at the controls. Eventually this prototype made approximately 50 flights, for a total of 30 hours, when it crashed in early 1943 just north of Rosamond Dry Lake, California. At the time of the fatal crash, pilot Max Constant was conducting aft C.G. stability and control tests, including stalls. A farmer who witnessed the crash thought he saw the wings alternately flashing in the sun, which may have indicated either a spin or tumbling motion. Post-accident investigation suggested the possibility that aerodynamic forces had been generated which developed full-aft forces on the control column. They must have exceeded Constant's strength, trapping him in the cockpit and preventing bailout.

N-9M FRONT AND REAR ASPECTS. Two 275-hp Menasco engines, driving rear-mounted propellers, powered the first three N-9M's. The air-cooled power plants were completely submerged within the wing.

48

N-9MB, THE "FOURTH" OF THE FLYING SCALE MODELS, in final assembly. The original specification called for a "crew of one pilot . . . provision made for an observer in restricted quarters normally occupied by a 50-gallon fuel tank." The "B" model was modified to accept a "second seat."

SUBMERGED N-9M ENGINE with extended rearward drive shaft to pusher propeller. Note the fluid-drive coupler between engine and propeller.

Subsequent engineering checks found all stall/spin characteristics within acceptable limits. However, to prevent the possibility of aerodynamic forces from overpowering the pilot, a one-shot hydraulic boost device was installed to push the control forward in an emergency. Flight tests were resumed without further incident.

The remaining three N-9M's flew hundreds of hours over a three-year test program at Muroc Army Air Base, providing valuable verification data for the XB-35, as well as giving pilots excellent training in the flight performance and handling characteristics of Flying Wing airplanes. The "Little Herbert" autopilot was also developed for the big Flying Wings in one of the N-9M's.

The first three N-9M's were powered by two submerged 275-hp, air-cooled, six-cylinder Menasco engines. The Menascos were mounted on their sides and drove extension shafts to the two-bladed Hamilton Standard pusher propellers via a fluid-drive coupler.

FLIGHT CONTROL SYSTEM (N-9M) consisted of a conventional control wheel connected to elevons, and rudder pedals operating split trailing edge rudders independently. Elevon surfaces (combined elevators and ailerons) deflected together for longitudinal (pitch) control and differentially in opposite directions for lateral (roll) control.

SPECIFICATION (NS-99) FOR N-9M asserted that its primary mission was to provide flight test information from which the maneuverability, controllability, and performance of the XB-35 airplane could be predicted.

TEST PILOT Max Stanley instructs Air Force pilot in the features of the N-9M control systems. The Air Force regarded the Northrop program as Confidential, since it was a true flying scale model of the future XB-35 bomber.

N-9M COCKPIT shows confined seating quarters, instrumentation, and controls facing the pilot. The seat is fixed. In event of emergency bailout, procedures required manual release of hatch, engine turn-off, and braking of the rear pusher propellers.

FLIGHT ECHELON OF THREE N-9M's photographed in early 1946.

The coupler helped reduce engine/propeller vibration problems and also allowed disengagement of the propellers from the engines to stop their rotation in the event of a bailout. The fourth airplane, identified as N-9MB, was fitted with a pair of 300 hp, air-cooled, six-cylinder Franklin engines. With the removal of a fuel tank from behind the pilot, the "B" contained sufficient space for an observer. The "second seat" was occasionally occupied by Bill Sears, Chief of Aerodynamics, or Jack Northrop. By 1945 this space was refitted with an extra fuel tank for extended range.

The N-9M's were of mixed wood and metal construction. The center section structure consisted of a welded steel tubing truss covered with wood and metal panels. The outer wing panels were fabricated primarily from wood with wood veneer covering. All N-9M's featured a tricycle landing gear. The first two N-9M's were painted yellow overall. The third (Model A) was painted blue on top and yellow on the bottom, while the fourth (Model B) had the reverse scheme, yellow on top and blue on bottom. These color combinations served as aids in identifying whether the top or bottom of the aircraft was being observed during the flight tests.

As with the N-1M Jeep, the N-9M's were capable of extremely rapid acceleration, shallow glide-paths, and a short turning radius that was spectacular.

N-9M

SPECIFICATIONS

WING SPAN . . . . .60 FT.

OVERALL LENGTH . . . . .17 FT., 10 IN.

OVERALL HEIGHT . . . . .8 FT., 7 IN.

WING AREA . . . . .490 SQ. FT.

TAKEOFF WEIGHT . . . . .7,100 LB

SPEED-MAXIMUM . . . . .257 MPH

SPEED-CRUISING . . . . .160 MPH

RANGE . . . . .500 MILES

SERVICE CEILING . . . . .21,500 FT.

POWER — (2) MENASCO C6S-4, 6-CYL, AIR COOLED,
          IN-LINE, 275 HP (N-9MA)
          (2) FRANKLIN 0-540-7, 6-CYL, AIR COOLED,
          OPPOSED, 300 HP (N-9MB)

P-61 BLACK WIDOW

In the summer of 1944, a new destructive force suddenly appeared in the night skies of the European and Pacific theaters of operation. It was Northrop's P-61 "Black Widow" Night Fighter, one of the best kept secrets of the war. Within a very few months this large, radar-guided interceptor would virtually sweep the night skies clear of enemy intruders. Toward the end of the war, it would also fly interdiction raids deep into enemy territory with pronounced success, scoring destructive strikes on supply convoys, troop columns, railroads, and airfields.

The origins of the P-61 go back to the blitz-torn skies over England in 1940. The extraordinary feats of the RAF during the "Battle of Britain" were witnessed first-hand by a team of U.S. Army officers, headed by General Emmonds. They were impressed by the singular achievements of British fighters flying day and night missions. But they sensed the need for a special-purpose aircraft to perform the night fighter role. Upon return to the United States, the team recommended immediate development of a totally new fighter. Approval was quickly followed by the issuance of a specification in the fall of 1940 calling for an airplane large enough to house the required bulky radar equipment and extra heavy armament.

For Northrop the real story of the P-61 does not lie in its outstanding overseas performance, nor in the number of kills it chalked up. Rather it lies in the company's ability to handle its first large-scale production order, and its versatility in responding quickly to change requests and to improve product quality at judicious stages. Over a period of four years, the P-61 proved to be not one airplane but no less than 13 different variations and models. The challenge turned out to be much more complex than anticipated. Northrop came of age with the P-61.

NATIVE MANPOWER lends a helping hand to a Black Widow in the South Pacific. The P-61 entered combat service almost simultaneously in both the Pacific and European theaters of operation during April and May of 1944. Initial deliveries were made to the 6th, 419th, and 421st Night Fighter Squadrons (NFS) in the Pacific. In Europe the first units to receive the Black Widow were the 422nd and 425th NFS.

53

UNVEILED JANUARY 8, 1944, in the night sky over the Los Angeles Coliseum, "something fast and dark flashing through the stabbing searchlights . . ." startled 100,000 spectators at an Army-Navy Show for war workers. Over the public address system came the announcement: "What you saw – if you looked fast enough – was America's newest fighting plane, the Northrop P-61 Black Widow."

ALL-OUT PRODUCTION of the P-61B at height of World War II. The main Hawthorne assembly plant, which was wholly owned by the company, was one of the first to be automated in the industry.

Design of the prototype airplane started in October 1940 when preliminary requirements were placed with leading U.S. aircraft manufacturers as a basis for the design of a night fighter. Jack Northrop submitted his preliminary design to the Army Air Corps on December 7, 1940, and received a contract for $1,367,000 on January 30, 1941, for two XP-61 airplanes.

A giant among fighter aircraft of the day, the XP-61 possessed the dimensions of a medium bomber. Grossing nearly 30,000 pounds, it had a wing span of 66 feet and a maximum speed of 370 mph. In the fashion of its namesake, the "Black Widow" was dressed in a glossy black finish with a red band around the fuselage (propeller disc warning) and red markings (serial numbers), and was equipped with a very deadly bite (cannons and machine guns).

The crew nacelle, located between the engines, completely housed a flying team of three: the pilot, the gunner, and the radar operator-gunner. All armaments were contained within the crew nacelle, and consisted of a General Electric remote-controlled turret containing four 50-caliber machine guns, a battery of four 20mm cannon in a fixed, ventral (belly) position, and a radar installation in the nose. Structure of the crew nacelle was of aluminum alloy of the stressed skin, semimonocoque type.

The wing consisted of a stressed skin, two-spar, cantilever structure composed of six panel assemblies: two inner, two outer, and two tip. All design fuel was carried in inner wing tanks immediately aft of the engine installations. Engine nacelles, which also housed the main landing gear, were extended aft by booms for support of the empennage. On the XP-61 and YP-61 models these booms were fabricated of welded magnesium alloy; extreme manufacturing and quality control problems inherent in the thin-gage magnesium weldments eventually led to redesign for aluminum alloy construction.

Test pilot Vance Breese conducted the first flight of the XP-61 on May 26, 1942, from Northrop Field. The flight was very successful, but the accelerated test program soon indicated the need for certain modifications. To improve pitch control, the horizontal tail surfaces were redesigned, and full-span trailing-edge flaps replaced the Zap-type flaps on the prototype. Retractable, spoiler-type ailerons were also added.

An order for 13 "Service Test" YP-61's and one static test airframe followed closely on the heels of the XP-61 contract. They were all delivered within 18 months of receipt of contract, during August and September 1943.

In a similar vein, the pressing need for night fighters in all theaters of operations prompted a 200-aircraft production order well before the first of the XP-61's took to the air. Delivery of the completed P-61A's commenced in October 1943.

Flight tests showed the P-61A to be an extremely docile and manageable air vehicle. Maneuverability was considered excellent for an airplane of its size and weight. The sheer weight of the aircraft, however, ruled out intentional violent maneuvers such as spins and snap rolls.

The "B" version was similar in every respect to the "A" except for a slight extension of the fuselage nose. Engineers and test pilots alike considered the performance characteristics of the "B" series aircraft as excellent. However, mounting reports from the combat zones pointed to a need for increased speed and higher altitude capabilities. To achieve this improved performance, the "C" and "D" models were developed. Principal modifications involved updating of the P&W engines and adding wide-bladed Curtiss Electric propellers and G.E. turbo superchargers. Maximum speeds were raised to 430 mph, and service ceiling was increased to 41,000 feet.

The XP-61E was an effort to develop a high-performance, long-range, escort fighter which incorporated the same basic features of the other models of the P-61 series. Two P-61B aircraft were selected for modification to XP-61E's. One of the main changes consisted of omitting the gun turret, cutting the top of the crew nacelle down flush with the wing and adding a large bubble canopy. The center and aft sections of the new crew nacelle contained additional fuel tanks and radio equipment, and the nose radar was supplanted by four 50-caliber machine guns which complemented the ventral battery of four 20mm cannon.

XP-61 LANDING. Development of two prototype XP-61 airplanes started in October 1940. Test pilot Vance Breese conducted the first flight of Number One on May 26, 1942, from Northrop Field (now Hawthorne Municipal Airport). The entire trailing edge was later rebuilt to incorporate full-span flaps; retractable ailerons were also installed, thus improving low-speed flying qualities.

FIRST PRODUCTION P-61A's carried the four-gun turret (50-caliber machine guns). Because of turret-induced buffeting problems encountered in the flight testing of the YP-61's, the remaining 163 production "A" aircraft and early model "B's" were completed as two-place configurations without the turret. Flight test reports revealed the interesting fact that the difference in speed between the turret-on and the turret-off was only 3 mph.

TURRETLESS P-61B version, of which 200 were built. The last 250 ''B's'' were provided with the dorsal turret and an improved fire control system. The two wing racks of the ''A'' were expanded to four on the ''B'', permitting carriage of 310-gallon fuel tanks or 1,600-pound bombs. In all, 450 model ''B's'' were produced.

FORTY-ONE P-61C's had been built when V-J day brought a cancellation of the remaining 476 aircraft. The ''C'' series differed from previous configurations by the broad chord of the high-activity propeller blades, the turbo supercharger air intakes under the 2800-hp engines, and carburetor air inlets on the engine cowls. The heavier P-61C could attain an airspeed of 410 mph at 20,000 feet.

NIGHT FIRING A P-61 armament package at the gunnery revetment facility. Four 50-caliber machine guns were mounted in the movable top turret; four fixed 20mm cannon, in the belly below the crew nacelle. The movable turret could be remotely controlled by the gunner or radar operator-gunner; it could also be locked to fire forward under the pilot's control; it could be swivelled by the rear gunner for a ''parting blast'' in case of a target overshoot.

The XP-61F was planned to be an improved two-place fighter aircraft similar to the XP-61E. A P-61C was scheduled to be modified into the XP-61F; however, the program was cancelled on 24 October 1945, and the scheduled airframe reverted back to the P-61C configuration.

Excluding the F-15 derivatives of the P-61E, the final model to be produced was the "G". Sixteen P-61B's were modified in 1945 as weather reconnaissance airplanes, and powered by P&W R-2800 engines. All armament and the night camouflage and special radio equipment were deleted. Speed of the P-61G was slightly faster than the original P-61B airplanes.

In summary, a total of 706 P-61 Black Widows were turned out (674 by V-J day) from the original two test aircraft through production models, plus 20 experimental and special-purpose modifications. For the more experienced aircraft companies in the U.S. this would have been task enough; but for a company like Northrop, which came into existence less than two years before the onset of World War II, it was a very creditable accomplishment.

XP-61D DEVELOPMENT started even before production of the P-61C. Two P-61A's were selected to accept new turbo supercharged engines for improved high altitude performance.

CONVERSION TO DAY FIGHTER was the objective of the XP-61E development. Two P-61B's were selected for modification: cutting the top of the crew nacelle down flush with the wing and adding a bubble canopy; supplanting the nose radar with four 50-caliber machine guns (above). The design of the canopies differed between the two airplanes: one rolled aft on tracks; the other was hinged along the side (below).

59

P-61 PRODUCTION

MODEL	NUMBER OF A/C	NOTES
XP-61	2	PROTOTYPES
YP-61	13	SERVICE TEST MODELS
P-61A	200	FIRST FULL-SCALE PRODUCTION
P-61B	450	MOST NUMEROUS PRODUCTION MODEL
P-61C	41	REMAINING 476 AIRCRAFT IN CONTRACT CANCELLED AFTER V-J DAY
XP-61D	2	MODIFIED P-61A'S
XP-61E	2	MODIFIED P-61B'S; ESCORT FIGHTER WITH BUBBLE CANOPY
XP-61F	—	MODIFIED P-61C; PROJECTED ONLY, CONTRACT CANCELLED
P-61G	16	MODIFIED P-61B'S; WEATHER RECONNAISSANCE 1945
XF-15	1	MODIFIED XP-61E (NO. 2)
XF-15A	1	MODIFIED P-61C
F-15A	36	PRODUCED FROM PARTIALLY MANUFACTURED P-61C; ORIGINAL CONTRACT WAS FOR 175 F-15A'S
F2T-1	12	SURPLUS P-61A'S USED AS NIGHT FIGHTER TRAINERS BY U.S. MARINE CORPS

P-61A

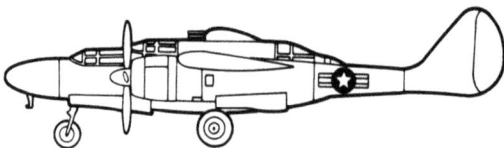

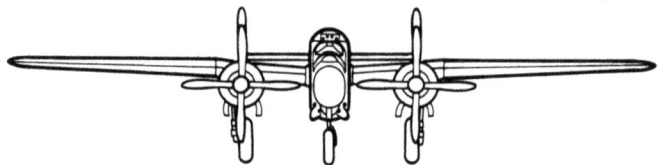

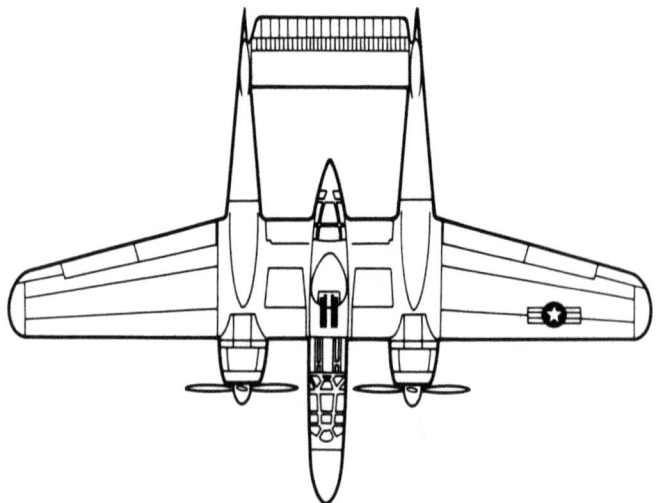

SPECIFICATIONS

WING SPAN . . . . .66 FT
OVERALL LENGTH . . . . .48 FT., 10 IN.
OVERALL HEIGHT . . . . .14 FT., 2 IN.
WING AREA . . . . .662 SQ. FT.
TAKEOFF WEIGHT . . . . .27,700 LB
SPEED-MAXIMUM . . . . .370 MPH
SPEED-CRUISING . . . . .200 MPH
RANGE . . . . .1,470 MILES
SERVICE CEILING . . . . .34,000 FT.
POWER — (2) P&W 2-2800-65, AIR COOLED, RADIAL, 2,000 HP
        (2) CURTISS ELECTRIC PROPELLERS
ARMAMENT — (4) 50-CAL GUNS
           (4) 20MM CANNON

XP-56 BLACK BULLET

Even before the outbreak of World War II, the U.S. military air arm was concerned about the advancement of German and Japanese fighter aircraft technology. It looked to new concepts, new designs to stay in the race. In order to prod domestic industry into action, the Army Air Corps opened an informal competition in late 1939. As a result, a wide variety of unique proposals came forward. Three of these "paper" designs were selected for development contract awards in June 1940. The winning contractors were Vultee, Curtiss, and Northrop. Northrop received $411,000 to proceed with the XP-56.

Each of the three contractors had submitted "pusher" designs, incorporating rear-mounted engines driving multi-bladed propellers. The general belief was that the pusher configuration offered lower aerodynamic drag, consequently superior flight performance, better pilot visibility, and more effective armament installation in the nose of the aircraft. Each contractor was to produce two single-seat airplanes.

The new 24-cylinder, liquid-cooled H-2600 (X-1800) engines under development by Pratt & Whitney were specified for each of the competing designs. But the program suffered a setback at the outset when H-2600 engine development was cancelled by Pratt & Whitney so that engineering efforts could be concentrated exclu-

sively on air-cooled power plants. In substitution, Northrop designers selected the air-cooled P&W R-2800-29 Double Wasp for the XP-56.

The Northrop XP-56 evolved into the first all-magnesium, all-welded airframe in history, and probably the first "pusher" with counter-rotating propellers and an air-cooled engine completely submerged in the fuselage. Northrop also perfected its patented "Heliarc" welding process during development of the XP-56. The airplane design was that of a tailless, swept flying wing, with both dorsal and ventral fins mounted above and below the engine immediately in front of the propellers.

The P&W Double Wasp engine was buried in the aft end of the stubby, podlike fuselage and was fan-cooled through two leading edge wing-root intakes. The engine drove two counter-rotating, three-bladed Curtiss Electric pusher propellers. The entire propulsion system was configured to increase power absorption with a relatively small propeller diameter for maximum ground clearance, and to reduce torque.

Since the propellers were located a short distance behind the pilot, and seat ejection was still in an early development stage, emergency bailout could be a frightening, if not fatal experience. Pratt & Whitney

FIRST OF TWO PROTOTYPE XP-56's. A variation of the all-wing concept, this aircraft had only a small dorsal fin on its stubby fuselage. Adverse yaw characteristics during the first flight brought about an enlarged stabilizer, which was installed like a glove over the original fin.

NUMBER TWO XP-56. First flew on March 23, 1944, from Northrop Field with a larger dorsal fin. Wingtip rudders were operated by air bellows to improve yaw control. This aircraft is currently in the Smithsonian Institution.

engineers alleviated the problem by means of an explosive cord wrapped around the engine gearbox. If the pilot were forced to jump, the cord could be first detonated, blowing away the propellers and the rear portion of the airplane, thus permitting a "safe" escape.

Intended as fighter-interceptors, the XP-56's were designed to mount four 50-caliber machine guns and two 20mm cannon in the nose. They were built in two slightly different versions, the first (S/N 1786) being originally distinguishable from the second (S/N 238353) by its small dorsal (upper) fin and by its lack of wingtip "bellows rudders." As with the N-1M Jeep Flying Wing, both XP-56 configurations had elevons and outboard lateral controls on the wing trailing edges.

Air-operated "bellows rudders" characterized Number Two airplane. In normal flight, the air travelled through a horizontal passage at each wingtip. When rudder was needed, the pilot moved the rudder pedals which operated a valve that diverted the airflow to the bellows. Thus the power of the airstream was used to assist in operating split-flap rudders at the wingtips.

Number One airplane first flew with a silver finish to protect the heavy-gage magnesium alloy skin. The only exceptions were the large propeller spinner and propeller blade tips which were painted yellow; the balance of the propeller blades and detail markings (serial numbers, etc.) were finished in black.

Number Two airplane was painted a green and gray camouflage finish. The dorsal and ventral fin tips, propeller blade tips, and serial numbers were finished in yellow. The balance of the propeller blades were black.

The prototype XP-56 was trucked to Muroc Dry Lake where it made it first flight on September 6, 1943. John Myers was the test pilot. The airplane exhibited adverse yaw characteristics, suggesting a need for more vertical stabilizer area. As a result, an enlarged stabilizer was "scabbed" over the original dorsal fin, improving the yaw tendencies during the subsequent flight tests. Later, during a high-speed taxi, short liftoff and landing at Muroc, the airplane turned completely over as a result of a tire blowout. The pilot, John Myers, escaped with minor injuries, but Number One airplane was demolished.

The second XP-56 took to the air on March 23, 1944, from Northrop Field with Harry Crosby at the controls. This model incorporated the greatly enlarged dorsal vertical stabilizer for improved directional stability, and the air bellows-operated rudders at the wingtips for greater yaw control. Flight characteristics were noticeably improved. However, the engine did not develop full power, and a nose-heavy or "down" moment precluded normal takeoffs at reasonable airspeed. Thus additional design development was indicated.

By this time, the Army Air Service requirements had changed with the introduction of the jet engine into new fighter applications. Further development was cancelled. Number Two XP-56 is currently in storage at the Smithsonian Institution.

FRONT AND REAR ASPECTS OF XP-56, (above) and (below) respectively. The pusher propeller design aimed at lowering aerodynamic drag. This first all-magnesium, all-welded aircraft was intended to be a fighter in the 400-500 mph class. It was designed to pack four 50-caliber machine guns and two 20mm automatic cannon in the nose.

ENGINE RUNUP of Number One XP-56 at Hawthorne. Wartime camouflage netting may be seen over structure at right.

XP-56 IN FLIGHT. Photograph is one frame of a motion picture film. Closely guarded confidentiality of the project precluded extensive photography of the XP-56 in flight.

XP-56

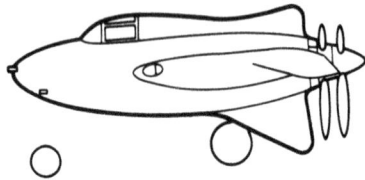
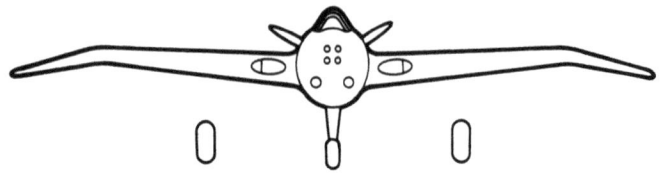

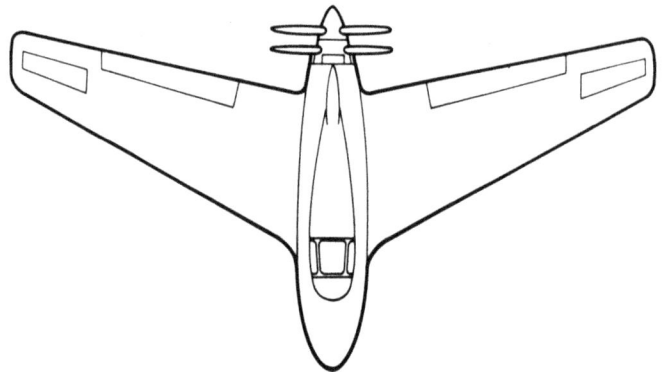

SPECIFICATIONS

WING SPAN . . . . .42 FT., 6 IN.

OVERALL LENGTH . . . . .23 FT., 6 IN.

OVERALL HEIGHT . . . . .9 FT., 8 IN.

WING AREA . . . . .307 SQ. FT.

TAKEOFF WEIGHT . . . . .11,350 LB

SPEED-MAXIMUM . . . . .467 MPH

SPEED-CRUISING . . . . .375 MPH

RANGE . . . . .450 MILES

SERVICE CEILING . . . . .33,000 FT.

POWER — (1) P&W R-2800-B, AIR COOLED, RADIAL, 2,000 HP
(2) CURTISS ELECTRIC COUNTER-ROTATING
PROPELLERS

ARMAMENT — (4) 50-CAL GUNS
(2) 20MM CANNON

MX-324/334 ROCKET WING

Details of the first U.S. military rocket plane only came to light in early 1947, fully four years after design conception. The MX-324/334 was one of the Army's most closely guarded projects of World War II. In its formative years it was known at Northrop only as "Project 12."

The bat-wing craft was still another member of the Northrop Flying Wing family. Small, 32 feet in span and 12 feet in length, it employed both rocket power and a prone pilot cockpit. The prone cockpit permitted the pilot to lie flat to withstand the "G" forces of far more violent maneuvers than were possible in a conventional airplane, and for reduced aerodynamic drag. Originally equipped with "elevons" alone, the final design included "brudders" (combination of air brakes and rudder) on the wing trailing edge. First flown under rocket power on July 5, 1944, by test pilot Harry Crosby at Muroc Dry Lake, the "Rocket Wing" indeed opened up new concepts of flight.

Originally conceived in September 1942 as a feasibility study for a future rocket-powered military interceptor, the idea brought Northrop an Army Air Force contract early in 1943. The plan called for the design and construction of three unpowered MX-324 gliders to test the aerodynamic qualities of the configuration. Later, before it was completed, the third MX-324 was converted into the rocket-powered MX-334. All three had the same dimensions.

Except for a welded steel tubing center section, all three airframes were built of plywood and painted yellow overall. The second MX-324 and the MX-334 featured a nonretractable tricycle landing gear fitted with large streamlined fairings. The nose gear was offset approximately one foot to the left to provide clearance for the prone pilot.

The powered MX-334 aerodynamic characteristics were first tested in 1943 with the two remaining gliders. The first glider was equipped with a pair of skids for a landing gear. Originally it was towed behind test pilot John Myers' Cadillac V-16 automobile to bring it up to launching speed. But the automotive speeds were too slow for safe flight. Number One glider was finally equipped with a detachable four-wheel dolly mounted on the skids. The dolly had been designed so that after the glider became airborne, the pilot could drop the dolly and make his landing on the skids.

Although a number of flights were made with the skid/dolly configuration, it was not completely satisfactory. Testing resumed with the second MX-324 equipped with the streamlined tricycle landing gear.

NO. 1 GLIDER VERSION. Two gilders were built to test the aerodynamic characteristics of the powered wing. Landing gear originally consisted of a pair of skids. A detachable four-wheel dolly was added later. No. 2 MX-324 was finally equipped with a streamlined tricycle landing gear.

MX-334 ROCKET WING. This configuration featured a 200-pound-thrust motor. First test flown by Harry Crosby, in a prone position, at Muroc Dry Lake on July 5, 1944. Note off-center nose-wheel to permit cockpit room for prone pilot. The MX-334 was towed to release altitude by a P-38 fighter.

FRONT (above) AND REAR (below) NO. 1 MX-324 VIEWS. Originally equipped only with "elevons," the final design incorporated "brudders" (combination of air brakes and rudder) on the wing trailing edge.

An incident occurred with the second MX-324 glider, when test pilot Alex Papana was being aero-towed over Muroc at 13,000 feet by a P-38 fighter. Papana accidentally pulled the release handle for the upper and lower cockpit hatches instead of the towline release. Without the streamlined enclosure the glider drag and buffeting increased dramatically. Quickly releasing the towline, Papana managed a hair-raising descent and successful landing.

Harry Crosby had an even more harrowing experience in the second MX-324 glider at Muroc while testing new full-length leading-edge flaps. During an aerotow to about 13,000 feet behind a P-38 fighter, Crosby found himself in the propwash of the leading plane as he released the towline, and stalled the glider. The glider flipped over into a spin, recovering in an inverted posi-

tion. The upside-down craft then started a steady glide toward the ground. Crosby jettisoned the hatches, unbuckled himself, and managed to climb up onto the wing center section. He then slid off the wing and opened his parachute. After the chute had opened, Crosby was shocked to notice that the inverted glider was flying in tight circles around him as they descended together. Fortunately, they never collided although both hit the ground in close proximity to one another.

The MX-324 might have survived the unmanned, inverted glide to the ground if the large vertical stabilizer had not first struck a nearby rocky hill, causing the glider to slam nose-first into the ground. The damage was too extensive to warrant repairs, and the glider never flew again.

MX-334 WING, April 1944. (Above) Profile view reveals unusually large wheel-and-strut fairings for aerodynamic streamlining. (Below) Test pilot Harry Crosby in prone position ready to take off in the vehicle without its rocket motor installed. Visible tow bridle was connected by a 300-foot towline to a P-38 fighter which carried the MX-334 to altitude (10,000 - 13,000 feet) where Crosby released the tow bridle and maneuvered in free flight to a glider landing.

Unpowered glider flights were resumed with the MX-334. Test pilot John Myers conducted the first at Muroc, California, on October 2, 1943. Later glider flights were performed by Alex Papana and Harry Crosby in the same machine.

During the rainy season, when Muroc Dry Lake became flooded, test flying was also conducted at Harper Dry Lake near Barstow, California, or at Roach Dry Lake, Nevada.

Racing against time to adhere to contract commitments and, especially, to keep abreast of similar developments in Germany, Northrop had joined forces with the Aerojet Corporation of Azusa, California, for installation of its XCAL-200 rocket motor, then under development. The Aerojet motor burned monoethylaniline fuel oxidized with red fuming nitric acid in a cast aluminum combustion chamber. It was capable of restarts in the air.

Finally on June 22, 1944, the installed rocket motor was fired for its maximum duration run of 3-1/2 minutes while the airplane strained at heavy stakes that secured it to the hard surface at Muroc Dry Lake. The following day test pilot Harry Crosby climbed into the prone cockpit resting his head in a special sling just behind the windshield built into the leading edge of the wing. He fired the rocket motor on and off as he maneuvered about, taxiing across the dry lake surface.

Then, on the morning of July 5, 1944, in the presence of Project Engineer Don Smith, ground crew members, and Army Air Force officers, Harry Crosby again strapped himself into the prone cockpit. The MX-334 was hooked to a P-38 twin-engine fighter by means of a 300-foot tow line. Captain Martin Smith was at the controls of the P-38. The launch was successful. Captain Smith brought the tow plane and the MX-334 across the dry lake at 8,000 feet. Crosby tripped the release dropping the towline. The wing was now in free flight. Crosby then pressed the rocket motor trigger built into his control stick and the 200-pound-thrust motor came to life. Smoke billowed out in a long black plume as the Flying Wing picked up speed under the thrust of its own rocket motor. *America's first rocket-powered airplane was an unqualified success.*

Following that first successful flight, a series of other launches were made to gather data about rocket-powered flight. One of the first known uses of telemetry was employed with the MX-334, relaying by radio the data gathered aboard the aircraft to recorders on the ground. Although these flights were profitable, the program itself was soon to be terminated. The war in Europe was drawing to a close. Additionally, rocket power technology was in its infancy, and the fuels were extremely dangerous to handle.

The MX-334 Rocket Wing with the original Aerojet XCAL-200 rocket motor is currently in storage at the National Air and Space Museum.

ROCKET POWERED FLIGHT OF MX-334 lasted only 3 1/2 minutes before the ''wing'' returned to the ground in glider fashion. The Army was experimenting in the use of rocket-powered vehicles as manned interceptors against raiding bombers.

MX-334

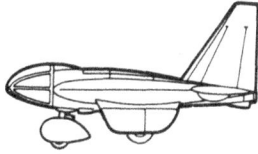

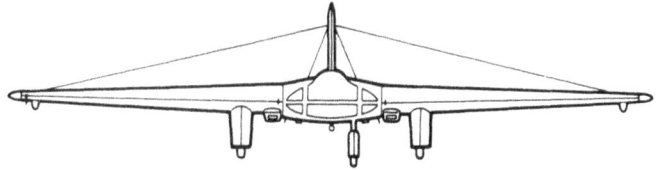

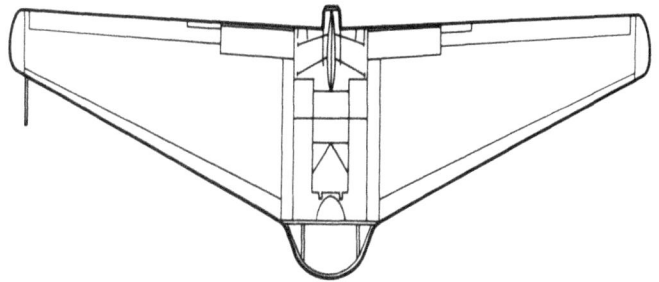

SPECIFICATIONS

WING SPAN . . . . .32 FT.

OVERALL LENGTH . . . . .12 FT.

OVERALL HEIGHT . . . . .7 FT.

WING AREA . . . . .244 SQ. FT.

TAKEOFF WEIGHT . . . . .2,500 LB

SPEED-MAXIMUM . . . . .300 MPH

RANGE . . . . .20 MILES

POWER — AEROJET XCAL-200, ROCKET MOTOR, 200-LB
        THRUST. 3½ MIN. BURN.

JB-1 (MX-543) POWER BOMB

Great Britain's harrowing experiences with the German-launched V-1 robot bombs prompted the U.S. air arm to consider the development of similar weapons. Late in 1943, Northrop was awarded an Army Air Force contract to design and develop a Flying Wing "Power Bomb." Under Project MX-543 and classified "Secret," two Model JB-1 air vehicles were produced. Don Smith was the Project Engineer.

The first airframe to be manufactured was a man-carrying glider, its unusual shape earning it the name "Bat." Except for the pilot's cockpit and canopy, the glider was the unpowered aerodynamic equivalent of the second, jet-powered version, and it was used to explore the design's flight characteristics. The wing span was slightly under 30 feet.

The glider center section, including the two stream-lined "torpedo-shaped" bomb containers, was fabricated of formed and welded magnesium alloy plate; the wing panels were made of riveted and spot-welded aluminum alloy sheet with magnesium wingtips. The pilot's cockpit was located in the space that would be used for the jet engine installations in the unmanned, powered model.

Test pilot Harry Crosby made the initial glider flights out of Muroc Dry Lake in 1944, using airplane tows to get airborne. Once again the glider flights demonstrated the high aerodynamic efficiency of the Flying Wing concept.

Following the successful glider flights, the second model JB-1A was equipped with a pair of General Electric Type B1 turbojet engines replacing the pilot.

The Power Bomb was designed as a ground-launched, pilotless airplane with a pre-programmed guidance system. This onboard system was theoretically capable of guiding the Power Bomb with reasonable accuracy to a target approximately 200 miles away, at which point it was to make a terminal dive into the target zone with its bomb load. The design ordnance consisted of two 2,000-pound demolition bombs, one in each wing root container.

JB-1 POWER BOMB. Two models were produced – a man-carrying glider called the "Bat" and a pilotless jet-powered vehicle. The streamlined "torpedo-shaped" containers were to house 2,000-pound bombs. Project Engineer Don Smith sat in the glider version for this picture to show diminutive size of the vehicle.

JB-1 FRONT VIEWS. The piloted version was lifted aloft as a glider by means of a tow aircraft. Tow hitches are visible at the tips of the two bomb containers. Only one man-carrying JB-1 was built to test qualities of the flying-wing design as a "buzz bomb."

JB-1 REAR VIEWS. The glider model shows the provision for the twin-jet power plants (400 pounds of thrust each) to be installed in the JB-1A's. The powered JB-1A, which was a ground-launched pilotless bomb, was flown on pre-set guidance control.

The ground launch method utilized a 400-foot track gaged to carry a sled on which the Power Bomb was mounted. Five 10,000-pound thrust rockets drove the sled along the track to achieve 160-mph takeoff speed for the Power Bomb. Inflight speed of JB-1A was to exceed 400 mph. But by the end of 1944, military attention had shifted to pulse-jet powered designs, and the JB-1 program was terminated.

The original JB-1 ''Bat'' glider was later donated to Northrop Aeronautical Institute for instructional purposes.

JB-1A

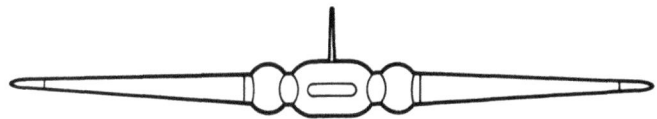

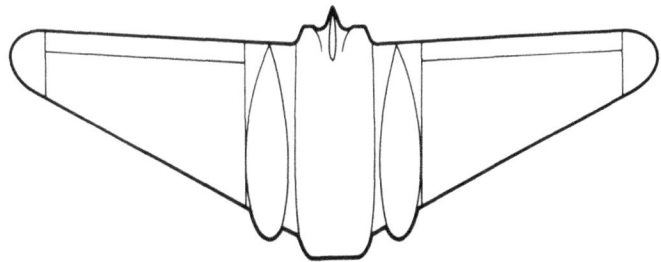

SPECIFICATIONS

```
WING SPAN .................................28 FT., 4 IN.
OVERALL LENGTH ..........................10 FT., 6 IN.
OVERALL HEIGHT ...........................4 FT., 6 IN.
WING AREA .................................155 SQ. FT.
LAUNCH WEIGHT ...........................7,080 LB
SPEED-LAUNCH ..............................160 MPH
SPEED-CRUISING .................427 MPH AT 5,000 FT.
RANGE ......................................670 MILES
POWER — (2) G.E., TYPE B1, 400-LB THRUST
ARMAMENT — (2) 2,000-LB BOMBS
```

JB-10 (MX-544) JET BOMB

The Army Air Forces' drive to keep pace with German V-1 robot bomb technology continued with the pulse-jet engine that was under development in the laboratories of the Ford Motor Company. The design was based on captured German models.

Encouraged by the previously successful JB-1 Power Bomb, the Army awarded Northrop a contract in late 1944 to design a pilotless Flying Wing Jet Bomb system incorporating the new Ford pulse-jet engine. The JB-10 was regarded as a closely guarded secret weapon known only as "Project 16" until the end of the war. The principal problem facing the designers of the JB-10 was its method of launch. Northrop engineers began by experimenting with launching sleds that could be used on a 300-foot section of standard railroad track. However, it soon became apparent that long lengths of track would make site selection extremely difficult under combat conditions. The concept also negated the use of mobile launchers such as truck/trailers, or LST invasion launchers.

Taking advantage of the latest state-of-the-art booster rockets, Northrop developed a 50-foot track platform from which a sled-mounted JB-10 could be propelled into the air. Backbone of the sled was a 14-foot-long aluminum tube, 12 inches in diameter, mounted on runners. With the JB-10 securely cradled on the tube, four "Tiny Tim" solid rockets at the rear of the sled were fired electrically. Rammed forward by the burning rockets, the JB-10 very quickly achieved the launch speed of 220 mph required for pulse-jet engine operation.

Once airborne, the JB-10 accelerated to its high-speed cruise of 426 mph. Guided by a primitive, preset, on-board guidance system, the "buzz bomb" was able to range up to 185 miles, at which point it dove into the target detonating its bombs.

Successful test launchings were conducted in secret at the North Base of Muroc during 1945 under the direction of Project Engineer Don Smith. Smith had

JB-10 JET BOMB. Wing center section was fabricated of the largest magnesium castings ever produced up to that time. Elevons and wingtips were magnesium. Northrop developed a 50-foot-long track platform from which to launch the pulse-jet bomb cradled on a sled that was propelled by four solid rockets.

been in charge of the previous JB-1 project. Design ordnance load consisted of two 1,825-pound warheads built as an integral part of the inner wing, one on each side of the internally mounted pulse-jet engine.

The JB-10 was fabricated of aluminum and magnesium using Northrop's "Heliarc" welding process. The entire 8.7-foot-span center section of the wing, including the bomb carriers, was built of magnesium castings. They were among the largest magnesium castings ever produced. The outer wing panels were made of welded aluminum alloy; the elevon controls and wingtips, of welded magnesium.

During the early pulse-jet engine tests in Northrop's Hawthorne laboratories, nearby residents were cautioned by Army officials to expect but not worry about the ear-shattering booms characteristic of the "stuttering stove-pipe" engine. However, not until after the war, in December 1945, did the magnitude and significance of "Project 16" come to public light.

Test launches were conducted at Eglin Field, Florida, and over 1,000 sleds and 24 JB-10's were delivered to the Army before the armistice halted any further production. The system was not known to have been employed in combat.

JB-10

SPECIFICATIONS

WING SPAN . . . . .29 FT., 1 IN.

OVERALL LENGTH . . . . .11 FT., 10 IN.

OVERALL HEIGHT . . . . .4 FT., 10 IN.

WING AREA . . . . .163 SQ. FT.

LAUNCH WEIGHT . . . . .7,084 LB

SPEED-LAUNCH . . . . .220 MPH

SPEED-CRUISING . . . . .426 MPH AT 5,000 FT.

RANGE . . . . .185 MILES

POWER — FORD PULSE-JET, 800-LB THRUST

ARMAMENT — (2) WARHEADS, 1,825 LB.

XP-79B (MX-365) FLYING RAM

No sooner had the development of the MX-334 Rocket Wing begun (1943) than the Army established requirements for an even more advanced Flying Wing fighter-interceptor. The criteria were based on a proposal previously submitted by Jack Northrop in 1942.

The secret new Wing was to be an all-magnesium, rocket-powered, prone-pilot fighter-interceptor capable of near sonic speeds. The prone-pilot concept had once again been chosen to raise the pilot maneuvering "blackout" threshold to 12 G's instead of the 8-G limit of an upright pilot. It also permitted a thinner, lower-drag wing for higher performance.

The XP-79B "Flying Ram" was built with heavy magnesium structure and steel armor plate, designed to enable it to dive on enemy bombers, slicing off tail assemblies to down them. In addition, the XP-79B had provisions for four fixed 50-caliber machine guns in the wing center section, two on each outboard side of the jet engines.

In January 1943, the company was awarded an Army Air Force contract for the design and construction of three prototypes designated XP-79. Each of the XP-79's was to be powered by a single 2,000-pound-thrust rocket motor which was under development by the Aerojet Corporation. Takeoff was to be boosted by two 1,000-pound-thrust JATO units. Considering the fighter state-of-the-art of the time, calculated performance was nothing short of spectacular: 518 mph at 40,000 feet altitude. Flight endurance, however, was limited to approximately 31 minutes owing to the high fuel consumption rate characteristic of rocket motors.

Unfortunately the above design never reached flight stage. Development of the Aerojet rocket motor was beset by a seemingly endless series of problems. In addition, proven turbojet engines were becoming available. Consequently, the military cancelled the first two aircraft, awarding Northrop a new contract to redesign the third of the three XP-79's for twin axial-flow, turbojet Westinghouse engines. This airplane was designated the XP-79B.

Aerodynamically, the XP-79B was a swept Flying Wing fitted with elevons and bellows-type rudders similar to those used on the XP-56 Black Bullet. The prone pilot controlled pitch and roll by means of a crossbar with hand grips at each end. The maneuvering brakes were operated by foot pedals, power-boosted by the air-operated bellows.

FLYING RAM XP-79B. Span, 38 feet. Length, 14 feet. Twin wing-mounted fins. Rudder "assist ducts" used the power of the airstream to aid in operating split flap rudders at the wingtips.

ONLY ONE XP-79B was built. (Above) Pilot lay prone in the cockpit to raise his blackout threshold. (Below) Large air intakes led to twin axial-flow turbojets, each capable of 1,400 pounds of thrust, one of the first applications of jet power in 1945.

As in the original XP-79 design, the structure of the "B" was fabricated of Heliarc-welded heavy plate magnesium. Skin thickness varied from 3/4-inch at the leading edge to 1/8-inch at the trailing edge, forming a very rigid semimonocoque structure with minimum internal bracing. The outer wing panels were made in two halves, an upper and a lower. These halves were then bolted together. Fuel was carried in the outer panels, the fuel tanks being formed by the wing skins themselves. A four-wheel, electrically retractable landing gear was mounted in the center section.

The pilot's compartment was a sealed cabin designed for a 2.75-psi pressure differential; however, the compartment was not pressurized in the prototype. Both upper and lower sealed hatches could be released by the pilot for an emergency bailout. The two 19-inch-diameter Westinghouse turbojet engines were installed on either side of the pilot's compartment. The windshield was formed of transparent acrylic plastic with a bullet-resistant glass panel located just aft of the windshield and in front of the pilot's face.

Armor plate consisting of 1/4-inch face-hardened steel was installed just inside of the leading edge of the wing at 45 degrees to the chord plane. The armor extended from the side of the pilot's compartment to the end of the fuel tank on each side. The thick magnesium alloy wing skins also served as armor protection and deflector plates against enemy gunfire.

The prototype XP-79B was trucked to Muroc in June 1945 to be prepared for flight tests. Harry Crosby was appointed test pilot. On September 12, 1945, following several days of preliminary taxi tests, Crosby made the first and only flight. Almost as a forewarning of events to come, one of the attending Army Air Force fire trucks crossed the marked runway area just as Crosby accelerated the XP-79B on takeoff. Crosby chopped power just in time to avoid collision, then reaccelerated and took off to about 10,000 feet. He made one sweeping circle over the launch area at extremely high speed, estimated to be over 400 mph.

On his second pass over the dry lake at 8,000 feet, Crosby made a climbing turn which became a roll and then a stall. The XP-79B fell off into a nose-down spin from which it never recovered. Observers watched Crosby jump at the last moment. He was struck by a portion of the rotating airframe. The chute never opened.

An accident investigation was unable to determine the cause of the fatal crash because of the total destruction of the airframe in the ensuing magnesium-fed fire. It was speculated, however, that a trim tab failure had occurred, preventing Crosby from making the spin recovery. Following the accident, the program was cancelled and no additional XP-79B's were produced.

TRUE MISSION of the experimental XP-79B was to down enemy bombers by using its reinforced wing leading edges to "ram" tail assemblies. The covert nature of its real role was omitted in the original aircraft description which mentioned only its fighter-interceptor mission.

XP-79B

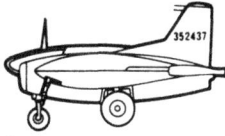
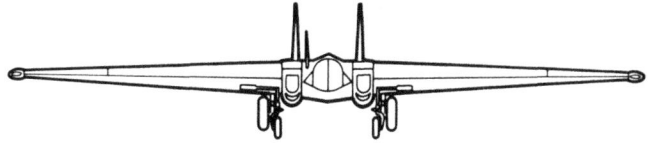

SPECIFICATIONS

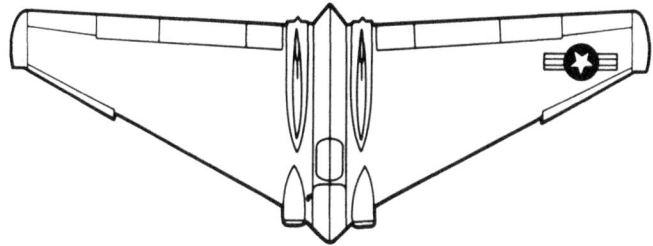

WING SPAN ....38 FT.

OVERALL LENGTH ....14 FT.

OVERALL HEIGHT ....7 FT.

WING AREA ....278 SQ. FT.

TAKEOFF WEIGHT ....8,669 LB

SPEED-MAXIMUM ....547 MPH

SPEED-CRUISING ....480 MPH

RANGE ....993 MILES

SERVICE CEILING ....40,000 FT.

POWER — (2) WESTINGHOUSE, MODEL B, 1,400-LB
      THRUST EACH

ARMAMENT — (4) 50-CAL GUNS

3

POSTWAR AND AFTERMATH

"INTRODUCTION OF THE JET ERA"

It was not long after the surrender of Germany in the West, and Japan in the East, that the U.S. aircraft industry was to feel the full impact of the war's ending. Military sales sharply dropped more than 90 percent; $21 billion in contracts were quickly cancelled. Could the industry survive? Had it been so wholly dependent on war-generated business that its underpinnings could no longer support a peacetime activity? Was it to face the same bleak outlook as post-World War I?

Unlike the milieu of the years following World War I, the political and socio-economic conditions of the late Forties were quite different. For one thing, the importance of airpower in national defense was now an accepted fact. For another, air transport was no longer an adventure, it was a practical reality with war-proven equipment and thousands of ex-military personnel already seasoned air travelers. Additionally, new technologies, such as jet propulsion, helicopters, and advanced aerodynamic concepts, would radically change all previous ideas about flying. Finally, new and challenging long-range military strategies, based on

guided missiles and atomic warheads, would appear on the scene.

Northrop's business backlog on July 31, 1945, stood at $141 million. By late August, following V-J Day, the backlog dropped to only $45 million, due principally to cancellation of P-61 production. As a result, the company began to implement a number of new aircraft programs and product diversifications planned long before war's end. Simultaneously, the XB-35 Flying Wing bomber came off the design board to assume new importance because of its excellent prospects for full-scale production. All of these activities helped to bridge the gap.

Two other programs assisted the company in transitioning from wartime production; they also had their beginnings before the end of the war. The more economically significant was an order for 175 F-15A Reporters. The F-15 was essentially a photo-reconnaissance version of the P-61E, and it was the first airplane to go into quantity production at Northrop following cancellation of the Black Widow. Indeed, it was one of the few warplane commitments considered of sufficient preacetime value to be retained after V-J Day. The second program, which was of some immediate help in reducing postwar layoffs, was a contract from United Airlines for the conversion of Army Air Forces surplus C-47 and C-54 transports into certified DC-3 and DC-4 Mainliners.

In line with the plan for diversification, the company formally established the Northrop Aeronautical Institute in November 1945. An outgrowth of a vigorous wartime training program, the school with its staff of 80 technical personnel taught engineering, manufacturing, and maintenance of aircraft. It was an unqualified success. First-year enrollment numbered 750 students. More than 1,000 were admitted the following year. The Institute assumed independence in May 1953, when it was sold because the company decided to concentrate on aircraft production. As a consequence of the sale, the school was merged with California Flyers in Inglewood where its name was changed to the Northrop Institute of Technology. Later it would be chartered as Northrop University.

Throughout this whole period, Jack Northrop never lost sight of his original design goal. Applying the lessons learned from the small Army-sponsored Flying Wings, he continued work on the huge XB-35 Flying Wing bomber, called "the airplane of the future." By January 1943, a large assembly plant had been completed at the east end of Northrop Field; fabrication of parts and tooling began at once. Three years later, the propeller-driven 172-foot Wing made its maiden flight from Northrop Field. The next stage was the transition to jet power. The spectacular jet-powered YB-49 versions shattered many flight records for speed and range. Patents covering several fundamental elements of the Flying Wing design were issued to the company between 1943 and 1947. The term "Flying Wing" was also registered as a Northrop trademark.

In 1948 a full-scale cabin mockup was fabricated as a commercial airline version of the jet-powered bomber. Unfortunately, the dream was never to materialize. It dissolved when the entire Flying Wing program would soon be cancelled because of budgetary and other considerations.

TEST PILOT MAX STANLEY (left) made first taxi test of XB-35 at Northrop Field, May 16, 1946. On June 25 he conducted the maiden flight to Muroc Army Air Base.

HAWTHORNE PLANT COMPLEX (looking east), early 1946, still showed the camouflage effects in force during World War II.

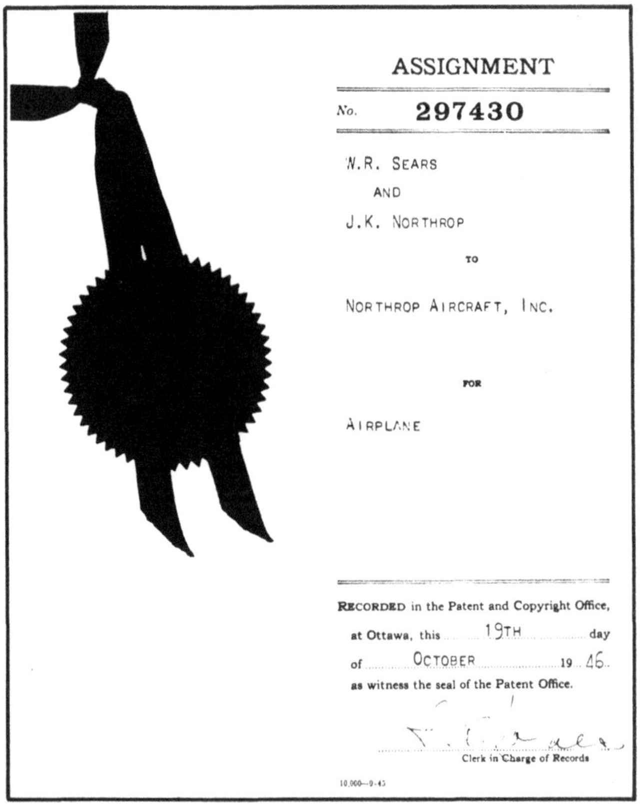

ASSIGNMENT

No. **297430**

W.R. SEARS

AND

J.K. NORTHROP

TO

NORTHROP AIRCRAFT, INC.

FOR

AIRPLANE

RECORDED in the Patent and Copyright Office,
at Ottawa, this _____19TH_____ day
of _____OCTOBER_____ 19..46.
as witness the seal of the Patent Office.

_____
Clerk in Charge of Records

10.000—9-45

JOHN K. NORTHROP and Dr. William R. Sears, Chief Aerodynamicist, assigned rights "in and to our invention" (Flying Wing) to Northrop Aircraft, Inc. on August 17, 1943, while applying for, and pending issuance of, a patent in the Dominion of Canada.

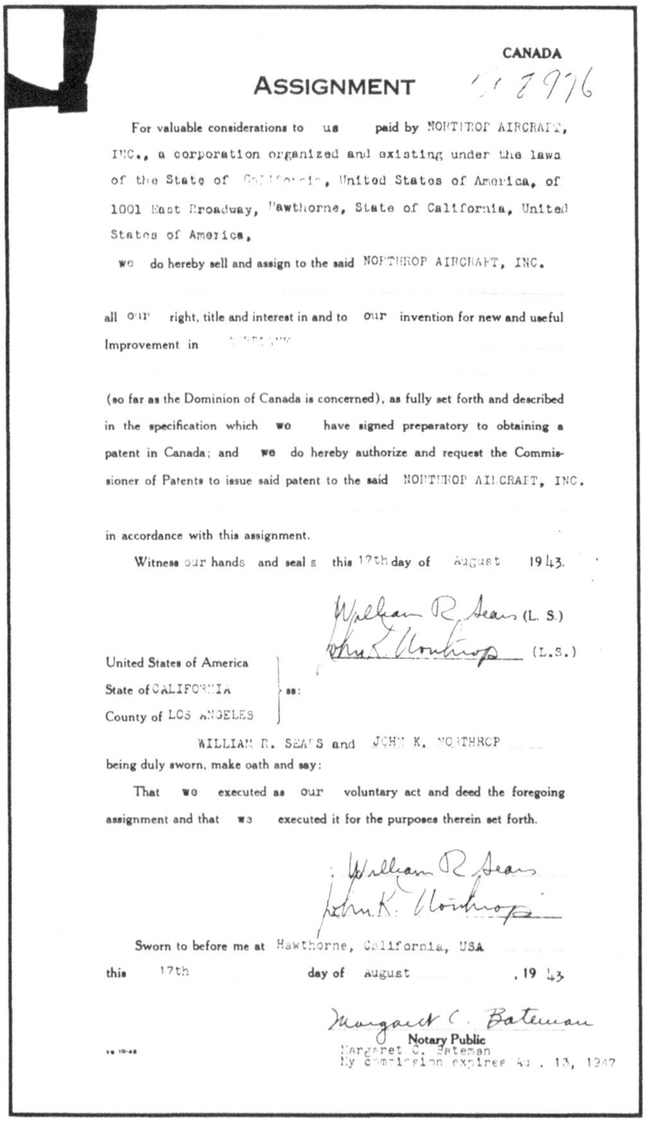

CANADA

ASSIGNMENT

For valuable considerations to us paid by NORTHROP AIRCRAFT, INC., a corporation organized and existing under the laws of the State of California, United States of America, of 1001 East Broadway, Hawthorne, State of California, United States of America,

we do hereby sell and assign to the said NORTHROP AIRCRAFT, INC.

all our right, title and interest in and to our invention for new and useful Improvement in _____

(so far as the Dominion of Canada is concerned), as fully set forth and described in the specification which we have signed preparatory to obtaining a patent in Canada; and we do hereby authorize and request the Commissioner of Patents to issue said patent to the said NORTHROP AIRCRAFT, INC. in accordance with this assignment.

Witness our hands and seals this 17th day of August 1943.

William R Sears (L. S.)
John K Northrop (L.S.)

United States of America
State of CALIFORNIA } ss:
County of LOS ANGELES

WILLIAM R. SEARS and JOHN K. NORTHROP being duly sworn, make oath and say:

That we executed as our voluntary act and deed the foregoing assignment and that we executed it for the purposes therein set forth.

William R Sears
John K Northrop

Sworn to before me at Hawthorne, California, USA
this 17th day of August , 19 43.

Margaret C. Bateman
Notary Public
Margaret C. Bateman
My Commission expires Ma 13, 1947

84

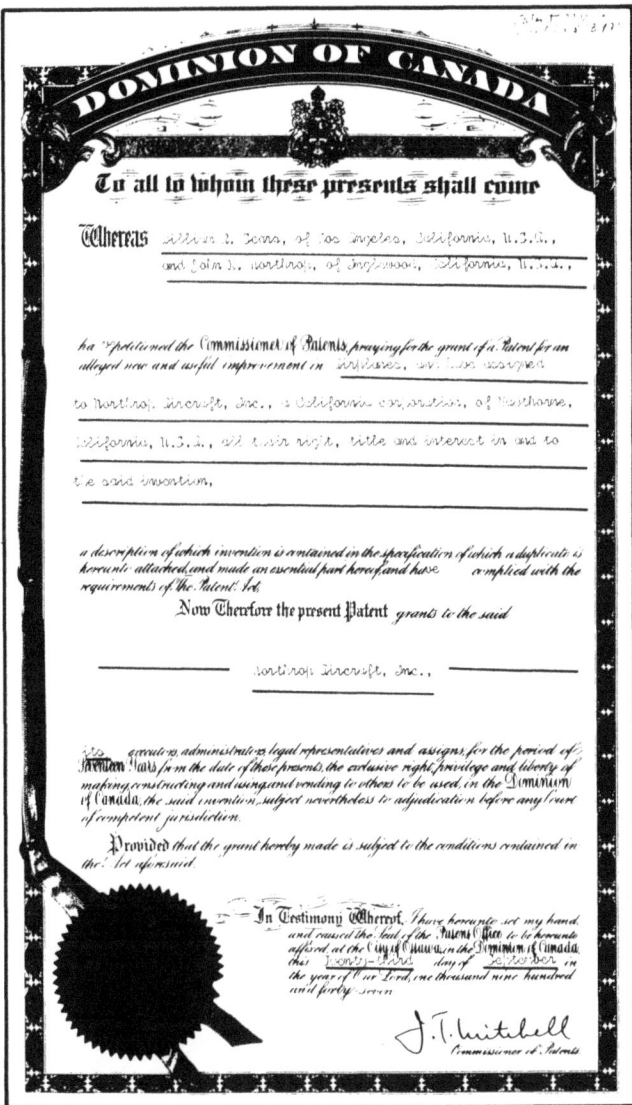

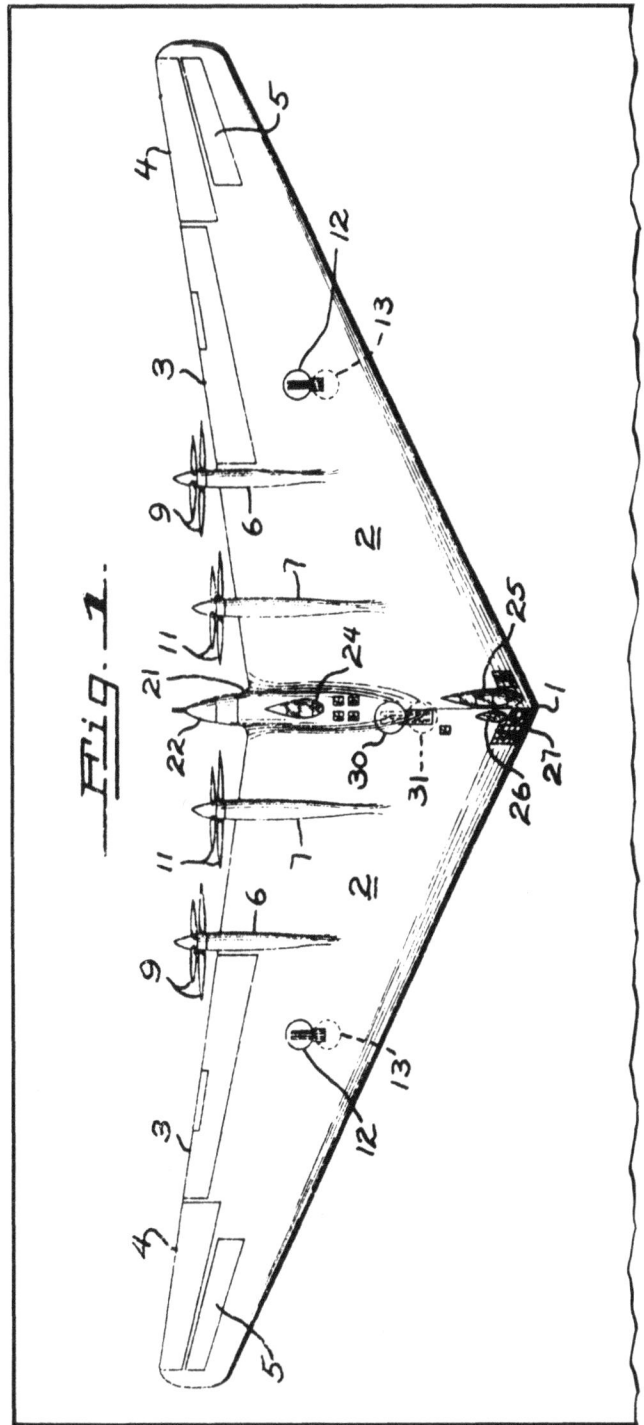

CANADIAN PATENT, petitioned December 15, 1943, was granted September 23, 1947. An excerpt from the specification of the petitioning patent shows the lines of the Flying Wing XB-35. Jack Northrop made worldwide applications for similar patents.

NORTHROP AERONAUTICAL INSTITUTE (NAI), later Northrop Institute of Technology (NIT), as it appeared from the air in 1946. The cluster of buildings in the center foreground would become an integral part of the entire plant complex bounded by Northrop Field (Hawthorne Municipal Airport) and Broadway. The building facing front is currently the administration center of the Aircraft Division, Northrop Corporation.

"OPEN HOUSE," December 1946. On display (clockwise from bottom right) are the F-15 Reporter, the N-23 Pioneer, two XB-35 Flying Wing Bombers, the ultrasmall JB-1 ("Bat") Power Bomb, and the P-61 Black Widow. The huge 172-foot Wings were assembled in the adjacent building, Plant 3. The building in the background served as the cafeteria for employees who worked in the east end of the plant complex.

The company's first postwar design for civilian use was the trimotor Pioneer. This was a short takeoff and landing passenger-cargo airliner intended for use in the primitive areas of the world, such as the jungles of South America. But when low-cost war-surplus transports began flooding the market, sales prospects evaporated. As a result, the Pioneer was redesigned as a military assault transport and Arctic rescue airplane. Twenty-three airplanes, designated the C-125 Raider, were built under Air Force contract.

Immediately after the war's conclusion, the Air Force had established a requirement for a new strategic missile. Experts of the day were convinced that such a revolutionary missile system — unmanned, automatically guided and expendable — was the key to any "push button" war of the future. In March 1946, Northrop was awarded contracts for the development of a strategic bombing missile of intercontinental range. The new missile was originally identified only as "Project MX-775" by the Air Force. The production version would be designated the SM-62 Snark.

The company quickly recognized the potential for the production of such a weapon, notwithstanding the formidable technical and development problems of guidance, airframe, and ground support. In 1950 a "Special Weapons" Division was established in Hawthorne to support the Snark, staffed by 3,300 personnel. Seven years later, the jet-powered Snark would become the first intercontinental guided missile to be put into operational status by the United States Air Force. Leading design experts were convinced that the Snark represented one of Northrop's foremost engineering achievements.

Jet engine technology was also taking hold in the immediate postwar period. As aircraft approached the speed of sound, Air Force officials turned to advanced research for answers to unknown and unexplored aerodynamic phenomena. One of their principal concerns was the undesirable compressibility effects experienced close to the sound barrier. They knew that part of the stability and control problem was related to the design of the horizontal tail surfaces, but neither laboratory nor wind tunnel could solve the complete mystery. Northrop offered its "Skylancer" design to investigate the problem in the air. The proposed aircraft was in the tradition of the Flying Wing, capable of transonic speed (Mach 0.9) at 35,000 feet altitude. The proposal was interesting enough to result in a contract for two X-4 "flying laboratory" airplanes equipped with NACA stability and control instruments. They performed many successful and problem-solving flights for both the Air Force and NACA, preparing the way for the design of supersonic aircraft.

SNARK ALOFT. First of the intercontinental guided missiles, SM-62 leaves launching cradle at Cape Canaveral, Florida. With booster rockets flaming, the Snark presented an awesome spectacle as it began long-range test flight over the Atlantic Ocean.

SLED RUNS at Muroc Army Air Base started after World War II in an "outdoor wind tunnel" environment to test airfoils at transonic and supersonic speeds. Later, the track was extended to determine the effect of severe deceleration forces on the human body.

COLONEL JOHN STAPP, "fastest man on earth," attained a speed of 632 mph on the 10,000 foot research track at Holloman AFB, New Mexico. Here, in 1956, Stapp is being prepared for run on Northrop-built rocket sled. Northrop personnel grouped around Stapp: (clockwise, from left) Tom Casey, Ralph Morgan, Jake Superata, Dr. Charles Lombard, and George Nichols.

In a similar research vein, the company supported Colonel John Stapp's renowned rocket-propelled sled experiments, first conducted at Muroc Air Force Base in California, later at Holloman Air Force Base in New Mexico. Northrop designed and built both the sleds and test facilities. Experts in acceleration/deceleration forces, company engineers spent seven rewarding years in this challenging field of aerospace medicine.

The company's first production jet aircraft derived from an Air Force requirement for a wholly new type of weapon system — an all-weather fighter interceptor. The twin-jet Scorpion was to be the last major design effort of a Jack Northrop-led engineering team. Designated the XP-89, the Scorpion would become the world's most heavily armed fighter interceptor of its day. Starting with two XP-89 (later XF-89) prototypes, ordered in May 1946, over 1,000 Scorpions would be delivered to the military air defense forces and would serve until the summer of 1969.

Increasing orders for the F-89 in the early Fifties, due to the Korean war, were impetus enough for Northrop management to convince the Air Force of the need for a new production flight and installation center at the Palmdale Airport. The Palmdale facility became operational in 1952, serving a function somewhat similar to that already established at the Ontario (California) International Airport.

In its continuing effort to generate new aircraft business, the company's engineering department proposed a wide variety of new designs. Some were aerodynamically conventional; others, radically advanced in configuration and performance. The more interesting, but unfulfilled, designs of the period were: variations of the large Flying Wing; advanced specialty fighters; a medium bomber; a test bed for the Turbodyne engine; antisubmarine warfare (ASW) aircraft; vertical takeoff and landing (VTOL) aircraft; and the "Fang" supersonic fighter.

Recognizing the growing prospect of Nuclear Energy for Propulsion of Aircraft (NEPA), the company corralled a small but workable team of scientists, each an expert in his individual atomic energy field. By 1950 the team had won a NEPA subcontract at Oak Ridge, Tennessee, working on the problem of how to shield the occupants of atomic-powered airplanes from radiation.

Product diversification continued to be emphasized. When the company was awarded a U.S. Ordnance Corps contract in 1951 to produce optical range-finders for tanks (a skill fallout from the Snark program), a new

PALMDALE, CALIFORNIA, INSTALLATION (above), was built by USAF to alleviate hard-pressed production facilities at Hawthorne. Palmdale in October 1954 (below) accommodated the assembly and staging of F-89D's. Over 1,000 Scorpions were delivered to USAF by Northrop into the Sixties.

factory was built at Anaheim, California. Richard R. Nolan, one of the founding "Northrop Group," was selected as manager.

In another major step toward diversification, the Radioplane Company of Van Nuys, California, was acquired in 1952. A leading manufacturer of target drone systems, Radioplane was established as a wholly owned subsidiary. Radioplane president Whitley C. Collins became a member of the Northrop Board of Directors.

In November 1952, company founder and president John K. Northrop informed the Board of Directors of his intention to retire from aviation. General Oliver P. Echols (USAF, Retired) became president, and Edgar Schmued, a prominent military aircraft designer who had been recruited to head the technical staff, was elected vice president in charge of engineering.

Early in 1953, Thomas V. Jones, a member of the staff of The Rand Corporation and an expert in planning and the economics of air transport, joined the company as assistant to the Chief Engineer, William Ballhaus. Within six years, Jones would become president of the Northrop Corporation.

Thus, in its fifteenth year, the company was in a reasonably healthy state. The backlog had climbed to a record $557 million, and employment had risen to more than 24,000 personnel.

B-35, B-49 FLYING WING BOMBERS

INITIAL VERSION OF XB-35 (underside) in flight, 1946. Four sets of counter-rotating propellers driven by Pratt and Whitney Wasp Major engines, developing 12,000 horsepower, push the 172-foot wing through the air. Wingtip slots permit delayed stall at high angles of attack for increased control. All control surfaces are on wing trailing edge. Three simulated gun turrets are visible; a similar number were installed topside.

The account of the Flying Wing Bomber is probably the most intriguing, and at the same time the most perplexing, in the annals of Northrop aeronautical history. In the first place, it represented the culmination of Jack Northrop's 20-year quest for an operational, revolutionary all-wing airplane. It was the most radically different airplane of its time. A quantum jump in performance, combined with ease of flying, quickly made it attractive for military operations, with the additional promise of future transport applications.

Secondly, it embodied the spirit and dedication of the employees who worked on it, and who were emotionally caught up in its daily trials and tribulations as well as its triumphs. Finally, it contributed to the ending of the propeller age and the beginning of the jet age.

What is perplexing is that this phase of near history has been the subject of a variety of publications, most of which have perpetuated or even inaugurated a number of inaccuracies about the big Wings.

Much of the confusion has undoubtedly been caused by the fact that of the 270 planned for production, only 15 basic airframes were manufactured, of which six actually flew in either the piston-engine or jet configurations. Confusion also arose from the plethora of model designations assigned to the Wings over a ten-year period. (Refer to table at the end of this text for data and remarks on each model configuration.) Whether XB-35, YB-35, B-35A, YB-49, RB-49A, RB-35B, EB-35B, YB-35B or YRB-49A, the reference was always to a profile that had the same characteristic Northrop "Flying Wing" look in the skies or on the printed page.

Still another contributing factor was the tumultuous political and budgetary backdrop surrounding military appropriations and allocations, resulting in fitful program startups and cutbacks. And lastly, the picture was clouded by the highly competitive environment of the postwar 1940's, during which Northrop's bomber versions of the Flying Wing were pitted against the Consolidated-Vultee B-36, and its photo-reconnaissance version against the Hughes F-11 and Republic's RB-12.

UNFINISHED NO. 1 XB-35 ROLLED OUT of Hawthorne's Plant 3 in July 1945. Its one-third flying scale model, the N-9M, is shown covered by tarpaulin immediately above right wingtip.

PROGRESSIVE STAGES of XB-35 and YB-35 assembly in early 1946. Lower photo shows No. 1 XB-35 just prior to official rollout, illustrated clearly flying-wing details with trailing edge controls serving as elevators, rudders, and aerodynamic brakes.

NO. 1 XB-35 being readied for taxi tests, April 1946, at Hawthorne. Left outboard engine is shown driving a six-bladed, co-axial, counter-rotating propeller for special tests and taxiing. This aircraft flew in June in its normal eight-bladed propeller configuration. Troubles with propeller governors and gearboxes plagued the early flight tests of both No. 1 and No. 2 XB-35's.

"OPEN HOUSE" CEREMONY for No. 1 XB-35, May 1946. As of this date, contract commitments called for 2 prototype XB-35 propeller-driven aircraft, 11 service test YB-35 propeller-driven aircraft, and 2 YB-49 jet prototypes – 15 vehicles in all with essentially the same Flying Wing airframe structure.

FIRST FLIGHT OF NO. 1 XB-35, June 25, 1946, from Hawthorne to Muroc Army Air Base (above). No aerodynamic problems were revealed. Max Stanley, who had been flying the one-third scale model N-9M, was at the controls. Pilot Max Stanley, flight engineer O.H. Douglas, and co-pilot Charles Fred Bretcher comprised the crew who were welcomed by Colonel Signa Gilkey, Muroc Commanding Officer, third left (below).

JOHN NORTHROP witnessed test flight of No. 1 piston-engine XB-35 from Muroc (later Edwards AFB) July 3, 1946.

The story of the Flying Wing is best told in two parts. The first segment discusses the aerodynamic features which made it the unique airplane of its time — unique from the standpoint of appearance but proven in principle through the two preceding decades of flight. The second part treats the chronological evolution and the various conversions of the Flying Wing Bomber throughout its changeable history in the 1940's and 1950's.

Northrop's Flying Wing Bomber was the aerodynamicist's closest approach to a practical airplane consisting of a pure supporting surface. It was an airplane in which nearly every exposed portion contributed to lift in return for the drag it created. Virtually all exposed parts were the wing itself. Drag was markedly decreased with the elimination of the fuselage, tail surfaces and exposed engine nacelles. Greater load-carrying, longer range, and increased speed were the direct end result.

Jack Northrop had led the teams that designed, developed and flew a long series of tailless aircraft since he founded the company in 1939. Company engineers were well steeped in the all-wing principle, carrying their studies still further in the wind tunnel. Test data suggested that significantly greater efficiency in the lift-to-drag ratio was theoretically possible for the Flying Wing Bomber. The following considerations were the main benefits:

- The low-drag, high-lift feature meant that in practice, the Flying Wing Bomber might transport a load 25 percent faster or farther than an aircraft of conventional design.

- The simplicity of fabrication presented few structural complications, and this could result in lower cost.

- The weight was more uniformly distributed because the engines, fuel, and cargo were carried in compartments all along the span. A more efficient structure might thereby be designed.

- For ease of loading and unloading, cargo (including bomb stores) could be placed in span-wise compartments, thus shortening turnaround time.

- For military purposes, the Flying Wing Bomber presented a smaller target.

All the Flying Wing Bombers, including the photo-reconnaissance version, were all-metal, tailless, multi-engine airplanes. The 172-foot wings were of the full-cantilever type consisting of riveted aluminum alloy, semimonocoque construction with stressed skin. Wing exterior surfaces were made smooth to reduce aerodynamic drag by the use of flush riveting and flush-type attachments.

The crew area was pressurized for high-altitude flight. Normal crew size varied from 15 specialists in the XB-35 to four in the YRB-49A reconnaissance bomber.

The electrically actuated, fully retractable landing gear was of the tricycle type. Each main gear had dual wheels, 5 feet 6 inches in diameter; the nose gear had a single wheel, 4 feet 8 inches in diameter.

The airplane control system featured the Northrop-developed elevons which combined the functions of ailerons and elevators and worked in either role as needed. Roll was created by the elevons working in opposition; pitch was generated by their working in unison. The elevons were hydraulically actuated.

Small electrically operated "trim flaps," moving segments of the wing located outboard of the elevons, provided aerodynamic trim. The trim flaps thereby minimized the upward deflection of the elevons and permitted them to be deflected over a greater range as elevators.

The rudders consisted of split flaps on the trailing edge at the wingtips. Operated one at a time, they provided directional control; operated together, they produced drag for speed control. On the jet versions, vertical fins were installed on the wings to replace the aerodynamic stabilizing effects of the four propellers and the associated shaft housings on the early versions.

Large split-type landing flaps were located on the inboard portion of the wing and were electrically operated. The elevons and rudder control surfaces were actuated by a dual full-boost hydraulic system. The dual system was composed of two independent sources of hydraulic pressure feeding separate actuators on each surface for safety. Additionally, as backup, an electrically driven hydraulic pump could supply pressure to elevon actuators in case of failure of both normal engine-driven sources. The elevon system also incorporated a force-producing device to provide control forces, or "feel," for the pilot. Although the aerodynamic controls were unconventional, a conventional control column with wheel and rudder pedals was installed in the cockpit.

YB-35, THIRD AND LAST of the piston-engine Flying Wings, takes to the air May 1948. This aircraft was equipped with new single-rotation, four-bladed propellers in place of the original eight-bladed, co-axial, counter-rotating propellers.

Wingtip slots in the wing leading edge near each tip were stall-delaying devices. The slots were provided with hydraulically actuated doors which automatically closed the openings for cruise flight and opened for low speed or whenever the landing gear was extended.

It was in September 1941, following an encouraging visit by Assistant Secretary of War Lovett, General H.H. Arnold, and Major General Oliver P. Echols, that the company submitted preliminary designs for its XB-35 Flying Wing Bomber to Wright Field. It had been postulated out of long military planning that England might possibly be defeated early in World War II. In such an eventuality, a bomber capable of flying nonstop to Axis Europe, and return, would be a necessity. Offering the prospect of 25-percent increased efficiency over conventional bombers, the XB-35 was cast for this role as an alternate to the newly proposed intercontinental XB-36.

The military specifications called for a bomber capable of carrying 10,000 pounds of bombs and flying a 10,000-mile mission with a 15-percent fuel reserve at the end of the flight.

Two XB-35 prototypes were ordered by the Army Air Forces in November 1941. As originally conceived, they were to be four-engine, pusher propeller-driven Flying Wings with a gross weight of over 200,000 pounds. Preliminary design work started in early 1942, but war-time commitments for the production of the Vultee Vengeance and the P-61 Black Widow made it necessary to seek engineering help outside the company. The Glenn L. Martin company was offered a contract to provide technical assistance. In addition to its engineering contract, Martin with its large bomber plant in Omaha, Nebraska, then received a letter of intent for the ultimate production of 200 B-35A's. A short time later, the Otis Elevator company, in a subcontract to Martin, joined the undertaking by providing assistance in the design of the wing structure.

In July 1942, the Mockup Board from Wright Field inspected and approved a Northrop mockup of the full-scale crew nacelle and a portion of the left wing. At this juncture a decision was also reached to build four 60-foot-span, one-third scale flying models (N-9M) to provide development data. These aerodynamic equivalents of the XB-35 also were to serve as trainers for Air

ASSEMBLY OF NOS. 1 & 2 YB-49 at Hawthorne "Crenshaw" plant. No. 1 is at the right, nearing completion.

Force pilots scheduled to fly the 172-foot bomber. The N-9M's were extensively flown and flight tested over the ensuing three years.

By January 1943, a new engineering and assembly plant had been completed at the east end of Northrop Field, and manufacture of parts for the XB-35 immediately started. Fabrication orders for 13 "Service Test" YB-35 bombers were then received to supplement the original XB-35 order. Two of these would later become jet-powered YB-49's and four would later be identified with the designation B-35A, and one with YB-35B.

A variety of development problems unique to pusher-propellers arose to plague the completion of the prototype airplane. The most severe impediment was the late delivery of the eight-bladed, co-axial, counter-rotating propellers and gearboxes, which when they did arrive proved functionally troublesome. As a consequence, the war ended before either of the two prototypes took to the air, and the Martin production program in Nebraska was cancelled.

No. 1 XB-35 took off from Hawthorne on its maiden flight June 25, 1946, after a ground run of only 3,000 feet. The three-man crew was made up of test pilot Max Stanley, co-pilot Charles Fred Bretcher and flight engineer Orva Douglas. Stanley was an experienced hand in the all-wing configuration; he had been flying the N-9M scale model and training Air Force pilots. Forty-four minutes later, the ship put down at Muroc Army Air Base after an uneventful 10,000-foot climb over the Sierra Madre mountains. This flight was successfully completed using the eight-bladed counter-rotating propellers. The second XB-35 was delivered to Muroc on June 26, 1947, in the same propeller configuration.

One of the first known applications of airborne television for flight-test data-recording occurred in the XB-35 program. On the first, second, and third test flights of No. 1 XB-35, a Navy-type television camera system was installed to pick up flight instrument readings. These TV pictures were transmitted to a P-61 Black Widow chase plane. In the P-61, a TV set located at the radar operator's station displayed the readings on the picture tube, and a motion picture camera facing the TV set then recorded the data on film.

YB-49 FEATURES to be noted are: rear crew nacelle with observation bubble, elevon on wing trailing edge (foreground), full landing flaps between crew nacelle and engines, and curved landing flaps under the jet engine nacelles.

SEALING CREW CABIN of YB-49 against leakage. Crew nacelle cabin was pressurized for flights to 45,000 feet. Crew members could easily stand erect with plenty of clearance in this portion of the cabin.

Prior to the first flight of the XB-35, there was a growing probability that the competing B-36 would be chosen as the last piston-engine strategic bomber in Air Force service. In addition, with the mounting interest in jet power, conversion of the YB-35 to jets appeared to be the next logical step. On June 1, 1945, the Air Force approved a Northrop-recommended change for installing sets of eight jet engines in each of two modified YB-35's, redesignated YB-49's. Although the new jet-powered bombers were expected to be significantly faster, the Air Force gambled on continuing production of the remaining 11 YB-35's since they would be longer-ranging and would have the ability to carry a 10,000-pound payload.

On October 21, 1947, the No. 1 YB-49 made its first flight out of Hawthrone with the same crew at the controls as on the XB-35. After a takeoff run of only 3,500 feet, the eight-engine jet reached Muroc in thirty-two minutes. Flight engineer Douglas later reported that since the flaps were not used for the landing, the "only trouble" encountered was slowing the YB-49 for the landing pattern. No. 2 YB-49 was delivered to Muroc January 13, 1948.

VERTICAL FINS provided directional stability and control of the YB-49. Two on each side bracketed clusters of four General Electric J-35-A-5 jet engines.

REAR VIEW OF YB-49. Wing span was 172 feet. The eight General Electric TG-180 (AF designation J-35-A-5) engines developed 32,000 pounds of thrust. Flight could easily be sustained with one or more inoperative. The Flying Wing could carry a 30,000-pound bomb load.

THREE FLYING WINGS at Muroc, January 1948. No. 1 XB-35 in foreground has already changed from its counter-rotating propeller configuration to a single four-bladed propeller. The two jet versions alongside were the only ones of that model built. Captain Glen Edwards (USAF) was to fly one of them five months later during the Phase 2 Acceptance Test series; all tests were essentially completed when the structural limits were exceeded on one final maneuver and the aircraft crashed.

NO. 1 YB-49 on its maiden takeoff from Hawthorne to Muroc, October 21, 1947 (above). Installation of four vertical fins provided directional stability by compensating for the absence of the propeller drive-shaft housings and the side force of the propellers themselves. Four inlets in the leading edge on each side of the wing admitted air to the submerged engines. The No. 1 YB-49 is shown taking off on a later flight test (below).

YB-49 IN FLIGHT. *Clean surface of upper wing was interrupted by air fences acting as physical barriers to prevent spanwise flow of boundary layer. The use of wing twist and mechanical slots which were sealed in high-speed flight and opened for low-speed condition were incorporated to delay stalls at higher angles of attack.*

Early YB-49 flight testing turned up inadequate rates of yaw oscillation damping, a condition that is vital for a stable bombing platform. As a corrective measure, a Minneapolis Honeywell Electronic Yaw Stabilization System, or "Little Herbert," was installed. This bombing autopilot made the YB-49 into a very stable platform.

Unsolved propeller governor and gearbox problems continued to dog the original two XB-35's to such an extent that the eight-bladed, counter-rotating propellers were replaced, as an interim measure, by four-bladed, single-rotation propellers of larger diameters. As expected, the new propellers were unable to utilize full engine power output. The penalties in performance were judged acceptable, while the company tried to work out the problems with the accessory manufacturers and the Air Force. All technical participants in the XB-35 project eventually agreed, however, that the dual rotation propellers had to be considered a necessity if the B-35's were to attain complete success.

Meanwhile, the two 500-mph class YB-49's continued flight testing at Muroc, consistently exceeding engineering performance forecasts. Air Force project officers declared the YB-49's to be among the "cleanest, most trouble-free and most ready to fly new bombers ever received from aircraft contractors." After flying the YB-49, General Roger M. Ramey, Commander, 8th Air Force, and one of the country's experts on heavy bombardment aircraft, described the airplane as "the fastest bomber I have ever flown," and "a fine ship with a real future."

Two years of testing the XB-35's and YB-49's at Muroc had convinced the Army Air Forces of the advantages of the all-wing bomber configuration. They had demonstrated outstanding performance capabilities in range, speed, and weight lifting. In January 1948, the Air Force publicly announced that the YB-49 was the longest-ranged jet aircraft in the world. On May 15, 1948, the third B-35 (a YB-35 Service Test model) was flown to the desert air base. Of 15 Flying Wing Bombers it was the fifth to join the Muroc fleet. Then an unfortunate incident in the program occurred. The Air Force was conducting a series of Phase 2 Acceptance tests with No. 2 YB-49. The date was June 5, 1948. The flight pattern was just north of Muroc. Quite suddenly, and out of range of official observers, the plane crashed after completing a number of scheduled maximum forward center-of-gravity tests. Post-crash investigation revealed that symmetrical structural failures had occurred in both outer wings, suggesting excessive uniform upward loading at the time of failure. The two outer wing sections had broken free of the main center section which housed the flight crew. All of the five-man crew were killed. Muroc was later renamed *Edwards Air Force Base* in honor of Captain Glen Edwards, flight commander of the YB-49.

Notwithstanding the unfortunate accident, the Air Force announced five days later its decision to put the unconventional jet-powered Flying Wing into production. The need for strategic reconnaissance bomber was paramount. Thirty modified versions of the YB-49 were ordered. These airplanes were designated RB-49A. Late in July 1948, the company announced that it was completing negotiations with Consolidated Vultee Aircraft in Texas to subcontract the major portion of 29 of the 30 RB-49A airplanes ordered by the Air Force. One RB-49A was to be built at Hawthorne by Northrop. Concerning the new RB-49A production arrangements, Vice President and General Manager Claude N. Monson pointed out that the Air Force had been seeking larger production facilities than were then available at Northrop Field for the production of the large Wings, and that the spacious bomber plant at Fort Worth was ideally suitable. Under terms of the subcontract with Consolidated Vultee, Northrop would direct and supervise the engineering, tool design and planning, and would be the prime contractor. Warren G. Knieriem was appointed to manage all Northrop activities at Fort Worth.

Although the exact cause of the wing failure was never determined, it was believed that the accident had been due to an excessive positive acceleration as would occur in a severe gust, pull-up, or pitch-up. Because the YB-49 was such a "clean" airplane, it would accelerate very rapidly, and the design limits or "red-line" speed might easily have been exceeded in the diving recovery from a test stall, or during a high-speed descent back to base. Later wind tunnel tests demonstrated that none of the Flying Wing Bomber configurations, including the YB-49, would tumble from any conceivable flight attitude.

Continued success with No. 1 YB-49 also prompted the Air Force to disclose, in November 1948, a plan whereby Northrop would convert the remaining 10 YB-35's to a new jet-powered configuration designated RB-35B. One of the 10 strategic reconnaissance bombers would be used as a static test airplane.

JACK NORTHROP (fourth from left) is taken on a routine test flight by pilot Max Stanley (left) in No. 1 YB-49 jet Flying Wing from Muroc in January 1948.

FULL-SIZE YB-49 CREW. Special test flight took this crew from Muroc on a run up inland California to Sacramento and return via San Francisco and the coast, September 18, 1948. (Left to right) Don Swift (tech rep engineer), Frank Schroeder (assistant flight engineer), Max R. Stanley (pilot), Stan Erbeck (assistant project engineer), O.H. Douglas (flight engineer), Charles Tucker (co-pilot), Colonel Gates (Wright Field observer), Roy Wolford (photographer).

AT THE TIME this photograph was taken at Hawthorne in late 1948, a USAF decision had been made to convert ten of the piston-engine Flying Wings (above) to an all-jet configuration.

Again the suddenness of change, so typical of the times under consideration, made itself felt. Facing sharp budgetary reductions and reassessing its own strategic requirements, the Air Force dissolved the Northrop-Consolidated Vultee arrangement. Likewise, the program for the conversion of 10 YB-35's to RB-35B's at Hawthorne was cancelled. These cancellations were intended to provide extra funds for B-36 and RB-36 bombers, as well as B-50 modifications, so that a long-range strategic force could be put into combat readiness in the shortest time possible.

As if in one last demonstration of its true capabilities, No. 1 YB-49 flew non-stop from Edwards Air Force Base to Andrews Air Force Base, Washington, D.C., in 4 hours, 25 minutes early in 1949. The distance of 2,258 miles was covered at an average speed of 511 mph. Unfortunately, this same airplane was destroyed one year later (March 15, 1950) during an excessively high-speed turn while taxiing on the runway at Edwards Air Force Base. The nose gear collapsed, flipping the

airplane completely over. All of the crew escaped unharmed.

The Air Force continued to keep the Flying Wing program alive, primarily because of the outstanding flight performance demonstrated by the two jet-powered YB-49's over a period of 24 months. It entertained a whole series of conversions from the YB-35 airframes to jet configurations.

The most unusual of the new designs was a combination of six jet engines and one gas turbine engine driving a propeller. This airplane, designated EB-35B, was to be an aerial "test bed" for the powerful XT-37 Turbodyne engine which had been sponsored and developed by Northrop since 1939. In the original proposed design concept, a single Turbodyne engine was to be mounted slightly to the left of center of the airplane, driving a large dual-rotation pusher propeller. The finalized design incorporated two Turbodynes, one on each side of the centerline, in addition to the six jet engines.

AS EARLY AS 1948, the Flying Wing Bomber in either the propeller or jet configuration was envisioned as a passenger and cargo carrier. Capable of accommodating as many as 80 passengers comfortably seated inside the wing with "window views" through the leading and trailing edge structures, the Flying Wing was hailed as "the airliner of tomorrow." Jerry Fairbanks, Inc. of Hollywood, California, made a short film highlighting the possibility of a 100-ton passenger-cargo transport in the 400- to 500-mph class.

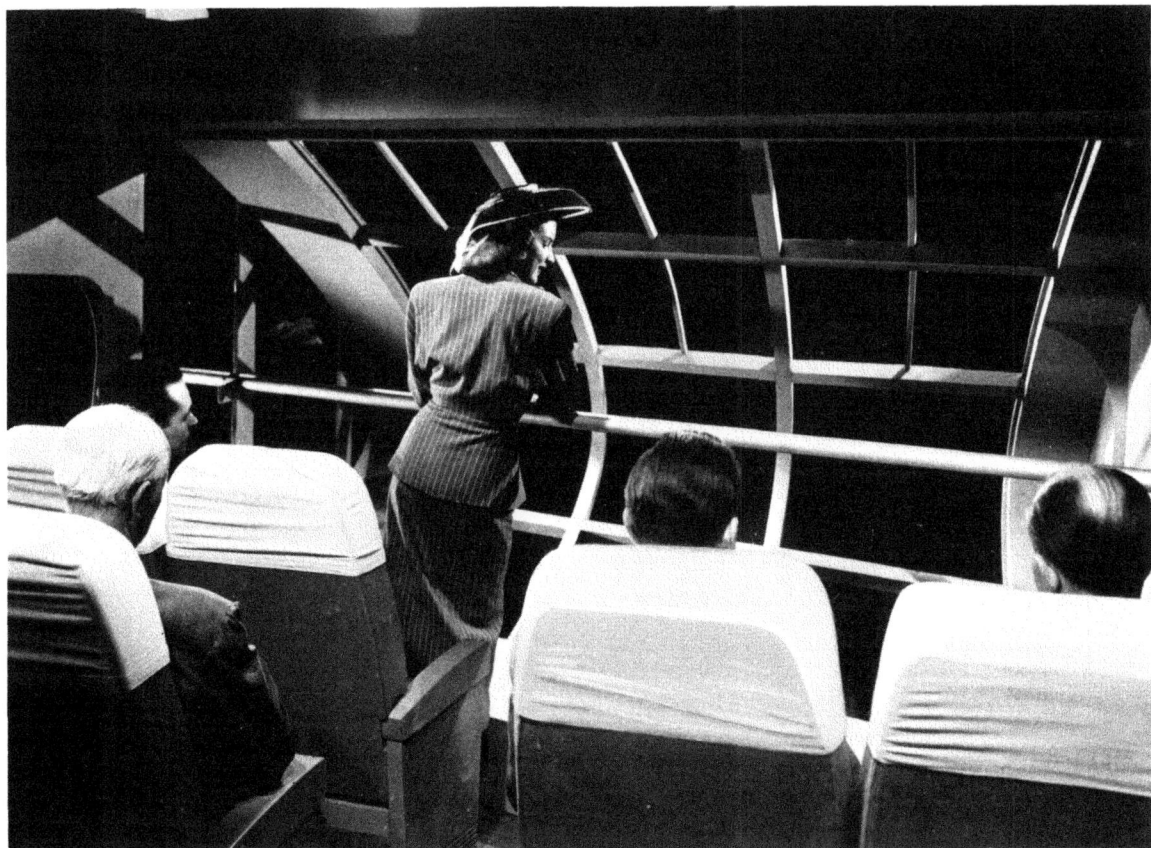

Six other YB-35's also were to be converted to a six-turbojet configuration. Four engines were to be buried in the wing and two suspended below the wing in streamlined pods. These airplanes were designated YB-35B's, earmarked for use in "advanced test work for Flying Wing-type airplanes." The eighth YB-35 to be converted was designated YRB-49A configured as above. This airplane, however, was to be equipped with special reconnaissance equipment. Four of the remaining piston-powered YB-35's were to be set aside to supply spare parts for the extensive new flight program planned for the eight converted YB-35's.

On October 28, 1949, the Air Force cancelled the major part of the YB-35 conversion program. The only portion of the contract left intact covered the completion and flight test of the single YRB-49A six-jet airplane. The rest of the YB-35's were ordered scrapped.

During the early months of 1950, the company proposed a variety of large Flying Wing concepts, none of which proved saleable. Some of these variations included a four-turboprop bomber, an escort fighter, the "Cargo Pack," and a Boundary Layer Control Flying Wing. In the same period, the single YRB-49A was completed and equipped with the latest long-range photo-reconnaissance equipment. On May 4, 1950, the YRB-49A made its first flight from Hawthorne to Edwards Air Force Base. At Edwards it began a series of flight tests, with emphasis on the photo-reconnaissance mission. In early 1951, the YRB-49A was flown to the Northrop facility at the Ontario International Airport where it was placed in dead storage. In October 1953, this last of the large Flying Wings was ordered scrapped by the Air Force.

29861-109 NORTHROP
PROGRESS REPORT; AC21721, SHIPS
N-1497, N-1496, AND N-1498, VIEW
OF WORK BAY LOOKING NORTH,
27 OCTOBER 1949, YB-35B, YRB-49A,
YB-35B

LAST OF THE MODEL CHANGES. In late 1949, the Air Force commissioned the last of the YB-35 airframe conversions. Ship in the foreground was being modified to carry two Northrop-developed Turbodyne engines driving rear-mounted propellers, plus six jet engines – four in the wing, and two externally mounted below the wing; it was designated EB-35B. Ship in the middle had the same six-jet-engine configuration; it was designated YRB-49A. Ship in the background was similarly jet-equipped; it was designated YB-35B. Only the YRB-49A was to fly after major portions of the Flying Wing program were cancelled on October 28, 1949.

TEST BED FOR NORTHROP TURBODYNES. The
EB-35B was configured to carry two of the 10,000-hp
Turbodyne engines driving conventional propellers, as
well as four jet engines within the wing and two mounted
on pylons underneath the wing.

CAMERA EQUIPMENT inside the centerline crew
nacelle of the YRB-49A (February 1950). Only one
YRB-49A reconnaissance bomber was completed and
flown during the early Fifties.

FAIRED RADOME INSTALLATION on the underside of the crew nacelle characterized the YRB-49A. The aircraft also
carried extensive camera equipment.

YRB-49A, SIXTH AND LAST OF FLYING WINGS to fly. A reconnaissance bomber of long-range (9,000 miles) capability, it carried two of its six jet engines (Allison J-35-A-19's) externally to allow for a greater fuel capacity within the wing structure. Each engine developed 5,000 pounds of thrust.

FLYING WING BOMBER RECORD

MODEL	FUNCTION	ENGINE	NUMBER ORIGINALLY ORDERED	NUMBER STARTED OR COMPLETED*	NUMBER FLOWN	FIRST FLIGHT DATE	REMARKS
XB-35	BOMBER	4-PISTON (BURIED)	2	2	2	6-25-46 6-26-47	
YB-35	BOMBER	4-PISTON (BURIED)	13	6	3	5-15-48	5 YB-35's BECAME B-35A
B-35A	BOMBER	4-PISTON (BURIED)	205	5	—	—	GLENN L. MARTIN 200 A/C
YB-49	BOMBER	8-JET (BURIED)	2	2	2	10-21-47 1-13-48	CONVERTED FROM YB-35
RB-49A	RECON- NAISSANCE	8-JET (6 BURIED/ 2 POD)	30	—	—	—	CONSOLIDATED- VULTEE 29 A/C
RB-35B	RECON- NAISSANCE	6-JET (4 BURIED/ 2 POD)	10	10	—	—	CONVERTED FROM YB-35
EB-35B	TURBODYNE TEST BED	6-JET/ 2-TURBODYNE (6 BURIED/ 2 POD)	1	1	—	—	CONVERTED FROM YB-35A
YB-35B	TEST	6-JET (4 BURIED/ 2 POD)	6	1	—	—	CONVERTED FROM YB-35
YRB-49A	RECON- NAISSANCE	6-JET (4 BURIED/ 2 POD)	1	1	1	5-04-50	CONVERTED FROM YB-35
TOTAL			270	28*	8		

*15 BASIC AIRFRAMES MANUFACTURED TOTAL

XB-35/YB-35

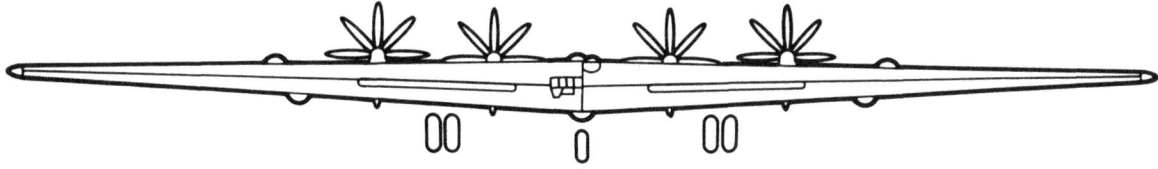

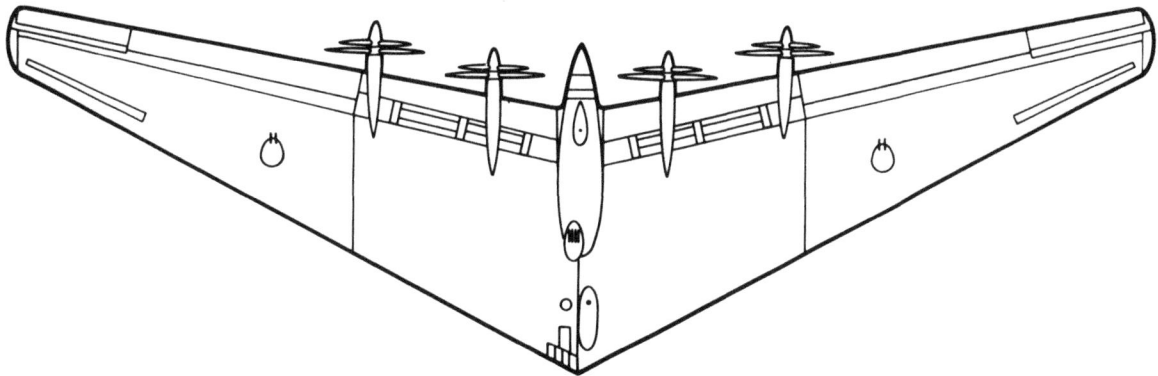

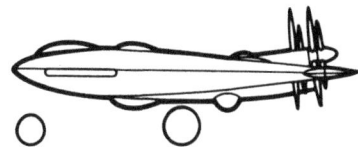

SPECIFICATIONS

WING SPAN . . . . .172 FT.

OVERALL LENGTH . . . . .53 FT., 1 IN.

OVERALL HEIGHT . . . . .20 FT.

WING AREA . . . . .4,000 SQ. FT.

TAKEOFF WEIGHT . . . . .209,000 LB

SPEED-MAXIMUM . . . . .391 MPH

SPEED-CRUISING . . . . .240 MPH

RANGE . . . . .10,000 MILES

SERVICE CEILING . . . . .40,000 FT.

POWER — (4) P&W WASP MAJOR, 3,000-HP MAX —
    (2) R-4360-17, AND (2) R-4360-21; HAMILTON
    STANDARD CONSTANT SPEED,
    FULL-FEATHERING, DUAL ROTATION,
    8-BLADED PROPS

ARMAMENT — 10,000-LB BOMB LOAD, (7) GUN TURRETS
    FOR (20) 50-CAL MACHINE GUNS

YB-49

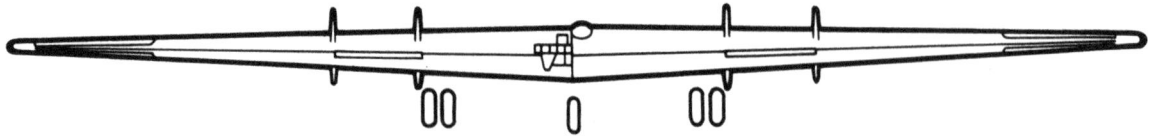

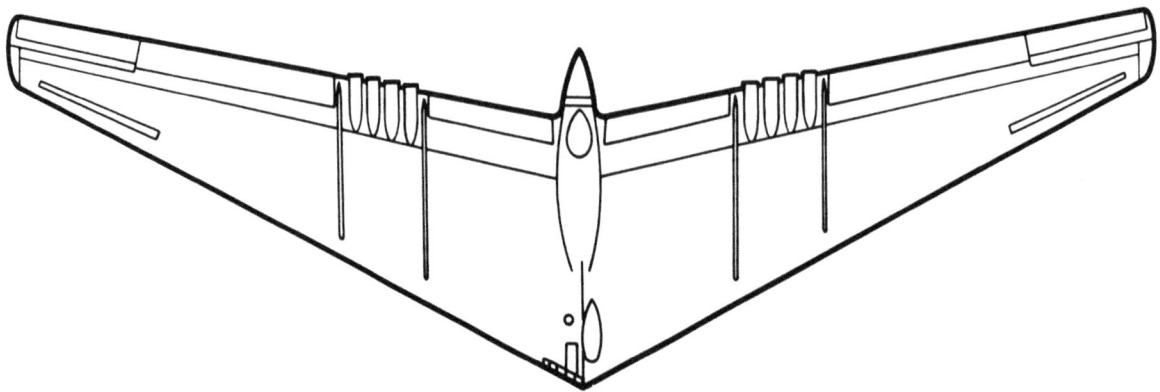

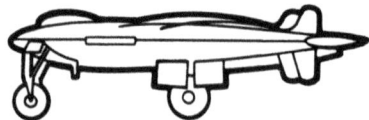

SPECIFICATIONS

WING SPAN . . . . .172 FT.

OVERALL LENGTH . . . . .53 FT., 1 IN.

OVERALL HEIGHT . . . . .15 FT., 2 IN.

WING AREA . . . . .4,000 SQ. FT.

TAKEOFF WEIGHT . . . . .196,193 LB

SPEED-MAXIMUM . . . . .493 MPH

SPEED-CRUISING . . . . .419 MPH

RANGE . . . . .3,155 MILES

SERVICE CEILING . . . . .40,700 FT.

POWER — (8) TURBOJET, ALLISON J-35-A-15, 4,000-LB
            THRUST

ARMAMENT — 16,000-LB BOMB LOAD

YRB-49A

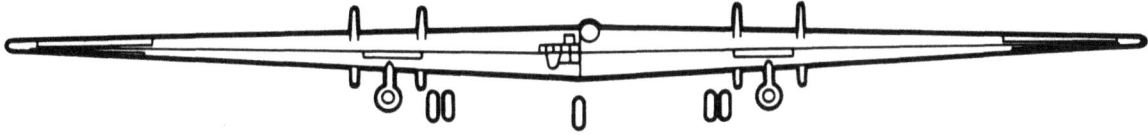

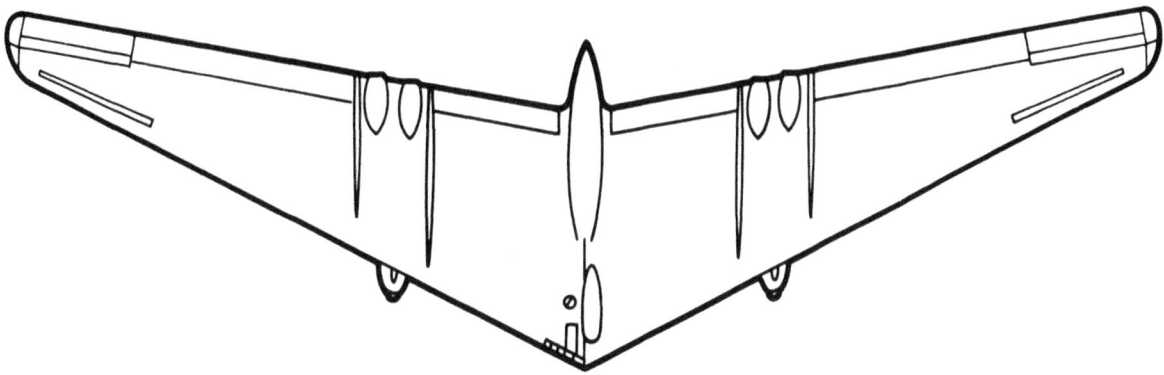

SPECIFICATIONS

WING SPAN . . . . .172 FT.

OVERALL LENGTH . . . . .53 FT., 1 IN.

OVERALL HEIGHT . . . . .20 FT.

WING AREA . . . . .4,000 SQ. FT.

TAKEOFF WEIGHT . . . . .206,000 LB

SPEED-MAXIMUM . . . . .440 MPH

SPEED-CRUISING . . . . .392 MPH

RANGE . . . . .2,625 MILES

SERVICE CEILING . . . . .42,600 FT.

POWER — (6) TURBOJET, ALLISON J-35-A-19, 5,600-LB
         THRUST

ARMAMENT — (6) 188-LB T-89 FLASH BOMBS

F-15 REPORTER

Most military aircraft production lines in the U.S. were brought to an abrupt halt after V-E Day. Those surviving met the same fate after V-J Day. One noteworthy exception was the Northrop F-15 Reporter, a photo-reconnaissance derivative of the P-61. The Reporter was the first airplane to continue in quantity production at Hawthorne after cessation of hostilities.

The Reporter contract was one of the few warplane commitments considered of sufficient value to be retained in peacetime service. The military visualized such potential uses as aerial mapping in soil erosion control programs and in geological research. In addition, a large-scale global mapping program was considered a possibility.

The original rationale for the F-15 was established a few months before the end of the war, when a long-range, photo-reconnaissance airplane was quickly needed by the Allied Forces to fix the locations and extent of Japanese home island fortifications and war industries. It was essentially an outgrowth of the earlier Escort Fighter recommendations by John Myers, Northrop's former chief of test pilots and at the time a special field representative in the South Pacific. The F-15 then may be considered a redesign of the experimental XP-61E escort fighter into an unarmed, camera-equipped airplane.

The Reporter design gained quick acceptance by the AAF in view of its excellent performance prospects and the ready availability of basic P-61 airframes. As a result, a requirement was established for 320 F-15 Reporters. An initial order for 175 airplanes was awarded to Northrop by the AAF in June 1945, even before the first prototype had been flown.

RANGE OF THE F-15 exceeded 4,000 miles with the addition of external fuel tanks. The aircraft shown above was one of two prototypes. This one was a modified P-61C, as distinguished by the turbo supercharger air intakes underneath the engines. The other prototype was a refurbished version of the experimental XP-61E day fighter.

114

MODIFIED P-61C INTO XF-15. Extensive rework in forward and central fuselage sections was required to make the conversion from the Black Widow night fighter configuration to a long-range photo-reconnaissance capability.

BELIEVED LARGEST PLEXIGLAS BUBBLE BLOWN. F-15 canopy slid fore and aft on tracks, afforded two crew members 360-degree vision.

The prototype XF-15 was a conversion of one of the experimental escort fighter airframes (XP-61E). The pre-production XF-15A was a modified P-61C. Only 36 F-15A airplanes were constructed from partially completed P-61C airframes before unexpected contract termination in 1947.

The basic aerodynamic and structural design characteristics of the F-15 were virtually identical to the P-61 series of night fighters. However, like the experimental XP-61E escort fighter, the photo-reconnaissance version carried only a crew of two housed under a large bubble-type canopy which slid fore and aft on tracks. The two-man crew consisted of pilot and co-pilot-navigator.

Either crew member could pilot the airplane or operate the cameras. Each seat could be reclined so that, alternately, the pilots could rest during fatigue-inducing missions of several hours duration. The F-15's long range was made possible by its large fuel capacity. In addition to the normal wing tanks, it carried a 500-gallon fuel tank located just aft of the rear crew member in the crew nacelle. Drop tanks could be installed for extended range.

In place of the forward guns featured on the P-61E, a special camera nose was installed on the F-15. As many as six cameras could be mounted in 24 optional arrangements, with the possibility of installing 17 different types of cameras.

MODIFIED NOSE on F-15 incorporated camera-viewing ports straight ahead, to the sides, and straight down.

F-15 MOVABLE, HINGED NOSE SECTION permitted ease of access for camera installation in a number of different configurations.

F-15

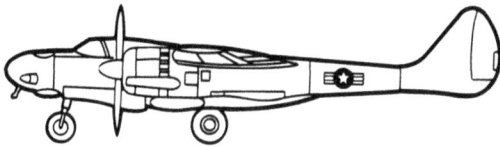

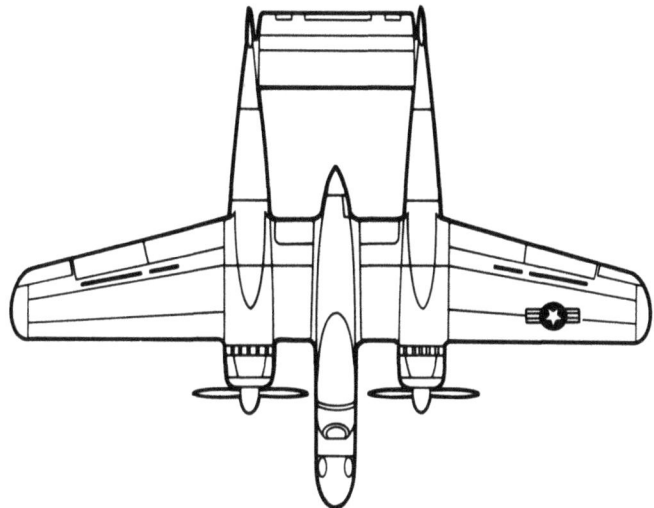

SPECIFICATIONS

WING SPAN	66 FT.
OVERALL LENGTH	50 FT., 4 IN.
OVERALL HEIGHT	14 FT., 2 IN.
WING AREA	662 SQ. FT.
TAKEOFF WEIGHT	32,190 LB
SPEED-MAXIMUM	440 MPH
SPEED-CRUISING	315 MPH
RANGE	4,000 MILES
SERVICE CEILING	41,000 FT.

POWER — (2) P&W R-2800-73, 2,800 HP
    (2) CURTIS ELECTRIC PROPS

N-23 PIONEER

The Pioneer trimotor passenger/cargo transport was the company's first postwar design for civilian use. The N-23 featured unusually short takeoffs and landings with economy of operation and minimum maintenance cost. It was designed and built with company funding for the express purpose of providing profitable air transportation to those areas of the world which, because of lack of modern airport facilities, had been denied any kind of air service. Industrial surveys concluded large portions of Central and South America, Alaska, Canada, China, and Africa to be likely candidates.

Unfortunately the Pioneer arrived on the market in competition with a flood of surplus World War II transports, and as a result it never went into production. Only one prototype was built. However, the basic N-23 design emerged later in an enlarged version called the C-125 Raider. The Raider was built for the U.S. Air Force as both an Assault Transport and an Arctic Rescue airplane.

The Pioneer made its first flight on December 21, 1946 at Hawthorne Municipal Airport. Max Stanley was the test pilot. After a flight of approximately 90 minutes, Stanley reported that the N-23 exhibited outstanding low-speed flight characteristics which he attributed in part to the full-span flaps and retractable ailerons that had been so successfully used on the P-61 night fighter. He also was impressed by the very soft landing which resulted from the oversized shock absorbers installed in the fixed "rough field" landing gear.

N-23 PIONEER in flight over Los Angeles. Full-span flaps and retractable ailerons, employed successfully on the P-61, gave transport unusual flexibility of performance.

SHORT TAKEOFF of the prototype N-23 Pioneer proved it could clear the runway well in front of the 500-foot marker. In these 1947 tests, John Myers actually took off in less than 400 feet from Hawthorne Field.

UNPAVED AIRSTRIP at Conejo Valley presented no difficulty to the trimotor Pioneer. John Myers, Vice President and Director of Sales, flew the airplane into and out of many Southern California fields normally used only by small personal craft.

119

Early in the flight tests, the Pioneer proved a capability for takeoff and climb on two engines. John Myers, Vice President and Director of Sales, flew the Pioneer into and out of many of the small Southern California airports normally adequate only for small personal airplanes. In short-field tests at sea level, the Pioneer took off in less than 400 feet and consistently landed in 600 feet with a 23,000-pound gross weight.

As a feeder or local service airplane, the Pioneer would normally be fitted with seats for up to 36 passengers, less cargo. As a cargo or "bush" airplane, the Pioneer could handle five tons of cargo with a maximum volume of 1,519 cubic feet. This meant a high percentage of useful load to gross weight (42%) yielding a low cost-per ton-mile and assuring a high earning potential.

A capacious cargo entrance was located near the center of gravity so that heavy objects did not need to be moved inside the airplane after loading. A passenger door was provided at the aft end of the cabin to facilitate simultaneous loading or unloading of passengers and cargo. A hatch in the underside of the nose permitted the loading of long objects such as pipe and timber, up to 36 feet in length. Quick-change fittings on the cabin floor were arranged so that seats might be removed and cargo hold-down rings installed within a few minutes. Hoist fittings could be provided in the cabin and on the wing to facilitate the loading of heavy objects where no ground equipment was available.

The N-23 airframe was of conventional riveted aluminum alloy (Alclad), stressed-skin, semi-monocoque construction. The extremely rugged non-retractable landing gear was of the three-point "tail wheel" design to help in executing short, rough field landings. For operation on extremely soft fields, provisions were made for the installation of dual main landing gear wheels. With this arrangement, an extra wheel and axle could be installed on the main strut in a few minutes. Late in the flight test program a strut was added as a brace between the horizontal stabilizers and the vertical stabilizer (fin).

Ready access panels were fitted over all areas requiring frequent inspection or maintenance. As one example, the entire leading edge of the wing was hinged to permit easy access to control cables, plumbing and wiring which were all routed through this area. The engine accessory cowlings similarly opened like an automobile hood. To minimize the requirement for spare parts, the maximum number of airframe components were made identical. Engine installations, horizontal stabilizers, and elevators were among the many items in this category.

WOODEN MOCKUP of N-23 Pioneer was fabricated in 1946 as Northrop's first post-World War II design venture into the commercial transport market.

TWO-PLACE COCKPIT featured more-than-adequate room and excellent pilot visibility. Windshield was specially designed to clear rain quickly, a hazard in tropical countries for which the Pioneer was developed.

The wings and empennage were designed for thermal (hot air) anti-icing. Four 250-gallon, bladder-type fuel cells were mounted in the inner wing structure between the 10% and 30% spars. The Pioneer was powered by three Wright Cyclone 744C7BA2 engines, each rated at 800 hp for takeoff. The Cyclones turned Hamilton Standard constant-speed, two-bladed propellers with a diameter of 9 feet, 1 inch. Each power plant installation was identical for ease of maintenance or replacement. Optional power plants included the completely overhauled, military surplus Pratt & Whitney S3H1 (R1340) engines as a low-cost alternative to the Wrights. The Pratt & Whitneys were rated at 600 hp for takeoff; calculated performance of the airplane was con-

sequently lower. The engine cowling was of the NACA full cowl type with two electrically actuated cowl flaps on the lower trailing edge of each engine cowl.

The prototype N-23 was destroyed after approximately one year of test flying. An experimental "scabbed-on" dorsal fin broke loose during yaw tests, severely damaging the airplane's tail surfaces. Although L.A. "Slim" Perrett, test pilot, managed to control the airplane long enough for flight test engineers John Atkinson and Eustace Hetzel to parachute to safety, he was obliged to jump last, too late to save himself.

WIDE STANCE AND OVERSIZED SHOCK ABSORBERS of the fixed landing gear made for soft landings in rough terrain.

N-23

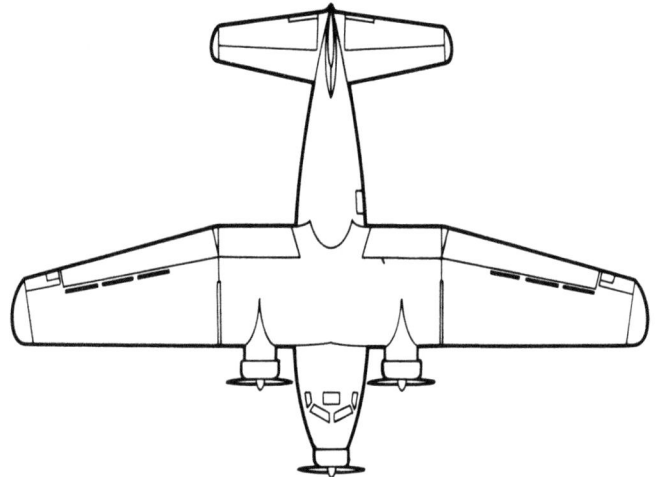

SPECIFICATIONS

WING SPAN . . . . .85 FT.

OVERALL LENGTH . . . . .60 FT., 7 IN.

OVERALL HEIGHT . . . . .17 FT., 10 IN.

WING AREA . . . . .1,100 SQ. FT.

TAKEOFF WEIGHT . . . . .25,000 LB

SPEED-MAXIMUM . . . . .193 MPH

SPEED-CRUISING . . . . .150 MPH

RANGE . . . . .1,750 MILES

SERVICE CEILING . . . . .21,000 FT.

POWER — (3) WRIGHT 744C7BA2 AIR COOLED RADIAL,
EACH RATED @ 800 HP, HAMILTON STANDARD
PROPELLERS

C-125 RAIDER

Designed to operate from improvised airstrips as airborne assault vehicles and rescue aircraft, the trimotor C-125 (Northrop designation N-32) was essentially a military development of the civilian N-23 Pioneer.

Expanding on the applications demonstrated in over a year of rigorous flight testing with the Pioneer, the C-125 incorporated a number of additional features. The more significant augmentations included increased cargo space; an underfuselage ramp/cargo door; larger wings with full-span double-slotted flaps and retractable spoiler-type ailerons plus small conventional ailerons for pilot "feel"; larger engines with reversible-thrust propellers; and JATO boosters for very short takeoff.

A $5.5 million contract was awarded to the company in March 1948 for the production of 23 aircraft. Thirteen of the order were to be equipped as Assault Transports for troop training (designated C-125A), and 10 were to be prepared as Arctic Rescue aircraft (designated C-125B). Both airframes were essentially identical except for internal equipment.

The C-125 made its first flight on August 1, 1949, at Hawthorne Field. Max Stanley was the test pilot on the successful 32-minute flight over the Pacific Coast area between San Pedro and Santa Monica. Shortly after the first flight, the prototype was prepared to start the Civil Aeronautics Administration Preliminary Type Certification Board inspections. These inspections were intended to certify the C-125 for future civilian transport use. However, certification was never completed.

The concept of the Assault Transport was new to the Air Force. The 13 C-125A's equipped for this task were to be used in a test program to evaluate their capability for establishing "air heads" — a job previously performed by gliders. Capable of landing with a full load in virtually the same space required for assault gliders, the new short-field C-125A's were expected to eliminate many of the difficulties encountered with assault gliders for establishing bases of operation in enemy territory. Unlike gliders which were committed to land once their tow ropes were dropped, the new C-125A's permitted assault pilots to select the most advantageous landing areas. When cargo or troops were discharged, the C-125 would be able to return to its base of operations. A further extension of the "assault" function was the C-125A performing as an Escape and Evacuation Transport.

LOADED FOR BASIC MISSION C-125B Raider had a cruising altitude of 10,000 feet and total flight time of 9 hours. Range was 1,260 nautical miles.

JATO THRUST of six units (equivalent to 6,000 pounds) permitted takeoff in less than 500 feet. Fully loaded, the C-125 Raider weighed 40,900 pounds.

EARLIER AND LATER ASSEMBLY. (Above) Progressive stages from fabrication of aluminum fuselage shell. (Below) Wing carrythrough center section with control flaps, landing gear, and engine installation.

FRONT AND REAR ASPECTS OF THE C-125 (above and below, respectively). Extra wheel-axle assemblies could be attached to the main landing gear by a simple jacking operation. The dual-wheel arrangement facilitated negotiation into and out of soft-surface fields.

The large rectangular fuselage of the C-125 could accommodate up to 32 troops or 12,000 pounds of cargo, or any combination of the two conditions. Recessed tiedown fittings were installed for a wide variety of loads. The cargo could be quick-loaded or unloaded through the 9-foot by 6½-foot underfuselage ramp door. This ramp, in conjunction with the unique tail wheel strut which also performed as a jack to raise the rear of the airplane off the ground, permitted handling of mobile and bulky equipment. A "door-within-a-door" formed a part of the loading ramp in its flight position and served for aerial drops of cargo and paratroops.

As on the Pioneer, the extremely rugged nonretractable landing gear was of the three-point, "tail wheel" design to help in executing short, rough field takeoffs and landings. The main gear struts were designed to accommodate extra wheel-axle units for operation from soft-surface fields. This dual-wheel arrangement ensured very low "footprint" pressure. Additionally, for missions of extremely long range, an attachment was provided on the landing gear strut so that the aircraft could be air-towed.

Although intended for use primarily on the Arctic Rescue version (C-125B), fittings came with all C-125's for specially designed, hydraulically retractable wheel-skis or a pair of floats (pontoons) for water operations. The Arctic Rescue configuration also carried a full set of navigation and communications equipment necessary for remote operations.

Like the Pioneer, the C-125 airframe was of conventional riveted aluminum alloy, stressed skin, semimonocoque construction. Ready-access panels were fitted over all areas requiring frequent inspection or maintenance. The entire leading edge of the wing was hinged to permit easy access to control cables, plumbing, and wiring which were routed through this area. The hinged leading edges adjacent to the wing-mounted engine nacelles also served as work platforms. Engine cowlings were hinged and secured with trunk-type fasteners for quick access, and all three power plant packages were interchangeable.

ACCESSIBILITY was built into all parts of the aircraft. Wing leading edges were hinged to expose cables, plumbing, and wiring. Leading edges adjacent to wing engine nacelles served as work platforms. Engine cowlings opened like automobile hoods.

LOADING THE RAIDER was simplified by the ramp door and hydraulically jacking up the tail wheel strut to provide clearance for vehicles and bulky cargo. Here L-5 airplane fuselage presents no problem.

FULL-SPAN FLAPS, extending the length of each wing, were made possible by the use of retractable ailerons, a feature introduced on the P-61 Black Widow. This arrangement, plus reversible-thrust propellers, allowed landings under 400 feet.

FIVE OF THE TWENTY-THREE RAIDERS produced for the Air Force. Numbers 620, 621, and 622 were C-125B's earmarked for the Air Rescue Service. In addition to the normal flight crew of pilot and co-pilot, the Arctic Rescue configuration contained equipment for navigator and radio operator.

INTERIOR VIEW. Troops and personnel carrier were normal cargo complements of the C-125A Assault Transport.

The wings consisted of five panel assemblies: a center section, two outer wing panels, and two wingtips. A total of 1,800 gallons of fuel was carried in four tanks. Two 500-gallon fuel cells were mounted in the wing center section, one behind each wing-mounted engine, and two 400-gallon fuel cells were mounted inboard in the outer wing panels.

A leading edge thermal anti-icing system consisting of four manifolded surface combustion heaters was installed to prevent ice formation on wing and tail surfaces. Cockpit windows and cargo hold were heated with warm air supplied by two additional heaters. Propellers were protected against ice formation by electrical resistance heating.

The C-125 was powered by three Wright Cyclone WAC-666C (R-1820-99) air-cooled radial engines, each rated at 1,200 hp for takeoff. The Cyclones drove Cur-

tiss Electric constant-speed, full-feathering, reversible, three-bladed propellers with a diameter of 12 feet, 2 inches. The C-125 was capable of takeoff and climb on two of its three engines. One optional power plant was the Wright Cyclone R-1810-101 rated at 1,525 hp for takeoff.

For very short-field takeoffs, the Wright engines were supplemented with six JATO units (three on each side), each rated at 1,000 pounds thrust for a few seconds. This boost in power permitted the C-125 to take off in less than 500 feet, clearing a 50-foot obstacle in less than 1,000 feet. For short field landings, the reversible-thrust propellers kept landing runs as short as 330 feet.

The last of the 23 C-125 Raiders was delivered to the Air Force by the end of 1950.

C-125A/B

SPECIFICATIONS

WING SPAN	86 FT., 6 IN.
OVERALL LENGTH	67 FT., 1 IN.
OVERALL HEIGHT	23 FT., 1 IN.
WING AREA	1,131 SQ. FT.
TAKEOFF WEIGHT	40,900 LB
SPEED-MAXIMUM	207 MPH
SPEED-CRUISING	171 MPH
RANGE	1,856 MILES
SERVICE CEILING	12,200 FT.

POWER — (3) WRIGHT CYCLONE R-1820-99, 1,200 HP
(3) CURTISS ELECTRIC PROPELLERS,
CONSTANT SPEED, FULL-FEATHERING,
REVERSIBLE

N-69/SM-62 SNARK

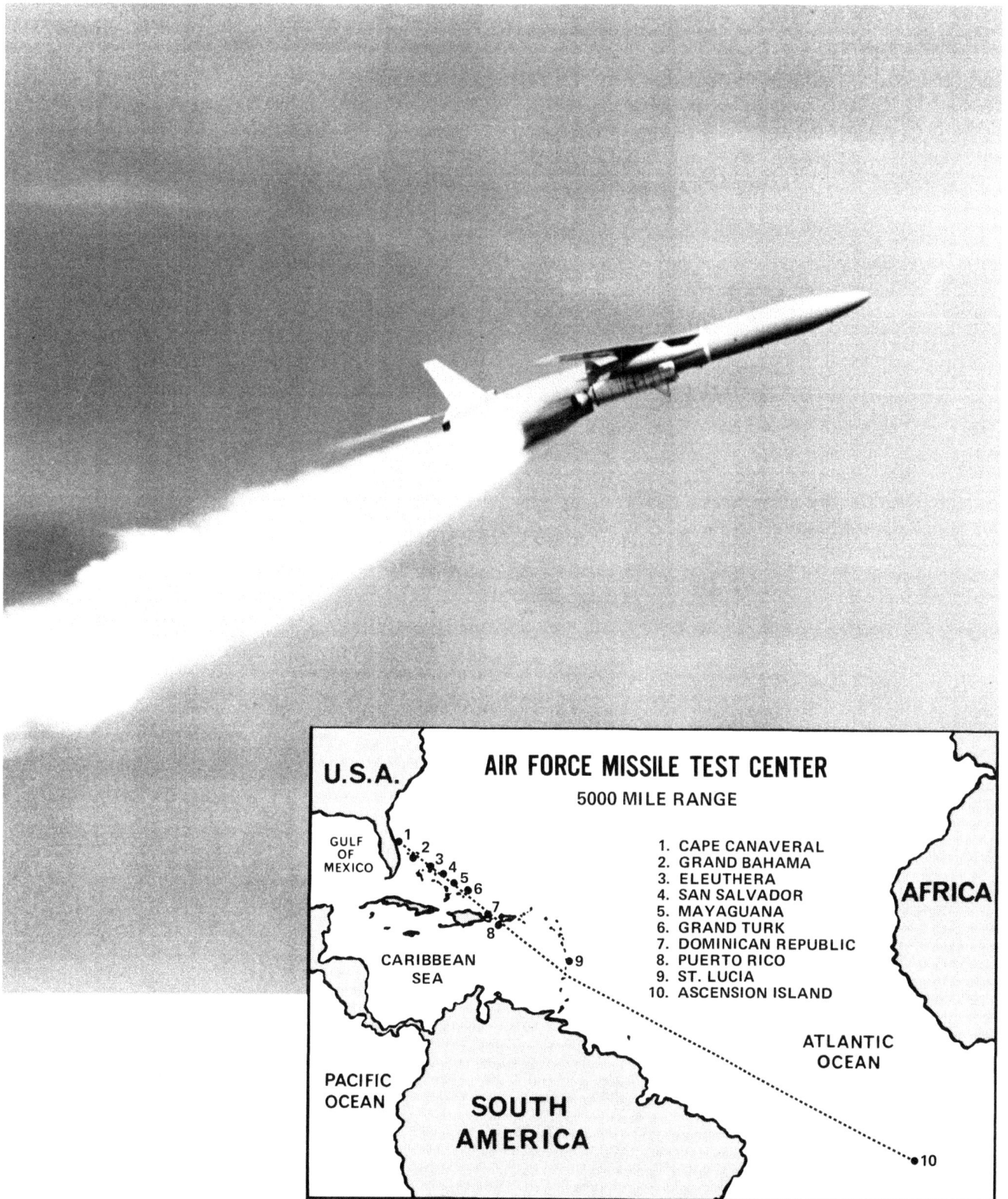

AIR FORCE MISSILE TEST CENTER

5000 MILE RANGE

1. CAPE CANAVERAL
2. GRAND BAHAMA
3. ELEUTHERA
4. SAN SALVADOR
5. MAYAGUANA
6. GRAND TURK
7. DOMINICAN REPUBLIC
8. PUERTO RICO
9. ST. LUCIA
10. ASCENSION ISLAND

10,500-POUND ENGINE THRUST takes over from boosters after zero-launch from Cape Canaveral, Florida. Boosters fell away after expenditure. Droppable fuel tanks on underside of wing helped sustain Snark Missile flight down the 5,000-mile Atlantic Missile Range (inset).

Aptly described in 1957 by leading design experts as Northrop's foremost engineering achievement, the operational Snark culminated a decade of intense research and development. It was the world's first on-line intercontinental guided missile, incorporating the first astro-inertial navigation system for guidance.

The eventual fallout from the Snark program was far-reaching, for it included the entire guidance system for the SR-71 strategic reconnaissance airplane, much of the technology used in the C-5 navigation system, and a host of other electronic and optical systems and components.

The name "Snark" had been originally suggested by Jack Northrop. It stemmed from a Lewis Carroll poem describing a mythical creature — part snake, part shark.

By the time the Snark had gone into service in 1960 with the Strategic Air Command at Presque Isle, Maine, it had been flown repeatedly from Cape Canaveral, Florida, to Ascension Island — a distance of 5,000 statute miles. Also worthy of note is that in the military training program, every test launch conducted by the Air Force was a complete success.

One Northrop-directed flight test in particular stands out. The program had moved into its final phase, missiles reaching out into longer segments of the Atlantic testing range. Milt Kuska, who had left California to become base administrator at Cape Canaveral, went to Ascension to supervise the observation post there for the first full-range flight. Sal Xifo was the flight test director. A missile was fired down range. Kuska sent back word that the missile had missed the target center by several miles, but the test people found this difficult to accept. They checked and rechecked their data. Finally they came to an astonishing conclusion — the charts were wrong; the map-programmed Snark was right! The cartographers had mislocated tiny Ascension Island. Northrop reassembled its data and presented it to the military. As a result, the maps were changed.

In subsequent flights, SM-62's proved time and again their ability to drop warheads on the designated target. Later, when the expanding U.S. space program produced sophisticated instrumentation capable of measuring the earth's true contour, the Northrop finding concerning the correct location of Ascension was confirmed.

PHOTOS OF THE SM-62, like the one above, were not released to the public until 1956, ten years after the company was awarded a contract to develop the first U.S. Intercontinental Guided Missile.

N-25, EARLIEST OF DESIGNS, being readied for rocket sled launch at Holloman AFB, New Mexico. Radio-controlled vehicle was recoverable by means of drag chute and fore and aft skids which were extended from the airframe. This design was precursor to the zero-launched N-69 series.

The Snark had its beginning in a study contract awarded to Northrop by the Army Air Forces shortly after the end of World War II. The Air Forces had invited bids related to the development of a subsonic air-breathing, long-range guided missile. Northrop's study, designated Project MX-775, was conducted in utmost secrecy. The results impressed Air Forces officials. In March 1946, the company was awarded a new contract to develop a strategic bombing missile of intercontinental range. The new missile was redesignated B-62. At the time no one fully realized the difficulties and problems that would have to be overcome. S.E. "El" Weaver, the twenty-third employee hired by Northrop in 1939, was assigned to head the project.

Three broad development phases comprised the engineering effort necessary to produce the Snark weapon system: (1) a guidance system capable of programming automatic missile flight along a prescribed trajectory; (2) a missile airframe suitable for long-range intercontinental strategic air operations; and (3) related ground support equipment. It soon became apparent to Weaver that the guidance system was beset with almost overwhelming problems, while the airframe and ground support areas fell within the range of reasonability. In 1946, the art of long-range automatic navigation was virtually nonexistent. An automatic star-tracking navigation system capable of guiding a strategic bombing missile with a 5,000-pound warhead to a target 5,000 miles away seemed like science-fiction. In those days human navigators were still having trouble finding Hawaii on routine flights from the United States.

Furthermore, as if to compound the ever-increasing technical problems, off-the-shelf electronic and optical components were nonexistent; vacuum tubes had not yet been replaced by transistors; solid-state devices in general were still years in the future; and computers were still huge and bulky. Weaver's first task was to assemble a team of experts in the fields of navigation, computers, electronics, and optics. A comprehensive study of the various guidance methods revealed that a stellar-monitored inertial system offered the greatest promise; its precision increased with duration of flight, and it was not jammable. However, to duplicate the observations and calculations of a human navigator with mechanisms and computers on board the missile was not feasible from cost and reliability standpoints. The practical solution to the problem was brought within reach by the development at Northrop of the "time-specified trajectory" concept. With the flight plan completely specified, the bulk of the computation would be done in advance on ground-based computers. Onboard equipment thus was kept to a minimum.

Feasbility of the "time-specified trajectory" method was established by test flights of a specially equipped P-61 Black Widow during 1948. Among the pilots on those early pioneering flights were Max Stanley and Fred Bretcher, both transferred from the Flying Wing program, and a former Army Air Forces pilot, Gil Nettleton, later to become Vice President of Northrop International. In early 1951, the time-specified trajectory concept was demonstrated by a nighttime system installed and tested in a B-29 airplane flying over a 1,200-nautical-mile great circle course. In late 1951 and early 1952, flights were conducted over a 2,100-nautical-mile range.

Research on daytime star tracking had been carried on since the inception of the missile program. Ground daytime star tracking was first accomplished in January 1948. Various airborne sensing and scanning systems were designed and tested; and during 1952 and early 1953, satisfactory experimental tests results were obtained. These results furnished the basic information necessary for a complete system design, which was designated Mark I.

Direct observation of guidance system operation under actual airborne conditions was the purpose of an extensive program of flight testing in manned B-45 aircraft initiated in 1953. When this program was concluded in August 1958, a total of 196 flights, involving approximately 450 hours of guidance operation and nearly 159,000 guidance-navigated miles, had been achieved.

The airframe design phase was divided into stages, each represented by a model configuration and dependent upon the previous stage for cumulative data. Out of these progressive development stages evolved the SM-62 production version. The first stage consisted of the design and testing of the N-25 missile (XSSM-A-3). Sixteen of these research vehicles were rocket-sled-launched at Holloman Air Force Base, New Mexico, to determine the launch and flight characteristics of the design. The thin, highly swept wing and long, slender fuselage of the N-25 contributed to low drag. Predicted stability and control were adequate without conventional rudder, elevators or horizontal stabilizers. Elevons, used first on the Flying Wings, provided the necessary control. Simplicity of structural design kept gross weight and cost to a minimum.

So that the N-25 could be flight tested prior to completion of automatic guidance development, a radio

N-25 IN FLIGHT. Northrop-developed elevons on wing trailing edges provided control. Vehicle attained a speed of Mach 0.9 in level flight, could remain in the air over 2-1/2 hours.

134

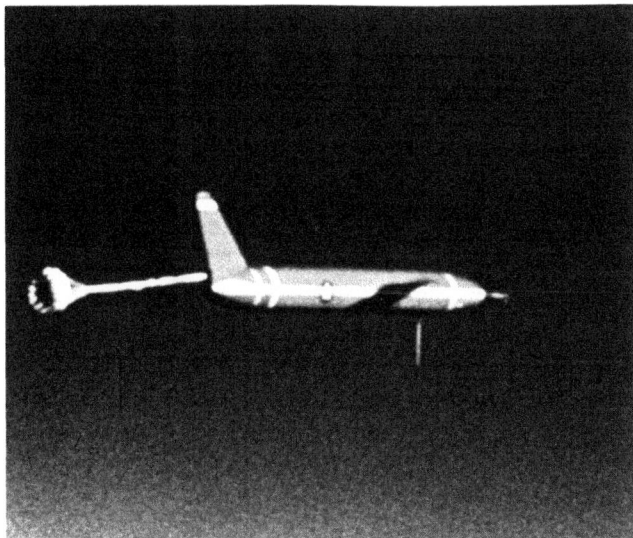

N-25 READY TO LAND. Radio command pops drag chute to reduce speed. Retractable skid landing gear made recovery possible on a small dry lake bed near the White Sands National Monument in New Mexico. Recovered vehicles were reflown as many as three times.

LAUNCHER OF N-25 was a rocket sled running along level tracks. Recovered N-25's were later modified and successfully launched at Cape Canaveral, Florida, to test the zero-launch technique which became feasible with the development of larger booster rockets.

control system incorporating a modified Sperry A-12 autopilot and command receivers was designed. Corresponding transmitters were provided for B-45 director aircraft and ground control stations. To permit recovery of these missiles, the design included retractable skid landing gear and a drag chute.

Twenty-five flights were made with the 16 N-25 missiles. Performance and flight characteristics were excellent. Speeds of Mach 0.9 in level flight and Mach 0.97 in a shallow dive were achieved, and a maximum flight duration of 2 hours and 46 minutes was accomplished.

During the N-25 flight test program in New Mexico, new missile range and warhead requirements were established by the Air Force. Although the basic configuration of the N-25 was proven at Holloman, the new requirements called for a larger and more powerful vehicle. The N-25 design was changed to the N-69 (XSM-62) configuration to meet Air Force specifications for increased range and higher warhead weight. The missile was lengthened from 50 to 68 feet, and the flying gross weight increased from 28,000 to 50,000 pounds. The wing was moved aft, and an external engine air intake replaced the N-25's flush duct. The autopilot was modified to keep it abreast of recent programs in guidance system design, and advances in booster rocket development made it possible for the N-69 to be designed for zero-length launching.

Like the N-25, the N-69 airframe was of semimonocoque, riveted magnesium and aluminum alloy construction. It was powered by a single Pratt & Whitney J-57 turbojet engine. The shoulder-mounted, highly swept wing incorporated elevon controls in lieu of a horizontal stabilizer.

As the N-25 program approached completion in the summer of 1952, the Northrop field test organization moved to the Air Force Missile Test Center at Cape Canaveral, where extensive ground facilities necessary to support the new N-69 test program were available. Downrange missile tracking and monitoring services for the N-69 flights were furnished by the AFMTC test range, extending from Cape Canaveral to Ascension Island off the coast of Africa.

Following the move to AFMTC, flight testing under Project MX-775 was resumed in November 1952, to be completed in September 1958. The AFMTC program consisted of four N-25 flights and 62 N-69 flights having such objectives as obtaining data on zero-length and short-rail launching techniques using JATO-type rocket motors, evaluating terminal dive and ballistic nose methods of warhead delivery, booster rocket performance, and warhead arming and fuzing operation; and demonstrating guidance, aerodynamic, airframe, and subsystem performance data.

Northrop established the N-69A, B, C, D, and E designations to denote changes in missile configuration and flight test purpose. Thirteen missiles were built to the N-69A and N-69B Performance Missile configuration, which were radio-controlled and recoverable. The flight tests had two purposes: evaluation of aerodynamic performance, and preliminary observation of the terminal dive maneuver. Flight tests of this configuration were completed in May 1955.

In that same month, flight test and wind tunnel test data indicated that the terminal-dive method of warhead delivery was not feasible because the prescribed dive trajectory could not be maintained with the available elevon control. As a result, the warhead delivery technique was changed at this time to a ballistic nose drop.

A ballistic nose had been under study as an alternate method of warhead delivery for the previous two and one-half years. In June 1955 Northrop proposed this program change to the Air Force, and concurrence was obtained in July 1955. The "ballistic nose" development team was headed by Roy Jackson (later Corporate Vice President and F-18 Program Manager) with Art Nitikman in charge of aerodynamics and Ralph Hakes, mechanical design. The ballistic nose was incorporated in the remaining N-69C missiles. The N-69C program was successfully completed in October 1956. Fifteen missiles were built as N-69C and modified N-69C Warhead Delivery Test Missiles with provision for a facsimile of the warhead. This configuration was fitted with radio control and was not recoverable.

Five of these missiles were flight-tested to evaluate terminal-dive warhead delivery, warhead arming and fuzing systems, and aerodynamic performance. One of the terminal dive missiles was also flown to evaluate the entry maneuver for the ballistic nose method of warhead delivery and to obtain aerodynamic and system performance data at high dynamic pressures.

The N-69D Guidance System Test Missiles were the first to incorporate the 24-hour Mark I guidance system and, in common with the N-69A configuration, it was recoverable through the use of radio control, skids, and a drag chute. The flight test objective for this series was to demonstrate Mark I guidance system capabilities. Although 20 missiles were initially programmed for use during this development stage, the tests were successfully concluded in November 1957 with the use of only 15 missiles. Eight of the N-69D missiles flown were successfully recovered; of these, three were subsequently reflown, three were used to flight-test guidance system and ground equipment modifications incorporated in the final operational configuration, and two were delivered to the Air Force for use as training aids.

The objectives of the N-69E Operational Concept Test Missiles were to demonstrate operational capability and establish compatibility of the prototype ground support equipment. Fifteen missiles were used in the flight test program, and one was delivered to the Air Force for training purposes. Flight tests were initiated in June 1957 and were completed in September 1958.

HIGHLIGHTS OF THE FLIGHT TEST PROGRAM

- August 6, 1953: first N-69 flight.

- September 26, 1955: first ballistic nose drop.

- September 13, 1956: first missile flight entirely under automatic guidance and control.

- November 14, 1956: first long-duration missile flight using daytime star tracking.

- June 20, 1957: first operational prototype missile (N-69E configuration) flown.

- October 31, 1957: first full test-range flight with warhead delivery.

- June 27, 1958: first launch of operational prototype missile by Air Force personnel.

F-89 AS A MISSILE DIRECTOR. Manned interceptor served as an inflight radio control of the N-69D Snark shown here after booster release. Occasionally a B-45 was used to direct the missile. The N-69D incorporated the 24-hour Mark I guidance system.

RECOVERABLE N-69. Square enclosure over the tail cone contained the drag chute which was released by radio command from a missile director aircraft or a ground control station. The N-69A, B, and D series were recoverable.

LAUNCHING PADS at Patrick Air Force Base, Florida. Three N-69C missiles positioned for firing down the Atlantic Missile Range. These Snarks, while fitted with radio control, were not recoverable. They were flight-tested to evaluate terminal-dive warhead delivery and ballistic nose drop.

N-69C READY FOR ZERO LAUNCH. Two solid propellant boosters initially lifted off a gross weight of 50,000 pounds before the Allison J-71 turbojet with its 7,000 pounds of thrust took over the flight of the Snark.

PRATT & WHITNEY J-57-P-3 engine ready for installation in an N-69D missile. The tail section, seen in the background, will be mated to the aft section once the engine is in place. The "D" version was used to test the guidance system and was recoverable by means of rear-deployed drag chute and landing skids.

PRATT & WHITNEY J-57-P-17 turbojet, with afterburner, was used in the operational production SM-62 Snark missile. This power plant developed 10,500 pounds of thrust.

FIVE THOUSAND-POUND WARHEAD (above) being installed in an operational SM-62 (right and below). Warhead was contained within a ballistic nose, which upon a signal from the guidance system separated from the missile proper and followed its own trajectory to the target.

TRANSPORTATION MODES. By 1958, after 10 years of development and testing, the SM-62 Snark was ready for shipment to the Strategic Air Command Base at Presque Isle, Maine. A wide assortment of vehicles and special equipment carried the missile to wherever it was needed.

The N-69E missile was substantially the same as the "D" version. A rudder was originally provided to trim out forces and moments produced by lateral asymmetries, but it was subsequently deactivated in favor of lateral asymmetrical compensation through the elevons.

In July 1957, the Air Force announced the award of a $73 million contract to Northrop for production of operational SM-62's. In September the Air Force announced the first operational squadron of Snarks would be assigned to the Strategic Air Command. An additional order for $50 million was announced in December 1958.

N-25

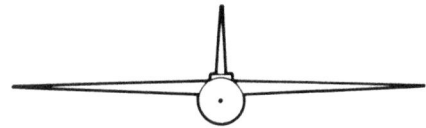

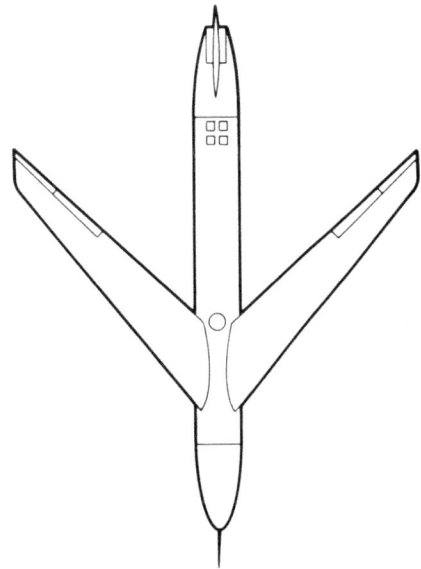

SPECIFICATIONS

WING SPAN . . . . 42 FT.

OVERALL LENGTH . . . . .52 FT.

OVERALL HEIGHT . . . . .12 FT.

WING AREA . . . . 280 SQ. FT.

LAUNCH WEIGHT . . . . .28,000 LB

SPEED-MAXIMUM . . . . .MACH 0.9

SPEED-CRUISING . . . . .MACH 0.85

RANGE . . . . .1,550 MILES

SERVICE CEILING . . . . .45,000 FT.

POWER — (1) ALLISON J-33 TURBOJET, 5,000-LB THRUST

In all, 51 production SM-62's were delivered. Prior to delivery to the Air Force, each big gray ''bird'' received an eight-hour performance checkout using some of the most sophisticated automatic ground test equipment developed up to that time. In all, approximately 350 different items were required for ground support.

Beginning with a ''blue suit'' launch in June 1958 at Cape Canaveral, six launches were conducted by Air Force personnel: two to demonstrate launch crew capability and four to evaluate the missile and ground equipment under the Employment and Suitability Test (E&ST) program.

Although the SM-62 Snark was a subsonic air breather, it fulfilled an important role for the Strategic Air Command as the first intercontinental guided missile until eventual replacement by the new generation of ballistic missiles.

N-69 (SM-62)

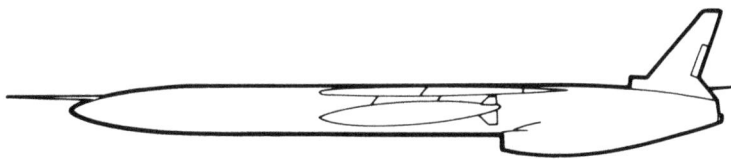

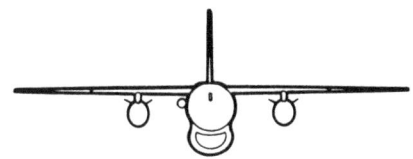

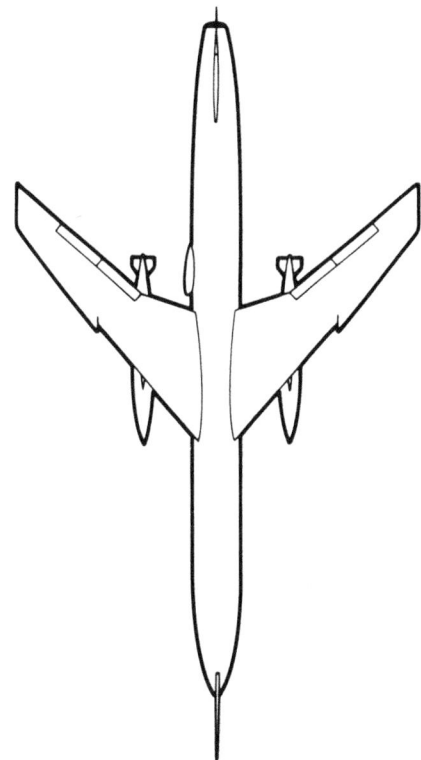

SPECIFICATIONS

WING SPAN	42 FT.
OVERALL LENGTH	69 FT.
OVERALL HEIGHT	15 FT.
WING AREA	326 SQ. FT.
LAUNCH WEIGHT	60,000 LB
SPEED-MAXIMUM	MACH 0.9
SPEED-CRUISING	MACH 0.85
RANGE	6,000 MILES
SERVICE CEILING	OVER 50,000 FT.

POWER — (1) P&W J-57-P-17 TURBOJET, 10,500-LB THRUST

ARMAMENT — 5,000-LB WARHEAD

X-4 SKYLANCER (BANTAM)

Jet propulsion technology was rapidly pushing fighter aircraft closer to the speed of sound (Mach 1) in the immediate period after World War II. But military investigators felt that only with more concentrated inflight research would routine supersonic flight become possible. They believed that many of the undesirable compressibility effects experienced near Mach 1 were caused, in part, by the horizontal tail surfaces of conventionally designed airplanes.

In early 1946, the company offered its Skylancer transonic (Mach 0.9) semi-tailless Flying Wing design as a research vehicle. On April 5, 1946, the Army Air Forces awarded a contract for two "flying laboratory" airplanes designated the XS-4, also known as the "Bantam." These research airplanes were to participate in a project exploring stability and control phenomena at high subsonic speed, one of a number of undertakings sponsored jointly by the AAF, Navy, and NACA (National Advisory Committee for Aeronautics).

The XS-4 was one of the smallest airplanes ever built for the AAF. The underlying idea was that the diminutive airframe would be most sensitive to the slightest aerodynamic reaction at transonic speeds. The wing span measured only 26 feet, 10 inches; overall length, 23 feet, 4 inches.

Equipped with two Westinghouse 1,600-pound-thrust jet engines, the XS-4 was thought to have sufficient power to explore the transonic speed range, but not to crack the sound barrier. Because of comparative jet engine fuel economy, the XS-4 was expected to be able to make longer flights than its sister rocket-powered research planes such as the X-1. With its close-coupled dimensions and low wing loading, it was also expected to be very maneuverable. These assumptions were proven to be true during the flight test program. Pilots equated the XS-4 with a highly responsive sports car in comparison to the other high-performance test airplanes under evaluation at that time.

X-4 BANTAM under test at Edwards AFB in late 1948. Northrop pilot Charles Tucker made first flight December 15, 1948. The small, swept-wing aircraft was intended only to continue research in aerodynamic phenomena at speeds near the speed of sound.

FRONT AND REAR VIEW OF THE X-4 show intake (above) and exhaust (below) of the two Westinghouse turbojet engines, producing 1,600 pounds of thrust each, more than adequate to power the 7,000-pound craft in the transonic range.

ART LUSK (right), project engineer on the X-4, converses with Jack Northrop at Hawthorne about first flight results of No. 1 aircraft, December 15, 1948. Work on the X-4 had been cloaked in secrecy for about two years since its contract date in early 1946.

The XS-4 also found favor because it was equipped with extremely effective dive brakes on each wing panel. They constituted a powerful control during landing and in the event a pilot had to "back out" of any high-speed difficulty. In addition, the XS-4 featured the Northrop-originated elevons which combined the functions of elevators and ailerons as used on all Flying Wings. All controls were power-boosted.

The white-painted prototype X-4 (designation changed from XS-4) was trucked to Muroc in late 1948. It made its first flight on December 15. Northrop test pilot Charles Tucker was at the controls. The second white X-4 first flew on June 7, 1949, also out of Edwards.

The following year General Albert Boyd, commanding officer of EAFB and veteran AF test pilot of high-speed aircraft, announced acceptance of the two X-4's. Air Force and NACA pilots subsequently conducted many stability and control flights until the entire research program was completed in April 1954. Among other Air Force pilots of repute to fly the X-4 were Chuck Yeager, Pete Everest, and Richard Johnson, while John Griffith and A. Scott Crossfield flew for NACA.

Designed only to explore the transonic speed region, the X-4's were unable to break the sound barrier. Many of the test flights did edge close to critical speed ranges, creating shock waves and other compressibility effects.

During Crossfield's first flight, for example, some interesting phenomena were experienced. He took off on December 6, 1950, accompanied by Pete Everest flying an F-86 chase plane. At Mach 0.88, Crossfield reported the X-4 as "capricious and delicate to handle." As he increased speed, he heard shock wave-induced sounds "like a freight train running over a steel bridge." Immediately, the compressibility effects became unmanageable. He quickly deployed his dive brakes to reduce speed, when he realized that both engines had flamed out. Diving the X-4 to regain flying speed and help restart the engines, Crossfield succeeded in relighting only one; but it was enough to bring the airplane safely back to base.

Both X-4's were of riveted, aluminum alloy, stressed skin construction. Integral fuel cells were built into the multicellular wing panels. The thin swept wing panels were fitted with large-area dive brakes on the inboard wing trailing edges. The elevons extended from the end of the dive brakes out to the wingtips. The fuselage pod incorporated a minimum-size cockpit to allow room for the elaborate instrumentation and the additional fuel carried behind the pilot's station. An ejection seat was installed; a blown "bubble" type canopy protected the pilot.

Both X-4 airplanes survived the flight test program, and both are currently on display. One is at the Air Force Academy in Colorado Springs, Colorado; the other, at the Air Force Museum in Dayton, Ohio.

X-4 IN FLIGHT. Strong dive brakes on the wing trailing edges, inboard of the elevons, served two purposes. They enabled the pilot to "back out" of any high-speed difficulty encountered during test, and they acted as a research tool by setting the brakes at various openings. The pilot had a wide range of glide approach angles (6 to 25 degrees), for testing sink rates, landing techniques, and landing gear strength.

NO. 1 AIRCRAFT ("6676") was retired in 1957 to the Air Force Academy, Colorado Springs, Colorado, for display. One of the smallest planes ever built for USAF, it was only 23 feet long.

147

X-4

6676

USAF

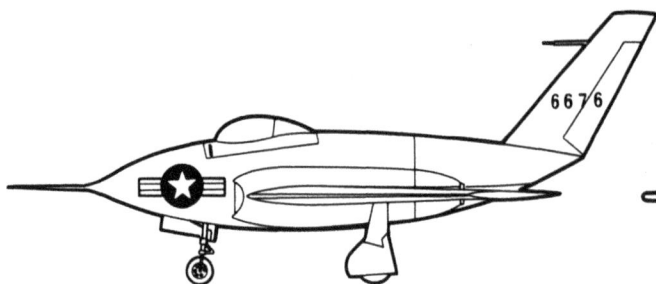

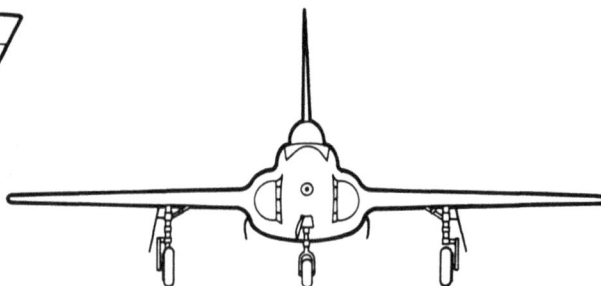

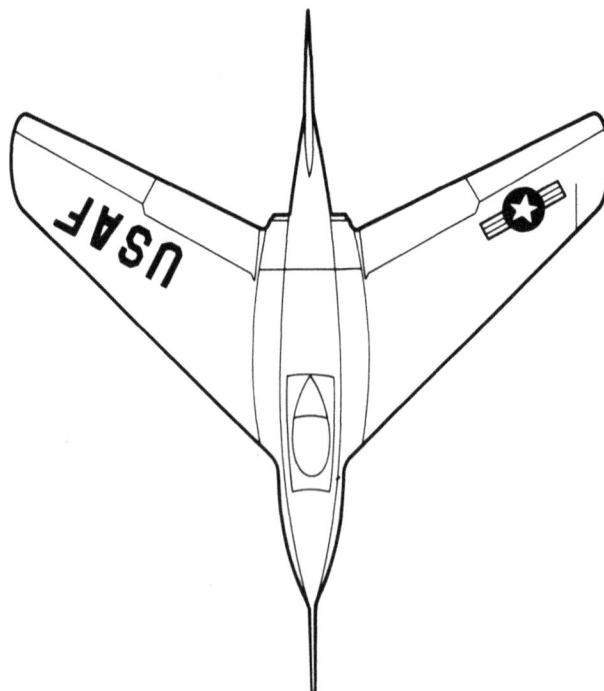

SPECIFICATIONS

WING SPAN ....26 FT., 10 IN.

OVERALL LENGTH ....23 FT., 4 IN.

OVERALL HEIGHT ....14 FT., 10 IN.

WING AREA ....200 SQ. FT.

TAKEOFF WEIGHT ....7,500 LB

SPEED-MAXIMUM ....680 MPH

SPEED-CRUISING ....330 MPH

RANGE ....320 MILES

SERVICE CEILING ....44,000 FT.

POWER — (2) WESTINGHOUSE, TURBOJET XJ 30-WE-7,-8, 1,600-LB THRUST

F-89 SCORPION

Jack Northrop's final major design effort and, fittingly, one of his most productive military designs, was the F-89 Scorpion all-weather fighter interceptor. The F-89 was developed as a modern successor to the radar-equipped P-61 Black Widow which had been manufactured in quantity during World War II. Ultimately over 1,000 F-89's were delivered to the Air Force and the Air National Guard. The Scorpion saw military service for nearly 20 years.

Design of the new fighter, which was to become the first airplane ever to fire an air-to-air nuclear weapon, started shortly after the end of World War II. At that time, U.S. defense planners established a requirement for an all-weather interceptor capable of guarding the United States, and particularly what was then the Territory of Alaska, against the possibility of bomber attack "over the top of the world." The fighter would have to operate in harsh climatic conditions, during periods of low visibility, and at night.

Leaning heavily on its experience with the P-61 and related electronic detection systems, the Jack Northrop team proposed a large, 40,000-pound twin-jet fighter in the 600-mph class. The fighter would carry a two-man crew consisting of pilot and radar operator, and pack six 20mm cannon in its radar-equipped nose. An extensive array of electronic navigation equipment made flight possible in any kind of weather.

Externally, all models of the F-89 were esssentially the same, with the exception of wingtip pods and radar gun-nose shapes. After the black-painted XF-89, all production models of the F-89 were delivered in their natural aluminum finish. Internally, the prime changes were the installations of successively more powerful turbojet engines.

NO. 1 XP-89, shown at Muroc without wingtip fuel pods, prepared for first flight on August 15, 1948. Shortly thereafter, the Air Force changed all "P" designations to "F".

149

ENGINE STARTUP of No. 1 prototype XF-89 at Muroc. While this airplane was painted a glossy black, production F-89's were delivered with the natural aluminum finish. The slender upswept tail suggested the name "Scorpion."

NO. 1 XF-89, with fuel pods installed on wingtips, was the forerunner of several different models of the ''89'' fighter interceptor, all with the same basic configuration – upswept tail, twin underfuselage jets – but carrying upgraded armament packages.

The F-89 was of conventional riveted aluminum alloy, semimonocoque construction with stressed skin. The two-man crew was seated in tandem on rocket-powered ejection seats. The cabin was pressurized, and a large bubble-type sliding canopy installed. Two Allison turbojet engines with afterburners were mounted side-by-side in the lower center fuselage separated by the main fuselage structural keel. Engines were on "swing-out" mounts, a feature which greatly simplified field service.

An unusually thin straight wing was designed for the F-89; it was adopted in lieu of the swept-back configuration then coming into vogue for the subsonic fighters of the day. This made for an efficient high-speed wing with all the superior low-speed flight characteristics of a straight tapered configuration. Low-speed stability was particularly important for inclement weather missions which demanded slow, instrument-approach speeds. The straight wing layout also provided optimum flight characteristics at high altitude and permitted mounting heavy stores on the wingtips. Multiple spars and thick wing skins made up for the lack of wing spar depth, and provided ripple-free aerodynamic surfaces for low drag.

Another singular feature of the F-89 was the split or clamshell ailerons known as "decelerons." When the decelerons were opened both top and bottom, a drag was created to slow the airplane down. The design feature was especially useful in combat situations where the pilot wanted to close rapidly on target, then decelerate to a "walk" while firing guns or rockets. The decelerons were also critical for braking the aircraft when it was occasionally put into a dive and achieved supersonic speed. The 42%-span decelerons were located just outboard of the 58%-span double-slotted landing flaps. All flight controls, including flaps, decelerons, elevators, and rudder, were operated by dual, engine-driven hydraulic power systems. As backup, an electrically driven hydraulic pump was installed. In addition, the rudder control took advantage of a yaw damping system, and a force-producing device gave the pilot elevator control "feel."

All F-89 models mounted nonejectable fuel pods at the wing tips. Internal fuel was carried in multiple wing bladder cells, in combination with self-sealing fuselage tanks.

The landing gear was of the tricycle type and extremely fast-acting; it could be retracted within four seconds by means of its high-pressure hydraulic system. The single main wheels had thin high-pressure tires (200 psi), so that they could fit within the wing panels; the nose gear was equipped with dual wheels.

F-89 "DECELERONS," a combination control feature perfected on the Black Widow P-61, performed the dual function of ailerons (in the closed position) and dive brakes (in the open clamshell position, shown above).

"QUICK FIX" external mass balances on first production-run "A" models alleviated flutter problem of horizontal stabilizer/elevator.

In May 1946, the Air Force awarded the company a contract for two prototypes designated XP-89. These airplanes were to be entered into competition with the Curtiss-Wright XP-87 Nighthawk at Muroc Air Force Base for a future production order.

The glossy black No. 1 XP-89 was rolled out of the Hawthorne plant in mid-1948 and trucked to Muroc where it was prepared for it first flight. It was at this point in time that the Air Force changed all "P" (Pursuit) designations to "F" (Fighter), and the Northrop airplanes were redesignated XF-89.

The XF-89 first flew out of Muroc on August 15, 1948. Fred Bretcher was the test pilot. Wingtip fuel pods were not carried on this first flight. The results of the ensuing test program marked the F-89 as a high-performance machine with unusually easy-to-fly and "forgiving" characteristics. In consequence, the Air Force awarded the company a production contract for 48 F-89A models in January 1949. One was set aside as a static test airplane.

A clearly recognizable and distinctive feature of the XF-89 was the upswept tail. This configuration kept the tail surfaces clear of both the wing downwash and the engine exhaust. Muroc ground crews soon dubbed the craft the "Scorpion," because the upswept tail reminded them of an angry scorpion. Later the name was officially approved by the Air Force.

No. 2 prototype, redesignated YF-89A to identify its function as a "service evaluation" airplane, was completed in early 1950. Programmed test flying was halted, however, when the original XF-89 crashed in February 1950 during a high-speed pass over Northrop Field. Test pilot Charles Tucker escaped with injuries but Arthur Turton, the flight test engineer, was killed. Post-accident investigation revealed that horizontal stabilizer/elevator flutter had induced structural failure resulting in the crash. Intensive studies and tests led to a "fix" which included the addition of large mass balances to the elevators. The changes corrected the problem; all F-89A airplanes were modified accordingly. Those still in fabrication also received internal equipment changes, including the introduction of the Lear F-5 autopilot and an ILS system, converting them into the "B" model.

HEIGHT OF "SCORPION" ASSEMBLY at Hawthorne. F-89D aircraft coming off line in this mid-1954 photograph were the result of a third production run contract. In all, 683 F-89D's were delivered to squadrons in the Continental Air Defense Command and the Alaskan Air Command.

The F-89A/B had provisions for two bomb pedestals on the wings for the carriage of 1,600-pound bombs. In addition, each wing had provisions for four rocket launchers, each capable of carrying two 5-inch HVAR rockets (16 total). The "B" model retained the F-89A nose configuration with a radar fire-control system and six 20mm cannons. Although the original XF-89 was equipped with 600-gallon fuel tip tanks, the subsequent A/B models were fitted with 300-gallon tanks.

The F-89C incorporated uprated Allison J-35 turbojet engines with a corresponding increase in the maximum allowable gross weight to 42,827 pounds. The F-89C was equipped with elevators with internal mass balances; all F-89A's and B's were retrofitted with the new elevators. Armament and fuel feed remained the same as on the "B" model. In May 1950, the Air Force ordered the improved F-89C into production with an initial order for 63 airplanes.

As tension mounted in the Far East, and U.S. mobilization plans unfolded with the outbreak of the Korean war, Washington ordered an acceleration in aircraft production. In September 1950, the Air Force authorized the company to proceed with plans to build and operate a flight and installation center at the Palmdale, California, airport. The new facility would alleviate hard-pressed production schedules, and allow final assembly and flight test outside of the Hawthorne area. It was expected to open operations in late 1952. A second contract was written for 100 additional F-89C airplanes.

The early "C" model aircraft turned up a disturbing problem soon after entering service with Air Defense squadrons. A series of unexplained crashes occurred as the result of wing structural failure in flight maneuvers. Consequently, all F-89's were grounded and an intensive investigation launched by the company. Analysis and tests disclosed that wing attach fittings were cracking and failing in certain flight regimes. Contributory to the condition was the phenomenon of aeroelasticity, which caused the wing to twist when subjected to aerodynamic loads. It was a new phenomenon, little understood in the early part of the Fifties. Within a short time Northrop engineers developed key structural changes which included strengthened wing attach fittings.

FLIGHT ECHELON OF SCORPIONS, bastion of America's air defense.

ONTARIO AIRPORT, California, (Above and Below) served as an F-89 staging area during the early 1950's until the newly built Palmdale facility was in a position to accommodate final checkout and flight acceptance. Aircraft were flown from Hawthorne to Ontario by Northrop ferry pilots. At the height of heaviest activity, during the F-89C wing modification, pilot Rod Close made a record nine flights during a 24-hour period.

155

F-89A ROCKET FIRE POWER. In addition to the six 20mm cannons mounted in the nose, the interceptor could launch a total of sixteen 5-inch HVAR's (high velocity air rockets) from eight underwing launchers. Armament was similar on the F-89B and F-89C.

F-89D ROCKET ARMAMENT was familiarly called "the Sunday punch." Pilot could fire 104 FFAR's (folding fin aircraft rockets) – 52 inserted in each of two wing pods – in clusters by selective mode.

A large-scale modification program was immediately started at Hawthorne, affecting close to 200 airplanes which had been in flight status. Airplanes on the production line were likewise modified, as were all subsequent airplanes. The modification program used the Ontario, California, facility as the production flight center. As a consequence of the structrual improvements, the F-89 become one of the safest airplanes in the Air Force inventory. By the time it was retired in 1969, the Scorpion had established new standards for low accident rates for operational fighters.

A major model change came with the F-89D. The most significant features were the addition of rocket/fuel pods to the wingtips, a new Hughes fire-control system, and the removal of the 20mm cannon from the nose. Each rocket pod carried 52 2.75-inch FFAR's, fired selectively or in salvo. This detection-armament arrangement firmly established the F-89D as the world's most heavily armed fighter of the mid-Fifties. In the 104-FFAR salvo mode, the rockets would fan out in overlapping patterns in the manner of shotgun blasts to blanket an area as large as a football field. The aft bays of each pod contained 300 gallons of fuel. The F-89D also featured more powerful Allison J-35 engines and a new maximum allowable gross weight of 46,780 pounds. This model seemed to satisfy Air Force needs during and after the outbreak of the Korean war. Orders for 194, 172, 240, and finally 77 were placed with rapid succession of one another.

The single YF-89E prototype was an F-89C airplane converted to incorporate two recently developed Allison YJ-71 engines. The function of the YF-89E was to perform as a "flying test bed" for the new engine which was in the 7000-pound thrust class, without afterburner. Only the one prototype "E" was manufactured.

The last model F-89 to be produced in quantity was the "H". It was the same as the F-89D except for revised rocket/fuel pods on the wingtips, and the installation of the latest Allison engines. The tip pods were redesigned to add three Hughes Falcon GAR-1 missiles (guided air-to-air) to each pod. The Falcons were mounted internally in each pod armament bay and swung out automatically on launchers in preparation for firing. The inclusion of the Falcons reduced the number of 2.75-inch FFAR rockets from 52 to 21 in each pod. On March 23, 1954, the Air Force gave the go-ahead for production of 156 fighter interceptors of the "H" model. Production versions of the F-89H were coming off the assembly line at the Palmdale facility by 1956.

YF-89D AIRFRAME was selected from the initial F-89 A/B production run. The aircraft had a new nose, and rocket pods replaced wingtip fuel tanks. Test pilot Ray Tenhoff conducted first flight of the prototype from Northrop Field to Edwards AFB (formerly Muroc AFB) October 23, 1951.

YF-89D showing rocket pods which replaced original F-89B fuel pods.

YF-89D in test flight from Edwards AFB.

WINTER SCENES. (Above) Alaskan climate was taken in stride by Air Force crews servicing the F-89C (later exchanged for the F-89D). (Below) Not Alaska but Palmdale in Southern California, where an unusual snowfall blanketed the facility during January 1955.

In a test at the Atomic Energy Commission's Yucca Flats, Nevada, test site on July 19, 1957, a modified F-89D fired an MB-1 nuclear-armed Genie rocket. Following this successful test, Northrop proposed an F-89J configuration to the Air Force. The new model would not require fabrication of new airframes at Hawthorne or Palmdale, but would result from the conversion of F-89D airplanes already in Air Force inventory. Although several armament/fuel pod variations of the F-89J were considered, the final production configuration carried two Genie MB-1 nuclear rockets and four under-wing Falcon GAR-2 guided missiles. Six hundred-gallon fuel tip tanks replaced the ''D'' model rocket pods. Ultimately, 350 ''J'' airplanes were delivered to the Air Force.

After serving with the regular Air Force, from Thule, Greenland, and Fairbanks and Anchorage, Alaska, to continental U.S. air defense bases, the Scorpion was assigned to domestic Air National Guard units. Phase-out came in the summer of 1969, when the last two squadrons were retired at Des Moines, Iowa, and Bangor, Maine.

An F-89J is on display at the Air Force Museum, Dayton, Ohio.

F-89H FEATURED a unique armament arrangement. Each F-89D wingtip rocket pod was configured to a combination of 2.75-inch FFAR's (21 instead of the usual 52) and three GAR-1 Falcon missiles. The Falcons were mounted internally inside the pod (top, outer center, bottom), swinging out of opened doors on individual launchers when ready for firing.

F-89J, LAST OF THE SCORPION MODELS, evolved from a plan to upgrade the F-89D armament package. The latest of two new armament arrangements is shown above – two MB-1 nuclear-tipped Genie rockets with provisions for four GAR-2 Falcon guided missiles. The F-89J became operational in January 1957.

EXPERIMENTAL ARMAMENT PACKAGE, T-110 rockets installed in the nose section of an F-89C, ready for flight by test pilot Lew Nelson. Another experimental armament package of mid-1952 was the Oerlikon gun.

F-89 PRODUCTION

MODEL	NUMBER OF A/C	NOTES
XF(XP)-89	2	
YF-89A	1	CONVERTED FROM NO. 2 XF-89
F-89A	48	INCLUDES 1 STATIC TEST AIRFRAME
F-89B	29	MODIFIED F-89A's
F-89C	163	
YF-89D	1	MODIFIED F-89B
F-89D	683	INCLUDES 1 STATIC TEST AIRFRAME
YF-89E	1	CONVERTED FROM F-89C
F-89H	157	INCLUDES 1 STATIC TEST FUSELAGE
F-89J	350	CONVERTED FROM SERVICE F-89D's

F-89D

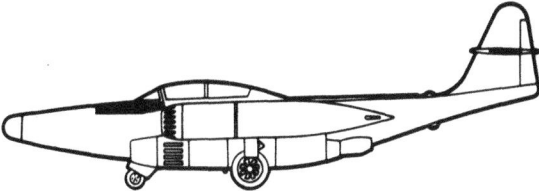

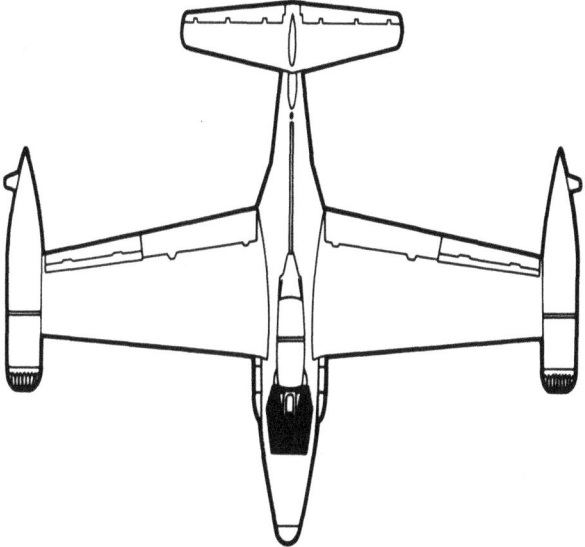

SPECIFICATIONS

WING SPAN . . . . .60 FT., 5 IN.

OVERALL LENGTH . . . . .53 FT., 10 IN.

OVERALL HEIGHT . . . . .17 FT., 6 IN.

WING AREA . . . . .562 SQ. FT.

TAKEOFF WEIGHT . . . . .46,780 LB

SPEED-MAXIMUM . . . . .630 MPH

SPEED-CRUISING . . . . .560 MPH

RANGE . . . . .2,600 MILES

SERVICE CEILING . . . . .51,000 FT.

POWER — (2) TURBOJET, ALLISON J35-A-35, 7,200-LB
       THRUST

ARMAMENT — (104) 2.75-IN. FFAR's

4

THE NEW AERODYNAMICS

"SUPERSONICS AND LFC"

Northrop management was well aware that military sales were the backbone of the company's future, but it also recognized the pitfalls inherent in the sole dependence upon a single customer. Realizing the potential for foreign sales in the NATO and SEATO countries as an alternative to domestic sales, teams of company executives and technical personnel visited the smaller nations in Europe and the Orient, as well as the continent of Australia. It was a major company effort to understand in depth foreign military needs and to establish credibility for Northrop's capabilities.

Reflecting the company's interpretation of the changing needs of the military, the N-102 Fang was a design case in point. A very small, supersonic, high-altitude day fighter, the Fang design incorporated a number of ingenious features for ease of access and quick field service. Although it did not progress beyond the mock-up stage, it had profound influence, during the middle Fifties, on the design of the lightweight fighters to follow.

Fortuitously, General Electric had been developing a small but powerful jet engine for missile application in 1955. In studying possible uses for this relatively simple, low-cost engine, Northrop engineers developed the concept for what was to become a family of lightweight, low-cost, supersonic military airplanes. The first preliminary design was for the single-place N-156 Freedom Fighter in 1956. It was patented by Welko Gasich, who was Chief of Advanced Design at that time. Lee Begin, also of Advanced Design, was given the responsibility for defining the original airplane configuration.

Although the Department of Defense ordered production of three N-156 prototypes, the Air Force showed no interest in this class of fighter for its own inventory. However, USAF's Air Training Command, which had initiated a requirement for a "TZ" trainer and which was faced with the need to train large numbers of jet pilots on a limited budget, was attracted by the low-cost, high-performance features of the N-156. In June 1956, the ATC ordered into production a two-place trainer version designated the T-38 Talon.

THOMAS VICTOR JONES (President, 1959–1976, currently Chairman of the Board and Chief Executive Officer). "It is Jones who has done most to bring economy and simplicity to the intricate and expensive field of aerospace" (Time, October 27, 1961).

THE F-5A AND THE TWO-PLACE F-5B appealed to the smaller nations of the world because of their low initial outlay, their ease of field maintenance, and their "honest" (actual vs promised) air defense performance. Over 1,000 went to 20 foreign countries by the early Seventies. Their stepped-up versions, the F-5E and F-5F, are enjoying a similar success for fundamentally the same reasons.

THE N-102 "FANG" MOCKUP. Under company and military security for four years, the N-102 emerged in 1956 as the forerunner of the N-156 and subsequent family of F-5 lightweight, low-cost fighters. Welko Gasich, then Chief of Preliminary Design and currently General Manager of the Aircraft Division, opted for quick, unhampered maintenance and turnaround by ease-of-access features.

By 1957, because of the high initial costs and high cost of ownership, fewer major weapon systems were being developed and produced. Therefore, the industry trend was leaning toward joint ventures. Northrop management's approach, however, was to reorganize its corporate structure to assume a more competitive posture. First, a corporate entity with responsibility for top-level planning and policy-making functions was established in new offices in Beverly Hills, California. Its original and largest organizational complex, covering aircraft and missile activities in Hawthorne, was designated the Northrop Division (later to become the Norair Division, still later the Aircraft Division). All electronics activities were grouped into the Nortronics Division located in the Hawthorne and Anaheim plants. The Radioplane subsidiary also became a separate division in Van Nuys, and Northrop International was established to direct overseas activities from the Beverly Hills offices. Late in 1958, the company acquired Page Communications Engineers, Inc., a leading designer

and installer of long-range networks. And on February 2, 1959, to reflect the changing character of its business, Northrop Aircraft, Inc. became Northrop Corporation.

Although Flying Wing development had been halted in the preceding period, the search for new ways to improve aircraft performance via reduced aerodynamic drag was continued on USAF R&D contracts and company funding.

Successful Low Drag Boundary Layer Control (later designated Laminar Flow Control) had been developed over a period of several years in the Northrop laboratories under the direction of Dr. Werner Pfenninger, eminent Swiss-born scientist. In June 1959, USAF awarded to Northrop the first of several contracts, culminating in the flight tests of two X-21A "LFC" research airplanes. The X-21A's demonstrated a scientific breakthrough by achieving laminar flow for 100 percent of the wing airfoil chord, resulting in a significant reduction in friction drag.

The corporation's aggregate military business materially benefited from two major contracts awarded to the Nortronics Division. The first was to develop the astro-inertial guidance system for the Air Force Skybolt missile (another Snark technical fallout). The second was to supply DATICO, the electronic checkout system for the Navy's submarine-launched Polaris missile system. Also significant was the first contract of the Radioplane Division (later the Ventura Division) for the Mercury space vehicle recovery parachutes, and eventually for the Gemini and Apollo programs.

By 1962 DOD and Military Assistance Program officials came to recognize the value of the supersonic N-156F as a replacement for aging U.S. jets that had previously been supplied to allied countries. As a consequence, the N-156F (subsequently designated F-5A) was ordered into production in April, along with the two-place F-5B trainer version.

Aircraft sales alone accounted for 29 percent of the Northrop Corporation business in 1962. Missiles, elec-

tronics, and communications systems — as a non-aircraft group — accounted for 61 percent; commercial or non-military projects, 7 percent; miscellaneous, 3 percent. Significantly, Northrop's international business was on the rise. Company products were employed in more than 22 countries, U.S. territories, and possessions.

Although cutbacks in DOD and NASA budgets were sharply curtailing previously awarded contracts throughout the defense community, expanding foreign sales helped to balance the scales at Northrop. Sales arrangements for the F-5A and F-5B with Norway, Spain, and Canada, as well as the assignment of a Tactical Air Command squadron to Vietnam, proved the validity of the original design concept. F-5's were also on order to Iran, South Korea, Greece, the Philippines, Republic of China and Turkey. Mounting sales of the T-38 to the Air Force not only served to brighten the economic present but also forecast a more promising future.

ONE OF TWO EXPERIMENTAL X-21A AIRCRAFT to test the company's Laminar Flow Control (LFC) concept. The promise of important advances in the range, payload, and flight endurance of "future transport and combat airplanes" was supported first by company funding, later by USAF contract.

CORPORATE OFFICES were moved from Hawthorne to Beverly Hills in 1957, "in a site that is geographically central to the company's various facilities throughout Southern California" (Annual Report, 1957).

N-156F PROTOTYPES lined up with T-38 Talons in 1960, one year after test pilot Lew Nelson took Freedom Fighter "94987" (foreground) on its first flight. A third prototype ("94989") never flew as an N-156F but did see service as the original YF-5A prototype.

ALL THREE YF-5A's (above and below) were formerly the prototype N-156F Freedom Fighters. One of the features which appealed to DOD and USAF officials was the aircraft's ability to land and take off from sod airfields. Old "89" above made 400 test flights until it retired to the Air Force Museum in 1970.

T-38 TALONS from Williams AFB in ceremonial formation over mountains near Yuma, Arizona. T-38's were mainstay of the Air Training Command; operational and safety records instilled confidence to inaugurate F-5 programs in Military Assistance Program (MAP) countries.

N-102 FANG

At the beginning of the Fifties, when the F-89 was just entering production, the company began to look to the future and explore a totally new, "next generation" class of fighters. The main thrust was directed toward a supersonic, lightweight — and at the same time simplified — day fighter with a high rate of climb and a high-altitude capability.

In 1952 Edgar Schmued, vice president in charge of engineering, initiated a program for the unique N-102, christened "Fang." Welko Gasich headed the preliminary design team. Although the N-102 never went beyond the mockup stage, it left its mark on future design concepts. It could rightly be considered the forerunner of the lightweight family of supersonic fighters and trainers which Northrop would pioneer in the years to come.

Less than half the weight of the twin-engine Scorpion, the Fang was conceived to develop the same amount of thrust (14,000 pounds with afterburner) with a single General Electric J79 turbojet. As a result, maximum speed of Mach 2.0 was possible, and a service ceiling of 60,000 feet was feasible.

Inaugurated in December 1952, the N-102 proceeded from complete preliminary design to mockup as a closely guarded proprietary research program. What designers were seeking was an economic solution to near-term (1958-60) Air Force requirements; but at the same time they took into account parallel Navy versions which could operate from small Jeep carriers. The Fang was initially proposed as a single-place day fighter; yet designers were quick to see the possibility of a two-place supersonic trainer by the simple expedient of exchanging the nose section forward of the main fuel bulkhead.

FANG MOCKUP showed provision for one turbojet unit. According to the N-102 specification, one of the major design aims was to accept any one of a number of planned engine installations, "utilizing tools, abilities and techniques generally available at any air base." Note underslung air intake.

N-102 FANG was classified as a lightweight day fighter, so designed as to be readily convertible into a fighter-bomber. Suggestive of the Mach 2 performance are the highly swept surfaces.

Among the many noteworthy aerodynamic features of the Fang were a thin delta wing with negative dihedral (cathedral), and an "all flying" horizontal swept tail configuration. A single jet engine was housed in the lower aft fuselage, coupled to an underslung air intake.

The tricycle-geared Fang was designed for riveted aluminum alloy, stressed skin construction, including corrugation-stiffened wing panels, and multiple spars and ribs. Its small size and lightweight structure contributed to the goal of a low gross weight. It was this low gross weight, when combined with high engine thrust, that enabled the fighter to attain superior speed, rate of climb, combat ceiling, and maneuverability.

A major design aim was to provide ease of conversion from one engine installation to another, all within the capability of an air base to which the Fang might be assigned.

This "power package" concept allowed for interchangeability of at least five different jet engines. The key lay in the engine mount design. The engine was suspended from the lower fuselage primary structure rather than forming an integral part.

Maintenance accessibility was emphasized in the detail design. Most of the fuselage interior was made accessible by means of removable panels or doors. The nose was hinged, immediately exposing radar, electronics, armament, and hydraulics. Windshield and cockpit canopy were similarly hinged for easy access to the cockpit and instrumentation areas.

Another quick-service item was the single-point refueling system whereby the large tanks behind the cockpit could be refilled in only 2.7 minutes. In a typical combat environment, in which armament, oxygen, and refueling operations would be going on simultaneously, the Fang could turn around in a remarkable six minutes!

The aircraft's basic armament was a single 20mm cannon with 600 rounds of ammunition. The cannon was located in the lower fuselage, below the cockpit, and was coupled to a fire control system consisting of a ranging radar and a computing sight. Alternate internal armament packages under consideration were: two 20mm cannon, two 30mm cannon, one 38mm rocket launcher, four 50-cal guns, 132 NAKA 1.5-inch rockets, and 32 Gimlet 2-inch rockets or eighteen 2.75-inch FFAR rockets. Various combinations of external armament could also be carried on the six wing-mounted pylons: Sparrows, Sidewinders, Ding-Dongs, napalm fire bombs, external fuel, missiles, rockets or other special stores.

A full-scale mockup of the Fang was fabricated from wood and metal in 1953. Northrop energetically sought support to build one prototype, but the time had not yet arrived for military planners to accept the idea of a small, lightweight, low-cost fighter. Even though the project was terminated, the all-white mockup was displayed at the Hawthorne plant as a breadboard device for new engineering ideas during the mid-Fifties. Finally, in 1956, the mockup was presented to the Northrop Aeronautical Institute for use by the school's engineering students.

N-102

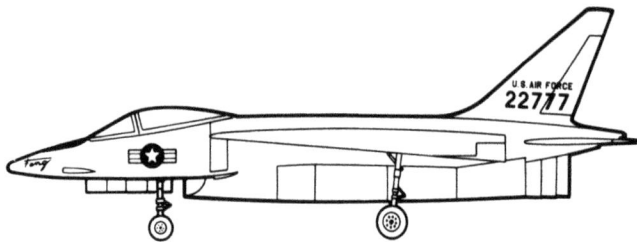

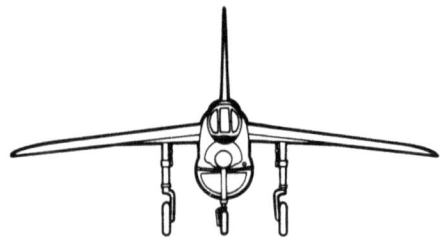

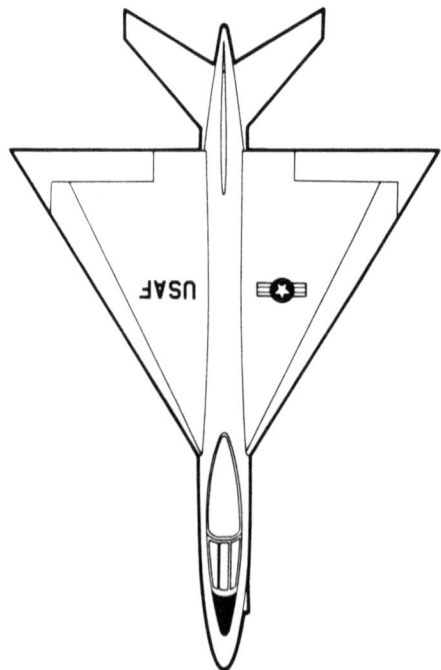

SPECIFICATIONS

WING SPAN	30 FT., 6 IN.
OVERALL LENGTH	45 FT., 10 IN.
OVERALL HEIGHT	15 FT., 10 IN.
WING AREA	366 SQ. FT.
TAKEOFF WEIGHT	18,760 LB
SPEED-MAXIMUM	MACH 2.0
SPEED-CRUISING	MACH 0.87
RANGE	2,030 MILES (FERRY)
SERVICE CEILING	59,300 FT.

POWER — (1) G.E. J79 TURBOJET, 9,290-LB THRUST (14,350-LB W/AFTERBURNER)

ARMAMENT — (1) 20MM CANNON

N-156 STUDIES

If one factor could be isolated as predominant over all others in influencing the N-156 design concept, it was "life cost." The term was originated by Tom Jones, deputy chief engineer in 1954. "Life cost" meant the total cost of a product over its entire life span. It lay at the heart of a design philosophy that would persist through the years.

In that time frame, the U.S. was seriously reassessing its defense posture following the lessons of the Korean war. Korea underscored the message that an outside threat to American security, somewhat minimized in the five-year period following World War II, was an ever-present possibility. It acted as a sharp stimulus to military preparedness. "The country was on a technological binge," Jones later explained. "But nobody mentioned that you only had so many hands and feet and could run in only so many directions."

Northrop sought an answer in a series of concentrated studies for a new type of manned weapon system. Out of these investigations emerged a totally new design philosophy. The decision was that a future fighter had to incorporate certain key features: it had to be small; it had to be lightweight and low cost, with high thrust-to-weight engines; and it had to lend itself to simple maintenance.

Several fighter and two-place designs were quickly developed. One of these was the N-102 "Fang" day fighter containing a number of design features that would be incorporated in the N-156. The timing was right because advanced lightweight, high-thrust jet engines were under development for missile application. Engineers and company management were quick to recognize their potential for manned aircraft under study. The new engines were small enough so that a "safety package of two" could be employed. In fact, the use of two small engines enhanced the weight savings compared to larger single-engine aircraft.

N-156F MOCKUP. When the Air Force authorized the building of three N-156F prototypes in 1959, the contract also covered the completion of a mockup. The new mockup was made up of a single-place nose mated to the "TZ" trainer (later T-38) mockup. The break is shown directly above the engine inlet.

The first full airplane design to accept the advanced engines was the original N-156, a single-place fighter proposed for the Navy. It was developed by an advanced design team headed by Welko Gasich. Key specialists were Robert Katkov and Art Nitikman, aerodynamics; Art Ogness, structures; Lee Begin, configuration; George Gluyas, performance. This short-coupled, T-tail, supersonic airplane of less than 10,000 pounds appeared to be ideal for operation from the small jeep carriers of the Navy. The proposal was short-lived, however, because of a Washington decision to mothball the Navy's entire jeep carrier fleet.

In this same time period, a company evaluation team made a tour of the allied nations of Europe and Asia to study their future airpower needs. It learned that a firm requirement existed for an airplane that was extremely versatile, easy and inexpensive to operate and maintain, rugged enough to function in less-than-ideal conditions, highly reliable, and so inherently safe that it possessed a low attrition of both machine and pilot. If it could also serve as a training vehicle, so much the better.

INITIAL DESIGN STUDIES were focused on a lightweight Navy fighter which could be operated from jeep carriers. Even though this requirement was nullified in 1954 with the mothballing of the small carrier fleet, company management proceeded ahead with an advanced version of the N-156F shown above.

AREA RULING, or the application of the Whitcomb theory of area distribution for reduction of drag, is clearly shown on the underside of an N-156F in flight. Pinching-in of fuselage at wing root enabled aircraft to accelerate from transonic to supersonic speed.

By applying the latest state-of-the-art design concepts to the N-156, Gasich's team settled upon a version with significantly improved capabilities, one that might satisfy foreign as well as domestic needs. New aerodynamic concepts were introduced: area rule (the pinching-in of the fuselage at the wing root), in-line components, cambered wing leading edges, and low horizontal stabilizer.

In January 1955, Northrop made its first presentation to the U.S. government for a tactical supersonic airplane based on the "life cost" concept. The proposal aimed at two versions designated N-156F, a single-place fighter, and N-156T, a two-place trainer. Coinci-dentally, or perhaps influenced by the Northrop proposal, the Air Force opened a competition for a super-sonic "TZ trainer" which would replace the aging T-33 subsonic jet then in service.

In mid-1955, the advanced design team applied further refinements to the N-156F and N-156T designs, offering a number of briefings to U.S. and foreign military leaders. In the meantime, the Air Force concluded that the N-156T would meet the "TZ trainer" specifications and issued a letter of intent in June 1956 that ultimately led to development and production of the T-38.

N-156F (Early Proposed Version)

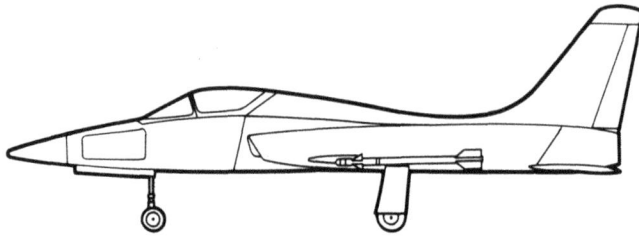

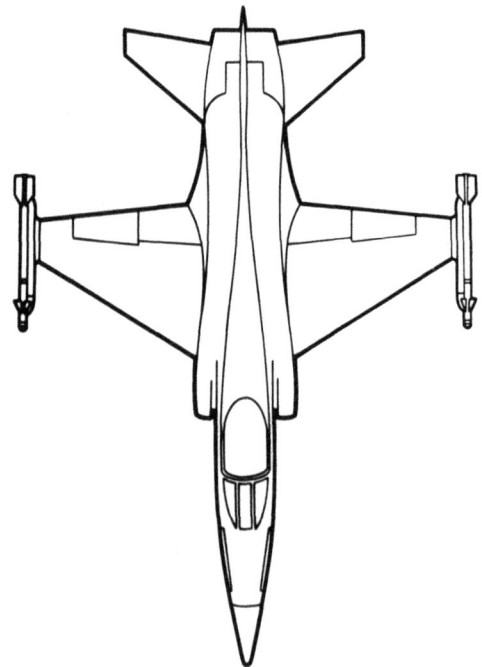

SPECIFICATIONS

WING SPAN .... 26 FT., 10 IN.

OVERALL LENGTH .... 39 FT., 2 IN.

OVERALL HEIGHT .... 12 FT., 10 IN.

WING AREA .... 170 SQ. FT.

TAKEOFF WEIGHT .... 11,370 LB.

SPEED-MAXIMUM .... MACH 1.3

SPEED-CRUISING .... MACH 0.88

RANGE .... 2,230 MILES (FERRY)

SERVICE CEILING .... 55,600 FT.

POWER — (2) G.E. J85-5 TURBOJET, 3,850-LB THRUST

ARMAMENT — (2) SIDEWINDER IR MISSILES

N-156T (Early Proposed Version)

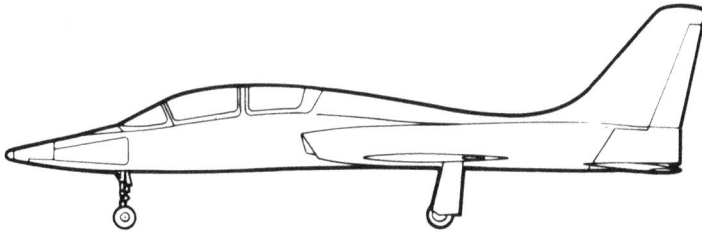

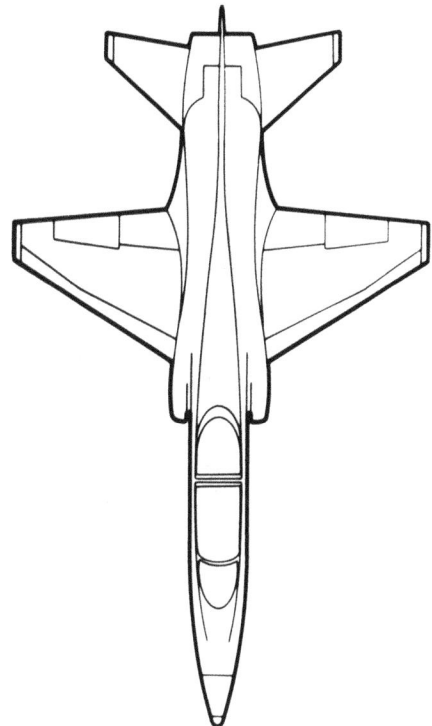

SPECIFICATIONS

WING SPAN	25 FT., 3 IN.
OVERALL LENGTH	42 FT., 8 IN.
OVERALL HEIGHT	12 FT., 10 IN.
WING AREA	170 SQ. FT.
TAKEOFF WEIGHT	10,900 LB.
SPEED-MAXIMUM	MACH 1.3
SPEED-CRUISING	MACH 0.88
RANGE	1,300 MILES
SERVICE CEILING	56,000 FT.
POWER — (2) G.E. J85-5 TURBOJET, 3,850-LB THRUST	

T-38 TALON

"YEAR OF FIRST FLIGHT."
Test pilot Lew Nelson made the maiden flight of the supersonic T-38 trainer out of Edwards Air Force Base on April 10, 1959. In all, Northrop produced 1,189 Talons for USAF, NASA, USN, and the Federal Republic of Germany.

1974

"YEAR OF ENERGY CRISIS."
USAF Thunderbird Demonstration Squadron transitioned from the F-4E Phantom to the T-38 Talon. In five months the Thunderbirds crowded in 35 aerial shows in 22 states before more than two million spectators.

Designed in 1956 as the first supersonic two-place trainer for the U.S. Air Force, the T-38 Talon was a direct derivative of the N-156 studies. Originally designated N-156T, then TZ-156, and finally T-38, it represented a major equipment change for the Undergraduate Pilot Training (UPT) program conducted by the Air Training Command.

In the early Fifties, the Air Force forecast a need for a trainer with performance characteristics more closely corresponding to those of its first-line tactical aircraft. The aging subsonic T-33 trainer in use at the time flew and handled differently from the contemporary and projected aircraft into which student pilots would transition immediately after graduation. The Air Force believed that the jump was too great and the training schedule too long. It required an aircraft especially tailored to improve the quality of training and simultaneously reduce transition time.

Fortunately, Northrop was fostering its own design program to develop a twin-engine, supersonic trainer that would provide maximum training effectiveness at low cost. To achieve this goal, the company was spon-soring studies looking into all facets of weight-saving opportunities possible with the new jet engines in the 7-to-1 thrust-to-weight ratio class. The end result was the N-156T Supersonic Basic Trainer designed for transitional flight training in these categories: supersonic flight familiarization; takeoff and landing techniques; multijet engine operation; aerobatics; night flying; and instrument instruction and cross-country navigation.

By May 1955, the Air Force had issued General Operation Requirement (GOR) 94, outlining the requisites for a "TZ" trainer. During the next few months, Northrop engineers applied further refinements to the N-156T design and presented a number of explanatory briefings to the Air Force. Finally, in March 1956, the company submitted a technical proposal to build the TZ trainer. On June 15, 1956, the Air Force returned a letter of intent authorizing development engineering for two prototype "YT" airplanes and one static test airplane. A series of low-speed wind tunnel tests was then conducted for aerodynamic refinement of the design, and a full-scale mockup was constructed under the designation TZ-156.

PROTOTYPE NO. 1 ("81191") removed from Advanced Production hangar, August 1958. Alongside is the N-156F mockup, the start of the F-5A program.

TRAINER MOCKUP. *The Air Force approved the TZ-156 design in October 1956 following the selection of Northrop's proposal to build the "TZ Trainer." The swept tail shown here was later redesigned to a trapezoidal shape. The Air Force converted the company TZ-156 designation to T-38.*

In October 1956, following a formal mockup board review, the Air Force approved the TZ-156 design. Tool design and manufacturing started in December, and the Air Force redesignated the airplane "T-38." Production go-ahead was received that same month for an initial order for four T-38A airplanes. Quickly following was a second production order for 13 T-38A's (hereinafter cited as T-38 since the "A" was the only model produced). T-38 fabrication had the advantage of the new NORAIL "moving assembly line" in 1958 at the Hawthorne facility, and production built up rapidly over the next two years.

The white-finished No. 1 YT-38 was trucked from Hawthorne to Edwards Air Force Base where it began taxi tests in March 1959. The first flight was made on April 10. Lew Nelson was test pilot. On the third flight, four days later, Nelson exceeded the speed of sound. No. 2 YT-38 made its first flight on June 12.

By fall the two prototypes had completed 100 flights, almost half of the entire flight test schedule. Milt Kuska, director of Flight Test Engineering, reported that the T-38 had encountered none of the major problems usually experienced in flight testing supersonic aircraft; not a single aerodynamic change was indicated throughout the program. The T-38 was rapidly achieving a reputation for outstanding flight handling qualities with "forgiving" flight characteristics. Maintenance was likewise proving very low.

In October 1959, the Air Force dispatched a letter contract for 50 additional T-38 airplanes. The contract also included provisions for raising the tooling production capability rate from two to 10 aircraft per month. Ten months later, the order backlog was again increased by 144 aircraft. In 1961, the production rate was lifted from 10 to 12 airplanes per month.

The flight test program was completed in February 1961 following a total of 2,000 flights. Air Force officials announced the tests the most successful ever conducted at Edwards. The first T-38 went to the Air Training Command at Randolph AFB, Texas, where it quickly proved its operational capabilities. The U.S. was now equipped with the world's first supersonic trainer embodying all the characteristics of first-line fighters. In August, another 144 aircraft were ordered.

FIRST SIX T-38's at Edwards AFB, June 1960. Nos. 81191 and 81192 were prototypes; the others were flown as "service test." The two aircraft at the end of the line were N-156F's, later redesignated YF-5A prototypes.

TEST INSTRUMENTATION occupied rear (instructor's) seat during the 1959-60 test and evaluation phase of the T-38 at Edwards AFB. Instrumentation package included oscillograph, photopanel, signal conditioning and camera.

ALL-MOVABLE ("FLYING") HORIZONTAL STABILIZER, observable above in YT-38 prototype. Speed brakes are shown open for deceleration. Main landing gear wheels tucked into fuselage as wings were kept thin for aerodynamic reasons.

T-38 TEST FORCE. In 1960, Air Force crews of the Flight Test Center, wearing Northrop-designed Talon patches, conducted Category II Flight Test and Evaluation at Edwards AFB.

HAWTHORNE ASSEMBLY LINE. T-38's shared same assembly line with single-place F-5A and two-place F-5B. At above station the center and aft fuselage sections were mated with forward fuselage section.

FIRST DELIVERIES TO USAF. These early production T-38's out of the initial contract order went to the Air Training Command in 1961.

183

Famed aviatrix Jacqueline Cochran brought worldwide recognition to the Talon in the fall of the same year. She flew a production T-38 to six new records for a woman flyer. She exceeded 800 miles per hour and flew a distance of 1,500 miles. Additional recognition came early in 1962 when Major Walter Daniel, a test pilot at Edwards AFB, broke four international time-to-climb records in a T-38. The most spectacular flight was his climb to 12,000 meters (39,372 feet) in only 95.74 seconds. The record flights were made at Edwards and at Point Mugu Naval Air Station, California.

T-38 production during the ensuing years held steady in response to incremental buys averaging 140 aircraft per year. In 1966 the Federal Republic of Germany purchased 46 Talons, and announced that it would conduct its entire student pilot program at Sheppard Air Force Base in Texas. The U.S. Navy joined T-38 users in 1969, when it procured five trainers for the Navy Test Pilot School, Naval Air Test Center, Patuxent River, Maryland.

The final T-38 was delivered to the Air Force on January 31, 1972, at the Palmdale facility. Overall, a total of 1,189 airplanes had been produced. The Talon has been instrumental in graduating 42,000 student pilots since its introduction. It also had achieved a very low accident rate, as compared to the overall Air Force rate. The T-38 required an average of only 10 manhours of maintenance per flying hour, or two-thirds of the originally projected rate, while maintaining a steady operational-ready rate of 80 percent.

Although the T-38 is most widely known for its remarkable record in the Air Training Command and will be the USAF Advanced Trainer until well in to the 1980's, it also has demonstrated its versatility in other roles for the Air Force, Navy and NASA: USAF Thunderbird Demonstration Squadron; support of Strategic Air Command missions; chase and test support for the Aerospace Research Pilot School; engineering flight test operations at Wright-Patterson AFB and Kelly AFB; range support missions at Eglin AFB; C-5 program support at Lockheed-Marietta; Air Force MOL program support at Los Angeles International Airport; astronaut flight readiness training and other space program missions at Ellington AFB; NASA support at Langley AFB; "aggressors" at Nellis AFB for USAF, and at Miramar and Oceana Naval Air Stations for the U.S. Navy.

T-38 FLIGHT LINE ACTIVITY at Williams Air Force Base in April 1967.

THE 1,000th TALON was delivered to the Air Force in January 1969. During an eight-year span Northrop was delivering to its customers an average of better than 10 trainers per month.

Structure of the T-38A Talon was essentially the same as in the N-156F fighter. It was predominantly of riveted aluminum alloy, semimonocoque with stressed skin; however, considerable use also was made of adhesive-bonded aluminum honeycomb and chemical-milled structural parts.

The thin dry wing was built as a single unit from tip to tip, with multiple spars and thick aluminum alloy skins. The trailing-edge flaps, ailerons, detachable wingtips and various sections of the wing were honeycomb-stiffened structures. The all-movable ("flying") horizontal stabilizer and rudder were likewise stiffened with honeycomb. Although the stressed skin fuselage was primarily of aluminum alloy construction, the canted, far-aft removable section surrounding the engine tailpipes and supporting the horizontal stabilizer was made up of a combination of different materials, including steel and titanium.

Six hundred gallons of fuel were carried in bladder-type cells located in the fuselage behind the twin cockpits. Each engine was supplied with fuel from separate systems; however, the instructor or student pilot could interconnect the two systems by actuating a crossfeed valve. The entire fuel tankage was serviced through either the gravity filler caps on top of the fuselage, or the single-point refueling fitting on the underside of the fuselage, which filled the tanks simultaneously.

The wide-stance tricycle landing gear was hydraulically actuated. The main gear retracted inboard into the fuselage, and the nose wheel retracted forward into the fuselage. The nose wheel was steerable with a hydraulic actuator which also served as a nose wheel shimmy dampener.

The hydraulically operated flight controls consisted of ailerons, rudder, and the all-movable horizontal stabilizer. Speed brakes located in the lower fuselage forward of the main landing gear doors were likewise hydraulically actuated. Wing flaps in the trailing edge of the wing were operated by electric motors. Dual hydraulic and electric systems provided backup safety.

T-38 COCKPITS and instrument panels.

VISIBILITY from rear (instructor's) seat.

An automatic rudder-aileron interconnect system was incorporated to improve roll characteristics at high speeds. Both the instructor and student were provided with realistic rudder and stick forces during maneuvers by an artificial "feel" system made up of springs and bobweights. A hydraulically operated stability augmenter system controlled both rudder and horizontal tail motion, damping short-period pitch and yaw oscillations and furnishing rudder trim.

Compressed air from the engines' 8th stage compressor sections provided cabin pressurization and conditioning, windshield and canopy defogging, inflation of canopy seals and anti-G suits, equipment cooling, and pressurization of the hydraulic reservoir. Each cockpit had its own manually operated canopy enclosure. The two canopies were automatically jettisoned if the pilots had occasion to operate their rocket-powered ejection seats.

The two General Electric J85-5 engines were mounted side by side in the aft fuselage. Installed on built-in overhead tracks with simple two-point mounting, the small and lightweight engines (525 pounds with afterburner) could be installed or removed with ease. An integrated power package, including gearbox, alternating current generator, and hydraulic pump, was mounted on the airframe forward of each engine. By disconnecting the engine drive shaft from the power package, each engine could be removed without disturbing the electrical or hydraulic system. Engine starting was accomplished using low pressure air from a ground-source mobile cart.

NASA selected the T-38 in 1964 for "maintenance of proficiency" in the astronaut program. The astronauts were already qualified pilots.

T–38A

U.S. AIR FORCE

USAF

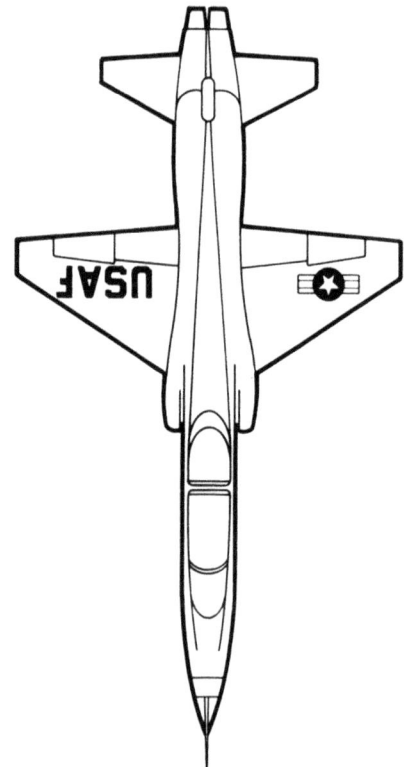

SPECIFICATIONS

WING SPAN . . . . .25 FT., 4 IN.

OVERALL LENGTH . . . . .46 FT., 4 IN.

OVERALL HEIGHT . . . . .12 FT., 10 IN.

WING AREA . . . . .170 SQ. FT.

TAKEOFF WEIGHT . . . . .11,600 LB

SPEED-MAXIMUM . . . . .MACH 1.3

SPEED-CRUISING . . . . .MACH 0.85

RANGE . . . . .1,000 MILES

SERVICE CEILING . . . . .55,000 FT.

POWER — (2) TURBOJET G.E. J85-5, 3,850-LB THRUST

N-156F FREEDOM FIGHTER

While the trainer version consumed most of the available engineering and manufacturing resources, President Whitley Collins did not lose sight of the N-156F. Early in 1958, he initiated the building of a prototype N-156F as a company-sponsored project. It was a gamble, but a well-timed gamble. U.S. defense officials began to recognize the logic of buying a new airplane more suited to " mutual assistance" programs for allied countries. Finally, in May 1958, the Air Force, acting on behalf of the Department of Defense, issued a letter of intent authorizing the company to build three prototype N-156F airplanes.

Work on the N-156F's accelerated. Commonality with T-38 parts and tooling shortened schedule time. As a result, No. 1 prototype made its first flight at Edwards Air Force Base on July 30, 1959, less than four months after the first flight of the T-38. Test pilot on both historic flights was Lew Nelson.

Following completion and flight test of the No. 2 prototype N-156F, work was halted on No. 3 prototype. The Air Force felt that the remaining tests would not require an additional airplane. The partially

completed third airframe was placed in storage. At the conclusion of the flight test program, when the need for this class of airplane at home or abroad was not in the immediate present, the program was temporarily halted.

A possible reprieve for the N-156F came the following year when the Army announced an interest in jets for close support of ground troops. In actual competition, the N-156F not only demonstrated outstanding capabilities in limited warfare situations, but also scored high marks for its maintainability and operational readiness. Unfortunately for the N-156F, the Army was denied jurisdiction over this class of warfare by the Department of Defense, and the competition was cancelled.

Finally in May 1962, all the effort expended in behalf of the N-156F found justification. The Department of Defense took an unprecedented step. It announced the selection of the N-156F as a defensive arm for favored nations under the Military Assistance Program (MAP). DOD assigned the procurement and management of the program to the Air Force.

N-156F PROTOTYPE NO. 1 rolled out of the Advanced Production Hangar on May 30, 1959. The "Freedom Fighter" was unveiled for the first time to visitors from over 40 foreign countries.

N-156F DESIGN PATENT was held by Welko Gasich (left), Chief of Advanced Design (presently General Manager of the Aircraft Division). Also instrumental in the success of the "Freedom Fighter" were Gerhardt Neumann (center), General Manager of General Electric's Jet Engine Division, and Ray Gardner (right), Northrop's N-156 Project Engineer.

IN FIRST FLIGHT at Edwards Air Force Base, July 30, 1959, test pilot Lew Nelson exceeded Mach 1 in a shallow dive in N-156F without afterburner engines. He reported, "Transition to supersonic, as with the T-38's, is so smooth you have to watch the instruments to know when it happens."

ARMY MARKINGS were painted on N-156F Prototype No. 1 when it was sent to Pensacola, Florida, in mid-1961 to participate in demonstration trials. The Army had jurisdiction over the close air support role of ground troops. The N-156F scored high marks for operational readiness and ability to operate from sod fields. The ground support mission shortly thereafter passed to the Air Force.

In October 1962, the company received a $20-million order and authority to produce both single- and two-place versions of the N-156. They were designated F-5A and F-5B, respectively. In order to put the first F-5A into the air as quickly as possible, No. 3 N-156F prototype was taken "out of mothballs" and rebuilt into the F-5A configuration. This airplane became the YF-5A. It was first flown on July 31, 1963, at Edwards Air Force Base by Hank Chouteau.

All three N-156F's were predominantly of riveted aluminum alloy, semimonocoque structure with stressed skin. Considerable use was also made of adhesive-bonded aluminum honeycomb. The thin wing was built as a single unit from tip to tip, with multiple spars and thick aluminum alloy skins. The leading-edge flaps, trailing-edge flaps, ailerons, detachable wingtips, and various sections of the wing were honeycomb-stiffened structures. The all-movable ("flying") tailplane (elevators) and rudder were likewise stiffened with honeycomb. Although the stressed skin fuselage was primarily of aluminum alloy construction, the canted,

far-aft section surrounding the engine tailpipes and supporting the tailplane was made up of a combination of materials, including steel and titanium. A 15-foot drag parachute was stowed just below the rudder in the aft fuselage.

Fuel was carried in bladder-type cells located in the fuselage behind the pilot's compartment. Single-point refueling permitted simultaneous pressure refueling of all tanks. Additional fuel could be carried in wing-mounted pylon tanks. Full-power controls were provided for the ailerons, tailplane, and rudder. A subsystem permitted Dutch-roll damping, and the rudder and ailerons were interconnected for programmed coordination.

The wide-stance retractable tricycle landing gear was hydraulically actuated. It had single main wheels retracting inwardly on the wing-mounted air-oil shock struts. The single, steerable nose wheel retracted forward into the fuselage.

Over 25 percent of the fuselage area was comprised of doors or removable panels, greatly simplifying access to the various systems and adding to the airplane's reputation for simple maintenance. The twin General Electric YJ85 turbojet engines were mounted side by side in the aft fuselage. Installed on built-in overhead tracks with simple two-point mounting, the small and lightweight engines could be installed or removed with ease. A cartridge starter was fitted to the right-hand engine; bleed air was then used to start the other. Supplementing the main power plants, four 1,000-pound JATO bottles could be mounted enabling the N-156F to operate from very short fields. After making 32 flights with the original non-afterburning YJ85-1 engines, No.

1 prototype was refitted with the specified afterburning YJ85-5 engines for a significant increase in performance.

As prototypes, the N-156F's were equipped with one Sidewinder infrared homing missile mounted on each wingtip. In addition, many combinations of external stores could be carried on the lower fuselage centerline, on the two underwing stations and on the wingtips. Proposed stores included the Sparrow (2), Falcon (2), Sidewinder (2), Bullpup (2), Zuni-pack (8), 2.75-inch FFAR (24), 50 caliber gun (4), Gatling 20mm gun pack, and a wide range of bombs up to 1,000 pounds each.

FREEDOM FIGHTER'S ARSENAL. Whether in the intercept, strike, ground support, or reconnaissance role, the N-156F could carry a variety of stores. The fighter had a high ratio of firepower (payload) per pound of aircraft weight.

N-156F

94987

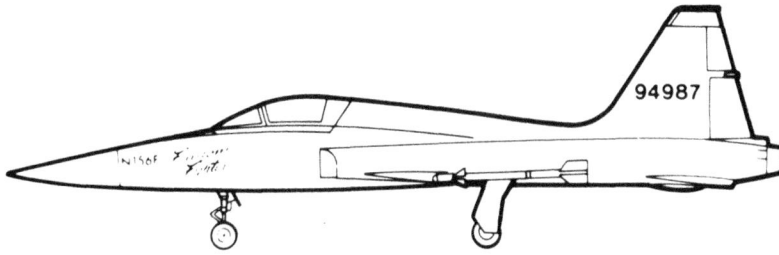

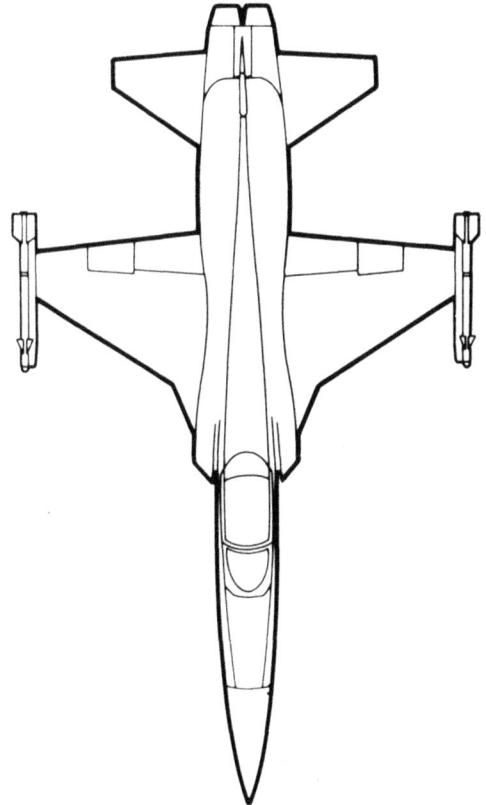

SPECIFICATIONS

WING SPAN . . . . .25 FT., 3 IN.

OVERALL LENGTH . . . . .45 FT., 1 IN.

OVERALL HEIGHT . . . . .13 FT., 1 IN.

WING AREA . . . . .170 SQ. FT.

TAKEOFF WEIGHT . . . . .12,190 LB

SPEED-MAXIMUM . . . . .MACH 1.3

SPEED-CRUISING . . . . .MACH 0.88

RANGE . . . . .2,230 MILES (FERRY)

SERVICE CEILING . . . . .55,600 FT.

POWER — (2) G.E. J85-5 TURBOJET, 3,850-LB THRUST

ARMAMENT — (2) SIDEWINDER IR MISSILES

X-21A LAMINAR FLOW CONTROL (LFC)

Long experimenting in the control of boundary layer air over wing surfaces, Northrop finally arrived at the first step toward a practical demonstration with the maiden flight of the X-21A on April 18, 1963. Jack Wells was the test pilot on the 75-mile flight from Hawthorne to Edwards Air Force Base.

For 14 years company scientists and engineers had been actively engaged in "boundary layer" research and development. If the layers of air passing over the surface of a wing in flight could be controlled, aerodynamic drag would be lessened and the efficiency of the airplane thereby maximized. This type of research became known as Laminar Flow Control (LFC).

The significance of LFC lay in its prospect for increasing either the range, payload, or flight endurance of large airplanes by 50 percent or more without increase in fuel consumption. The control was created by a boundary layer suction system inside the specially designed X-21A wings. This elaborate system of thin slots, ducts, and induced suction could eliminate up to 80 percent of the friction drag attributed to air turbulence over the wings of conventional airplanes. LFC operated during the cruise portion of flight. It had no relationship with other forms of boundary layer control that provided high lift during landing and takeoff.

EXTENSIVE MODIFICATION of the two Douglas WB-66D fuselage structures was required to accept the LFC wing and elaborate air suction system. The X-21A program, which was managed by Don Warner, currently Vice President of Engineering in the Aircraft Division, had reached this stage in October 1962.

MATING WING TO FUSELAGE (above and right) to create the No. 1 X-21A. Major modifications were made to the original WB-66D airframe, and the wing was entirely new.

NEW J79 TURBOJET ENGINES (left) were mounted alongside the aft portion of the X-21A fuselage instead of the original underwing locations. The fuselage was strengthened to accept the added structural weight. The top of the fuselage was aerodynamically faired.

NO. 1 X-21A takes off from Edwards Air Force Base where it was subsequently flown in demonstration tests at altitudes up to 45,000 feet and speeds up to Mach 0.8.

Whatever success LFC has attained in the scientific world belongs to Dr. Werner Pfenninger, a Swiss-born scientist who began his investigations in 1936. Dr. Pfenninger joined Northrop in 1949 and immediately inaugurated a low-drag boundary layer control research program. Milt Kuska (later Vice President, F-5 Programs) was manager in charge of the design phase; Don Warner (later Vice President, Engineering) was manager of the fabrication and flight test phases.

Working under Air Force contract and having recourse to vastly improved wind tunnels, Dr. Pfenninger was able to conduct tests which convinced him that boundary layer suction could be made to work in flight. Over 200 flights of an F-94 jet fighter with a 69-slot "glove" airfoil on its wing attested to the feasibility of LFC on large straight wings; more extensive wind tunnel testing further demonstrated that LFC could be successfully applied to swept wings as well.

The demonstration X-21A was a modified Air Force WB-66D Weather Observation airplane. It was one of two that were rebuilt expressly for LFC flight testing. No. 2 X-21A, which flew in August 1963, differed only in the addition of electrical de-icing and extra test instrumentation.

The two redesigned Douglas WB-66D's were fitted with new and larger wings at Hawthorne. The span was increased from 72 feet 6 inches to 93 feet 6 inches, and the overall area enlarged from 780 to 1,250 square feet. Two General Electric J79 turbojets replaced the original J71 engines, and the new power plants were mounted on the aft fuselage. Nacelles containing suction devices were installed beneath the wings.

The mechanics for achieving LFC were little short of staggering. Seventeen thousand linear feet, or over three miles, of paper-thin slits were sawed into the outer wing skins, running spanwise from root to tip, top and bottom. Interior to each slit, a small plenum chamber gathered the incoming air and channeled it through very small holes into ducts that led to the underwing nacelles. The wing contained no less than 816,000 metering holes and 68,000 tributary ducts!

Within each wing-mounted nacelle, two suction compressors were driven by bleed and bleed-burn turbines operating on air from the main propulsion engines. The suction system discharged all "inhaled" air from the rear of the two pods, thereby generating additional thrust.

The Northrop research and development program for LFC resulted in a number of novel manufacturing and tooling techniques. They were necessary to accomplish the fabrication of the unorthodox wing structures. The requirement for smooth, wave-free external surfaces prescribed an assembly operation that built the wing from the outside mold line inward. Contoured bonding fixtures of aluminum plate stock were machined on a numerically-controlled profile mill to .002-inch wave-free accuracy. Wing construction used honeycomb and metal-to-metal thermoset bonded surface skins, employing adhesive tapes especially designed for the stringent requirements.

Drilling of the 816,000 suction holes was automated. A self-propelled, track-mounted, electronically controlled feed-and-speed drilling tool, with automatic indexing to .25-inch spacing, made 90 holes per minute. Other specialized methods were developed for milling

the plenum chambers and sawing the fine intake slits. "Computer designing" techniques were used to determine the sizes and discharge rates of 22 different-size tributary ducts to equalize airflow from various sections of the wing.

When the two X-21A airplanes were ready for flight demonstration at Edwards, they embarked on a schedule requiring tests at altitudes of between 25,000 and 45,000 feet, at speeds up to Mach 0.8. In addition to the pilot and two flight observers, the X-21A's carried two flight engineers in the lower fuselage under the wing center section. Each flight engineer was seated at a bank of instruments to control and monitor LFC suction in one of the wings. Supplementing the Air Force contract, the flight test evaluation program was supported by funding from the Federal Aviation Authority (FAA). Applications of LFC to commercial transports were thought to be promising.

X-21A DEMONSTRATION TESTS proved that the aircraft could remain in the air far longer with the LFC system operating than without it. Spanwise "air-breathing" slits in the outer wing skin were the entry into an intricate network of slits, bleed holes, plenum chambers, ducts, and compressors – all to maintain laminar flow near the surface of the wing. The chordwise strips shown were flight test instrumentation.

Although extensive wind tunnel work had been previously performed on the demonstration wing configuration, an unanticipated phenomenon appeared after initial flights at Edwards. Turbulent air at the wing leading edge was being shunted outboard before curling aft and was "dumping" across the wing surface. The air "contaminated" leading edge flow, and had the effect of breeding turbulence across the forward sections of the wing. Eventually, the LFC team scored a breakthrough when it discovered that by adding an extension incorporating chord-wise slits to the wing leading edge and ducted to the suction system, the slits served to control the outboard movement of air. The leading edge slits induced the air to become laminar and to pass directly over the wing where the LFC system suction pumps could draw it through the spanwise slits. When the condition was corrected, LFC results immediately improved. During the months following system improvement, the percentage of wing area with laminar air flow was continually increased. At the conclusion of the X-21A flight test program, LFC was consistently being achieved on 73 percent of the upper, and 75 percent of the lower, wing surfaces. One-hundred percent chord laminar flow was achieved in areas away from local discontinuities such as control surfaces. In a typical flight demonstration, the X-21A had sufficient fuel for two hours and 25 minutes flying time without LFC. With the LFC system operating, the flight time was increased to approximately four hours using the same amount of fuel.

Following the accomplishment of LFC on the X-21A wings, additional tests were conducted to explore the impact of rain, sleet and snow on the system. Other tests were run to determine the effects of maneuvers, turbulent air, humidity, clouds, and the impingement of dust, dirt, or insects. The results of these investigations suggested that contamination from the atmosphere might raise maintenance costs in a military service environment. This problem dimmed immediate prospects for any practical application of LFC. Another factor was the concurrent development of the long-range turbofan jet engine. The turbofan was proving that it could furnish the range and endurance through a more conventional method. As a consequence, further development of LFC was set aside in 1964.

LOW-PRESSURE COMPRESSOR (above) in the forward part of the X-21A wing nacelle, and high-pressure compressor (below) in the aft were driven by an air turbine motor and a gas turbine motor, respectively. Turbine and compressor exhausts were discharged aft via co-axial jet nozzles. The two-stage pumping system was developed by AiResearch Manufacturing Division of Garrett Corporation.

How the term LFC came into being makes an interesting historical sidelight. In 1960, when the project was just getting under way, a name suitable for both the program and the experimental aircraft was actively solicited. Northrop sponsored a contest among members of the Aviation/Space Writers Association to suggest a name for Dr. Pfenninger's "low drag boundary control technique." The winning name — Laminar Flow Control or LFC — was submitted by Arthur Kranish, Washington-based columnist of the trade journal Western Aerospace.

X-21A

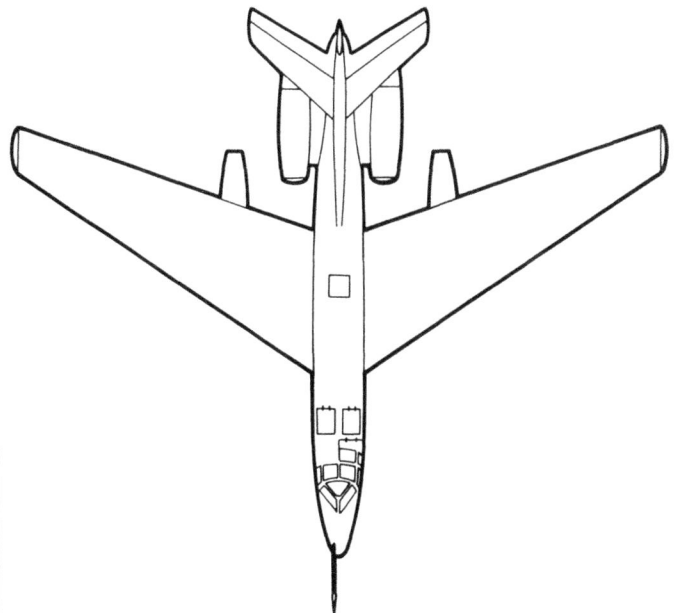

SPECIFICATIONS

```
WING SPAN . . . . . . . . . . . . . . . . . . . . . . . . . . . . .93 FT., 6 IN.
OVERALL LENGTH . . . . . . . . . . . . . . . . . . . . . .75 FT., 6 IN.
OVERALL HEIGHT . . . . . . . . . . . . . . . . . . . . . .23 FT., 7 IN.
WING AREA . . . . . . . . . . . . . . . . . . . . . . . . . . . .1,250 SQ. FT.
TAKEOFF WEIGHT . . . . . . . . . . . . . . . . . . . . . . . . .83,000 LB
SPEED-MAXIMUM . . . . . . . . . . . . . . . . . . . . . . .MACH 0.85
SPEED-CRUISING . . . . . . . . . . . . . . . . . . . . . . . . . .MACH 0.75
RANGE . . . . . . . . . . . . . . .2.4 HRS NORMAL/4 HRS WITH LFC
SERVICE CEILING . . . . . . . . . . . . . . . . . . . . . . . . . . . .45,000 FT.
POWER — (2) G.E. J79-13-7 TURBOJET, 9,400-LB THRUST
```

F-5A, F-5B TACTICAL FIGHTERS

After an extensive evaluation of several contemporary fighter aircraft, the Department of Defense (DOD) selected the N-156F in May 1962 to modernize the air force inventories of selected countries participating in the Military Assistance Program (MAP). At that time, two of the three prototypes had already completed their flight test program at Edwards Air Force Base. The third, a partially fabricated airframe, had been placed in storage. DOD assigned the procurement and management of the new "Freedom Fighter" program to the Air Force.

In October, the program was formalized with an initial order for two versions of the N-156F. These single-place and two-place tactical fighters were designated F-5A and F-5B, respectively. Aft of the cockpit, both were identical. The two-place F-5B was also able to fulfill a training role similar to the T-38. The initial production order authorized 71 F-5A's and 15 F-5B's under the MAP program.

The F-5 was the first military weapon system designed and developed by the United States specifically to meet the military conditions and requirements of the MAP countries. Primary emphasis was placed on achievement of outstanding operational capabilities while maintaining supersonic performance, superior handling qualities, and low acquisition and operational costs.

To achieve these goals, designers took advantage of the same new technological features and "second generation" aerodynamics which had been applied to the predecessor N-156 and T-38 aircraft. Noteworthy features were the use of two small jet engines with very high thrust-to-weight ratios; a small, lightweight airframe; area-ruled fuselage and tip tanks for transonic drag reduction; forebody camber also for transonic drag reduction; wing leading edge camber, for improvement of cruise characteristics; a low-set horizontal stabilizer with cathedral; improved directional stability; and Dutch roll damping. Low operational costs were ensured by the use of simplified systems, easy access to internal installations, and a ruggedized airframe.

NORWAY SELECTED the F-5A (above) and F-5B in 1964 after a series of evaluation flights of several types of aircraft conducted by Norwegian Air Force at Edwards AFB. Initial procurement was for three squadrons in the 1966-67 time period.

F-5B ROLLOUT. Two-place fighter version made its appearance in February 1964, and was then transferred to Edwards AFB for flight test.

Completion of the No. 1 prototype was expedited by taking the partially completed N-156F out of storage and rebuilding it into the new configuration. This airplane became YF-5A No. 1. Test pilot Hank Chouteau made the first flight at Edwards AFB on July 31, 1963.

Although the F-5A airplane was essentially the same as it progenitor, the N-156F, some important improvements were incorporated: greater thrust with General Electric J85-13 engines, and seven external locations for armament and additional fuel in place of the five stations on the N-156F. The stations included one centerline pylon, four pylons under the wings, and provisions for two fuel tanks or two Sidewinder missiles on the wingtips. The F-5A also incorporated a more rugged landing gear with wider-tread tires for operation from umprepared fields.

These features endowed the F-5 with the capability of a dual-role fighter, able to penetrate into hostile territory with more than 6,000 pounds of ordnance. In its primary role as a tactical fighter, the F-5 could provide close support of ground troops, strike and interdiction of enemy communications and supply lines, and surveillance of enemy territory. Equipped with two 20mm cannon in the nose and Sidewinder missiles on the wingtips, the agile F-5 was a highly effective interceptor in the air-to-air role. By means of a special nose section and camera installation, and extra fuel, the F-5A also could be converted into an RF-5A long-range reconnaissance airplane.

A total of eight F-5A/B test airplanes were used in the development and demonstration flight test program. Three were the original N-156F prototypes, and five were new airframes, one of which was configured as an F-5B. The prototype two-place F-5B made its first flight in February 1964 at Edwards AFB.

Although the success of the "Freedom Fighter" has customarily been ascribed to its designed-in, cost-effective performance, another factor made a significant contribution to the airplane's lower unit cost, and increased quality and reliability. That other factor was a unique three-dimensional production line at Hawthorne originally developed for T-38 production under the direction of Bob Lloyd, Director of Manufacturing Engineering at that time, and known as NORAIL (Northrop Overhead Rail Assembly and Installation Line), it was one of the newest and most modern aircraft production facilities in the world. It consisted of twin lines totaling 1,600 feet in length, accommodating the simultaneous assembly of three different aircraft-the F-5A, the F-5B, and the T-38. "The NORAIL system was designed expressly to capitalize on the accessibility and ease of maintenance that are an inherent part of the F-5 family design," said Jack Mannion, Manager of Manufacturing and Materiel, in 1964. "Because of the similarity in size and configuration of the F-5A, B, and T-38, the airplanes have many similar parts; some are common to all three, particularly aft of the cockpit sections."

BY JANUARY 1963, a single assembly line was already accommodating early T-38 production orders. Ceiling tracks, running lengthwise and crosswise, facilitated hoisting and lowering of heavy assemblies.

HAWTHORNE ASSEMBLY

NORAIL SYSTEM

THE FOLLOWING YEAR, 1964, a dual assembly line (F-5 on left, T-38 on right) was operating at the main Hawthorne plant.

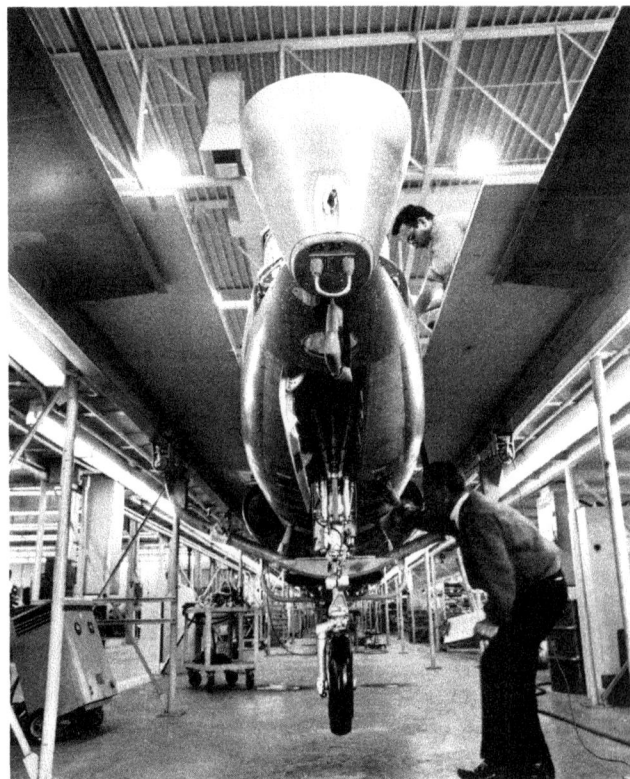

UPPER AND LOWER DECKS allowed simultaneous work at both levels. NORAIL (Northrop Overhead Rail Assembly and Installation Line) facilitated production operations.

WING ASSEMBLY accomplished in fixtures with different-level work platforms. Main NORAIL twin-assembly line can be seen in the background.

NORAIL SYSTEM moved components, held in fixtures attached to overhead rail, from station to station. Here the forward fuselage fixture rotates to permit easy access.

FLAT BED TRAILER at last NORAIL station received finished fuselage, wing assembly, and boattail section for transport to Palmdale. At Palmdale the aircraft was final assembled and the engines installed.

203

IN EARLY DAYS, 1961, the Palmdale facility mated the main assemblies shipped from Hawthorne to complete the aircraft.

PALMDALE ASSEMBLY

EIGHT YEARS LATER, 1969 (same area as above) Palmdale had its own NORAIL system, was able to perform some subassembly and final assembly, thus relieving the production burden on Hawthorne.

TWO-PLACE F-5B and T-38, alongside one another, reveal similarity in aerodynamic lines and configuration. Visible differences are the F-5B's wing leading-edge movable flap for greater maneuverability in combat, ordnance carriage, and the leading edge extension at the wing root.

These factors permitted the simultaneous movement of F-5's down one NORAIL line, and T-38's down the other. While assemblers standing on the floor were working on the lower portion of the fuselages, others on the deck above worked on the top portion. The forward fuselage sections were slung in a cradle that could be rotated in a complete circle, making cockpit work a stand-up procedure.

When the first MAP order took effect, the built-in flexibility of the NORAIL system enabled the assembly rate to jump from 12 airplanes per month to 22. As production accelerated at Hawthorne, the list of recipient MAP countries likewise grew. The list expanded to include Iran, South Korea, the Philippines, Turkey, Greece, and the Republic of China.

The attractiveness of the F-5 to non-MAP countries became evident early in 1964, when the Norwegian government announced the direct purchase of three squadrons of F-5A and F-5B aircraft with special features for the rugged operating environment in Norway. Ten months later, the Spanish Air Force announced a production-under-license order for 70 fighters designated SF-5A and SF-5B. Under the terms of the licensing plan, Northrop and Construcciones Aeronauticas S.A. (CASA) would cooperate in production.

In July 1965, Canada became the third non-MAP country to enter into a direct purchase arrangement for F-5's. These aircraft, designated CF-5, were to be constructed in Canada by Canadair Ltd. of Montreal under license to Northrop. The CF-5 had more powerful General Electric J85-15 engines and inflight fueling capability. Other features included two-position nose gear for quicker takeoffs, arresting hook, armor plate, and anti-icing. Later, also under license to Northrop, Canada produced F-5's for The Netherlands and Venezuela.

SKOSHI TIGER

"SKOSHI TIGER," refueling over Wake Island, on way to Vietnam in 1965. Within three months of readiness alert, twelve F-5A aircraft were modified in the U.S., crews trained, trans-Pacific flights made, and first combat sortie launched.

BOMB DROP. F-5A on mission of a 4 1/2-month combat evaluation. Twelve aircraft flew 2,600 sorties over a period of 150 days. Operational-ready rate: 85 percent. Abort rate: 1.5 percent.

BATTLE SCORES (bomb drops) painted on nose of F-5A redeployed from Vietnam. The single-place fighter had been modified to latest configuration in addition to being equipped with jettisonable pylons, armor plate, and refueling probe, before flying to Southeast Asia.

RETURNED TO U.S., camouflaged ''Skoshi Tiger'' undergoing further nighttime tests at Edwards Air Force Base.

The U.S. Air Force launched a program in 1965 to evaluate 12 F-5 aircraft in the Vietnam environment of limited war operations. These F-5's, sometimes labeled F-5C's, were more commonly identified as "Skoshi Tigers." Before proceeding overseas, the Skoshi Tigers underwent wartime modifications: jettisonable pylons, aerial refueling system, armor plate, camouflage. Operations ended early in 1966 after a four-and-one-half month tour of active duty in the combat zone. The trial evaluation definitely established the F-5 as a superior tactical fighter in a limited warfare environment, and one that sustained a high operational-ready rate with minor field maintenance.

By 1966 Ethiopia had become the latest allied nation to modernize its air force with MAP F-5 aircraft. The addition of Morocco and Thailand to the list of recipient MAP countries brought the roster of F-5 users to 17. By 1974 no less than 20 countries were operating over 1,100 F-5A and F-5B aircraft. The tactical fighter's reputation was firmly established as a cost-effective weapons system.

Between 1964 and 1965, the F-5A captured 85 percent of the weapons delivery meets in which it was entered. These formal contests took place both in the United States and in foreign countries, and against a variety of first-line fighters.

Structure of the F-5A and F-5B was essentially the same as that of the N-156F. It was predominantly of riveted aluminum alloy, semimonocoque with stressed skin. Considerable use was made of adhesive-bonded aluminum honeycomb and chemically-milled structural parts. The thin wing was built as a single unit from tip to tip, with multiple spars and thick aluminum skins. The leading-edge flaps, trailing-edge flaps, ailerons, and various sections of the wing were honeycomb-stiffened structures. The all-movable ("flying") horizontal stabilizer and rudder were likewise stiffened with honeycomb. Although the stressed-skin fuselage was predominantly of aluminum alloy construction, the aft section surrounding the engines and supporting the horizontal stabilizer was made up of a combination of different materials, including steel and titanium.

SPANISH AIR FORCE received its first SF-5B in May 1968 from Construcciones Aeronauticas S.A. (CASA). CASA had licensing agreement with Northrop to build SF-5A's and SF-5B's at its plants in Getafe, near Madrid, and Seville.

Fuel system simplicity reduced the pilot's fuel management task to a minimum. Internal fuel was contained in rubber-impregnated nylon fabric cells in the fuselage behind the cockpit area, containing a total tankage of 585 gallons. External tanks at the wingtips, inboard wing stations, and fuselage centerline totalled 550 gallons. Single-point refueling of internal and external tanks was accomplished through a pressure fitting on the underside of the fuselage. External tanks were pressurized to supply the two separate fuselage systems as fuel was consumed. The fuselage systems normally supplied each engine independently; a crossfeed was provided for single-engine operation.

As on the N-156F, the wide-stance tricycle landing gear was hydraulically actuated. Two independent 3,000-psi hydraulic systems were operated from engine-driven pumps. By means of dual and tandem actuators, the output of both left and right systems was used to power the primary flight control surfaces. The primary flight controls-ailerons, rudder, and all movable horizontal stabilizer-were operated by conventional stick and rudder controls. Secondary flight controls consisted of hydraulically operated speed brakes and electrically driven, three-position, leading-and trailing-edge wing flaps. An electro-hydraulic stability augmenter system controlled both rudder and horizontal tail motion, damped short-period pitch and yaw oscillations, and provided rudder trim.

Engine compressor bleed air pressurized and conditioned the cockpit, defogged windshield and canopy, inflated canopy seals and pilot's anti-G suit, cooled equipment, and pressurized the hydraulic reservoir. Each cockpit in the F-5B had its own manually operated canopy closure. The two canopies were automatically jettisoned if the pilots elected to operate their rocket-powered ejection seats.

Over 25 percent of the fuselage area was comprised of doors and removable panels. This greatly simplified access to the various systems and added to the airplane's reputation for simple maintenance. During periods of accelerated operations, only fuel and ordnance were required after each flight; all other inspection or replenishment normally was accomplished on a once-daily basis.

CANADA became the third country to acquire the F-5 by direct purchase, after Norway and Spain, and the ninth in the list that added the tactical fighter to its defense inventory. Canada and Spain operated under licensed manufacturing agreements with Northrop.

CANADAIR MANUFACTURING FACILITIES. Canada produced F-5A's and F-5B's for herself as well as for The Netherlands and Venezuela.

FIRST CF-5A to roll off the Canadair production line in Montreal, Canada, February 1968. It was immediately flown to Edwards AFB to participate in a flight test program.

The two General Electric J85-13 engines were mounted side by side in the aft fuselage. Installed on built-in overhead tracks with simple two-point mounting, the small, lightweight engines (each 570 pounds with afterburner) could be installed or removed with ease. Three skilled ground crewmen could remove and replace an engine in twenty minutes. An integrated power package, including gearbox, alternating current generator and hydraulic pump, was mounted on the airframe forward of each engine. By disconnecting the engine drive shaft from the power package, each engine could be removed without disturbing the electrical or hydraulic system.

The F-5A was equipped with two nose-mounted 20mm cannon. Although the "B" model carried no nose armament, both the single-place and two-place had seven external store stations, accommodating a full spectrum of tactical ordnance and/or fuel for extended missions. For example, four Bullpup missiles, or four rocket pods, could be carried, the latter providing seventy-six 2.75-inch FFAR rockets or sixteen 5-inch HVAR rockets. Sidewinder missiles could be mounted on the wing tips, and many other combinations of external stores could be carried up to a maximum of 6,200 pounds. In the photo-reconnaissance version of the F-5A, four 70mm cameras were mounted in the nose along with the two 20 mm cannons.

After seven years of test and development flying at Edwards AFB, the original YF-5A was retired. In August 1970, this prototype (tail no. 94989) was sent to the Air Force Museum, Wright-Patterson AFB, Ohio, for display.

Following more than eight years of production, the last of the F-5A's was delivered in June 1972.

REPUBLIC OF CHINA was a recipient of the tactical fighter in the late Sixties. Later, it became a coproducer of the F-5E version under agreement with Northrop.

TACTICAL AIR COMMAND (TAC) F-5A's and F-5B's in flight echelon with camouflaged, combat-tested "Skoshi Tigers." Air Force pilots of the 4441st Combat Crew Training Squadron, Williams AFB, Arizona, familiarized pilots from user countries in the performance of the "Freedom Fighter."

F-5A

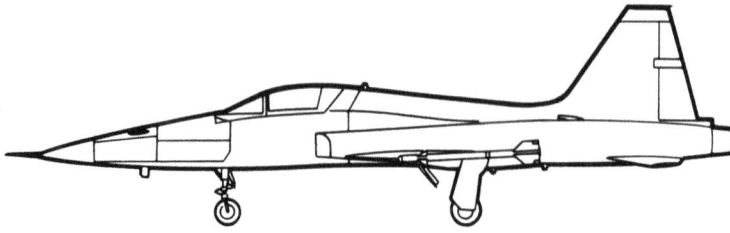

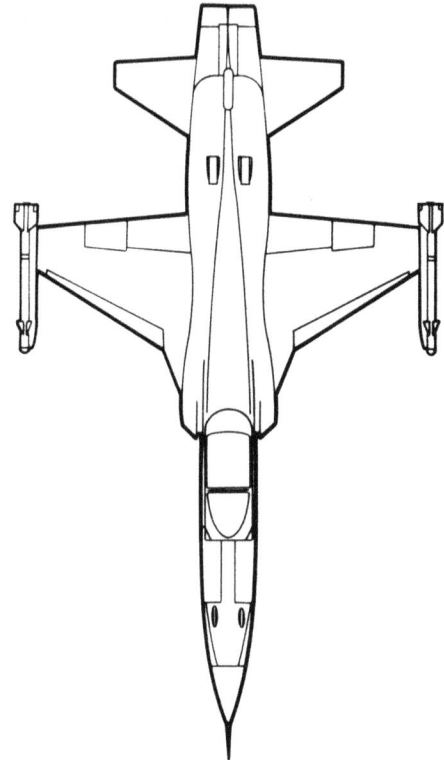

SPECIFICATIONS

WING SPAN . . . . .25 FT., 3 IN.

OVERALL LENGTH . . . . .46 FT., 11 IN.

OVERALL HEIGHT . . . . .13 FT., 2 IN.

WING AREA . . . . .170 SQ. FT.

CLEAN TAKEOFF WEIGHT .13,170 LB

MAX. TAKEOFF WEIGHT . . . . .19,860 LB

SPEED-MAXIMUM . . . . .MACH 1.4

SPEED-CRUISING . . . . .MACH 0.84

RANGE . . . . .1,400 MILES

SERVICE CEILING . . . . .50,000 FT.

POWER — (2) G.E. J85-13 TURBOJET, 4,080-LB THRUST

ARMAMENT — (2) 20MM CANNON;
              (2) SIDEWINDER IR MISSILES

F-5B

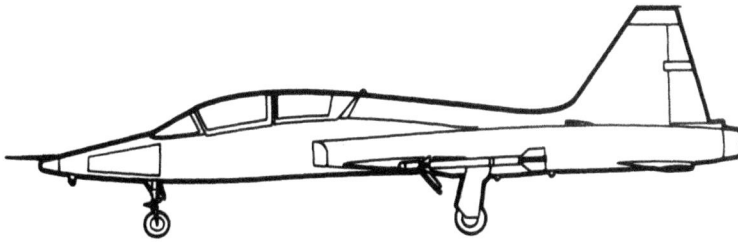

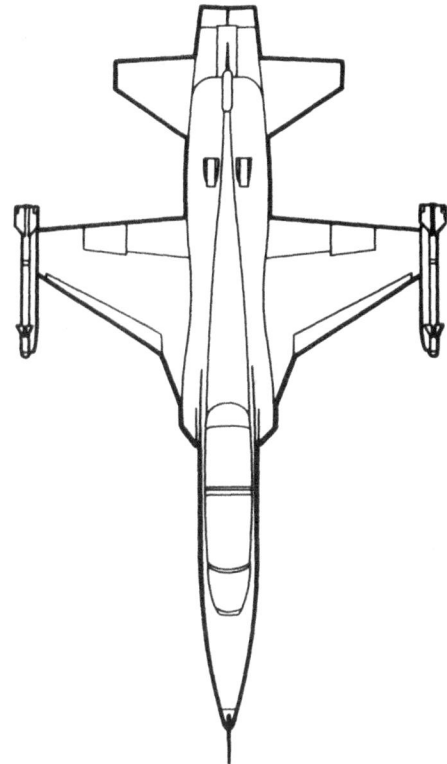

SPECIFICATIONS

WING SPAN . . . . .25 FT., 3 IN.

OVERALL LENGTH . . . . .46 FT., 1 IN.

OVERALL HEIGHT . . . . .13 FT., 2 IN.

WING AREA . . . . .170 SQ. FT.

CLEAN TAKEOFF WEIGHT . . . . .12,530 LB

MAX. TAKEOFF WEIGHT . . . . .19,510 LB

SPEED-MAXIMUM . . . . .MACH 1.34

SPEED-CRUISING. . . . . .MACH 0.84

RANGE . . . . .1,400 MILES

SERVICE CEILING . . . . .50,000 FT.

POWER — (2) G.E. J85-13, TURBOJET, 4,080-LB THRUST

ARMAMENT — (2) SIDEWINDER IR MISSILES

5

THE INTERNATIONAL LOOK

"THE COMPETITIVE AGE"

In early 1965 the aerospace industry once again faced a slowdown in new defense procurement. The government had requested industry to "take vigorous measures in finding ways to reduce costs and save defense dollars." Aerospace managers busied themselves seeking ways to channel skills and resources into commercial enterprises. But many officials were equally wary of the hazards of plunging into new ventures, particularly when they meant conducting both defense and commercial business under one roof. Memories of similar efforts in the post-World War II era with their catastrophic results were still fresh in mind.

Northrop reemphasized its determination to stay in the tactical fighter field which would be its primary thrust over the next two decades. This would be augmented by a broadening of its manufacturing base by major subcontracting of cargo/transport subassemblies. To keep its technological leadership "razor sharp" the company would continue to seek research and prototype projects.

Fortunately for Northrop, military sales continued to increase for both the T-38 supersonic trainer and the

F-5 tactical fighter. In particular, earlier F-5 sales efforts in foreign markets were now beginning to pay off.

In 1966, the commercial picture loomed even brighter. The company embarked on one of the most ambitious and challenging undertakings in its first quarter century of existence. It joined with The Boeing Company to produce the main passenger fuselage section of the 747 airliner.

The new program was established entirely on a risk-sharing basis with Boeing. Northrop's task was to do the detail design and build the 153-foot long, 21-foot wide fuselage section. Boeing and Northrop signed the largest contract in aviation history for airframe assemblies — a $450 million order for 201 shipsets.

The decision to proceed with the program represented a major step into the commercial aircraft business. More than 4,000 new employees had to be hired and trained for the program, and a modern new 500,000-square-foot assembly plant had to be designed and built.

BUSINESS WITH THE BOEING COMPANY started with Northrop's first birthday, 1940, and has continued to date. (Top) 1,660 aft fuselage sets (KC-135, 707 combined) delivered on schedule. (Center) Outer wing panels for same aircraft. (Lower left) One of three all-titanium wing test sections fabricated for Boeing's proposed Supersonic Transport. (Lower right) SST test cabin.

THE BOEING
AFFILIATION

NEW PLANT 3, operational in May 1967, built expressly to expand the Aircraft Division's large airframe assembly (747) capabilities. (Center) Interior of Plant 3. (Lower right) Upper bonnet section of the 747 fuselage. (Lower left) 747 skin handling via overhead monorail in Plant 1.

FROM HAWTHORNE, CALIFORNIA TO EVERETT, WASHINGTON. Since 1968, specially designed railcars have been carrying Northrop-built fuselage panels to The Boeing Company for the final assembly of its 747 airliner (opposite, above). Northrop fabricated the 153-foot long, 21-foot-wide main passenger section. Other contractual commitments included fabrication of wing fairings, cargo doors, and flooring. The California-based company started shipments for the short-body Special Performance 747SP in 1974 (photo inset and opposite, below).

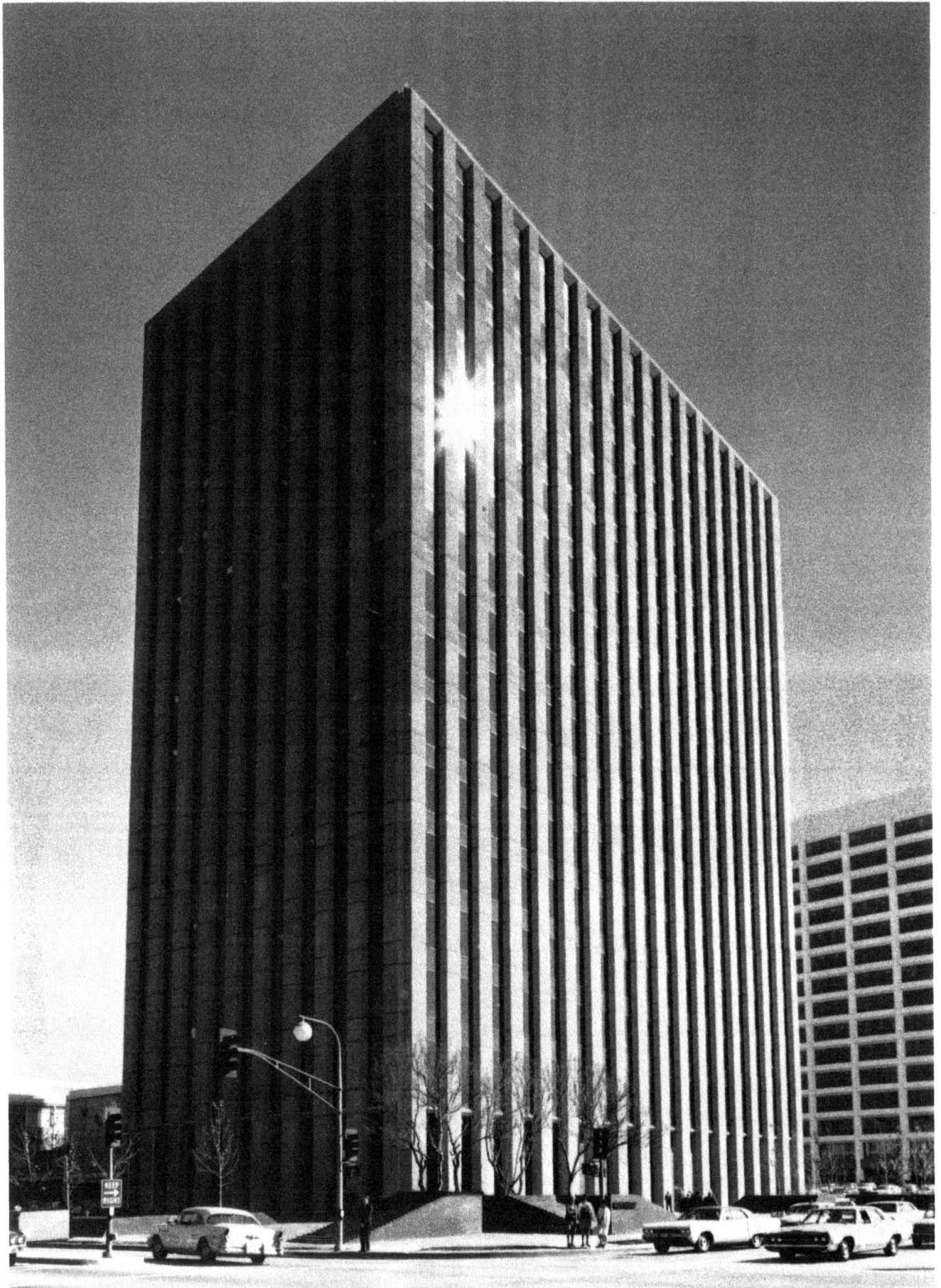

NEW CORPORATE OFFICES in Century City, Los Angeles, were occupied in October 1970.

Although the magnitude and risks of the 747 program were new to the company, the association with Boeing was not. It could look back on a long and successful record of subcontract tasks for the Washington State-based firm. Beginning in 1929, William E. Boeing and John K. Northrop had founded the original Northrop Aircraft Corporation to produce the Alpha airplanes. The Boeing association had resumed in 1939 and extended through World War II when Northrop subcontracted sections of Boeing's famous "Flying Fortress" bombers. Later, Northrop manufactured parts for the Boeing B-50 bombers as well as C-97 tankers, wing surfaces for the KC-135 tankers, and finally 707 and 720 commercial airliner subassemblies into the Seventies.

By mid-December 1975, Northrop had delivered via special railway car, 274 shipsets, including freighter versions of the 747. Total business was approaching the $1 billion mark when the company agreed to produce the fuselage for the 747SP (Special Performance) airliner, a shorter-body version of the basic aircraft, designed for long-range, lower-passenger-density routes.

As of May 1976, total 747 deliveries amounted to 293 shipsets, including 13 SP's.

Northrop was also actively associated with Boeing during the life of the proposed Supersonic Transport (B-2707). As early as mid-1965, in anticipation of a subcontract arrangement in the exciting SST program, the company's research organzation began to perfect a "thin film" brazing process to enable fabrication of honeycomb sandwich structures in a new lightweight titanium alloy. Boeing then asked Northrop to build three all-titanium wing test sections representative of the outboard wing sections. The company also produced a full-scale test cabin section, fabricated entirely of titanium and containing 700 machined, welded, and formed parts. It was a forerunner of the aircraft forebody (the flight control cabin and articulated nose section) which Northrop would produce under contract if Boeing built two prototypes under a cost-sharing arrangement with the U.S. Department of Transportation. The entire SST program, however, was cancelled in March 1971 due to discontinuance of U.S. government support.

SST ARTICULATED NOSE and crew compartment was proposed for production by Northrop. Boeing mockup demonstrated utility of nose-down position to give pilot maximum visibility on landing. Nose shell in normal flight configuration afforded aerodynamic streamlining.

In the mid-Sixties the National Aeronautics and Space Administration (NASA) had configured manned research vehicles to help solve certain aerodynamic problems in controlling future spacecraft during the critical period between reentry and landing. These space experts turned to Northrop to build two wingless "lifting bodies," vehicles which were capable of achieving lift from body shape alone. The first was a NASA Ames Research Center design for a 5,000-pound craft which was designated M2-F2. The second was the HL-10 lifting body to be built in accordance with a NASA Langley Research Center design concept. The HL-10 configuration featured a rounded top surface and a flat bottom surface, which was the reverse airfoil of the M2-F2. Both the M2-F2 and the HL-10 flew many successful research missions.

The single-place F-5A and two-place F-5B twin-engine fighters continued to find favorable reception not only in the Far East but in Europe and the Middle East as well. By 1970 the list of nations operating the F-5A and F-5B had grown to seventeen.

In the fall of 1969 the Department of Defense decided to open to competition an aircraft that would be a relatively low-cost successor to the F-5A in meeting the needs of allied nations in Southeast Asia. Having applied the various research technologies to improve its original F-5 configuration, Northrop entered the F-5A-21. The advanced General Electric engines provided a 23 percent increase in thrust over the earlier -13 engines, resulting in significantly improved performance. The new fighter also incorporated more advanced avionics, including air-to-air radar, and a lead computing optical sight.

On November 20, 1970, the Air Force announced Northrop the winner of the International Fighter Aircraft competition. Two months later, the new F-5A-21 was redesignated the F-5E, and later named Tiger II. The F-5E was to find a receptive market overseas not only as a replacement for the "A" but also as a front-line fighter in those countries which were receiving Northrop aircraft for the first time. Commitments for the F-5E exceeded 450 even before the delivery of the first aircraft. In 1973 the production rate reached 15 per month; in mid-1975, 18 per month. In that same year $49 million was funded for development of the two-place F-5F as a companion fighter-trainer for the "E."

The A-X (Attack, Experimental) program had started in 1967 when Northrop received, as one of four aerospace firms, a contract to conduct exploratory studies of a tactical aircraft specifically designed for close air support of ground troops in a limited-war operation.

M2-F2 LIFTING BODY built in 1965 for the National Aeronautics and Space Administration (NASA). The M2-F2 and HL-10, also built by Northrop, made 78 successful flights, of which 45 were conducted under rocket power.

Northrop and Fairchild Industries were selected in December 1970, each to build two specialized close air support aircraft (A-X) over a 26-month development period, which included a competitive flyoff at Edwards AFB, California. The Northrop entry was designated A-9A. Walt Fellers, Bob Bratt, Jerry Huben, and Don Heinze were awarded the basic A-9A aircraft design patent. Although the A-9A achieved competitive performance and weapon delivery characteristics, it was not selected for the production contract.

Experience with the F-5 abroad gave the company an intimate understanding of the air force needs and the economic and industrial capabilities of many of the free countries of the world. To satisfy these needs, Northrop engineers designed the multirole N-300 in the late Sixties. The N-300 eventually evolved into the Cobra air superiority configuration, which was based on the concept of multination development and production participation in the new aircraft.

By 1972 the company had invested one million engineering manhours, 5,000 hours of wind tunnel testing, and one full-scale mockup in the P530 Cobra. The Cobra had now developed into a twin-jet, Mach 2-class, air superiority fighter with added capabilities for close support, interdiction, interception, and reconnaissance.

It was in this same time frame that USAF established a Lightweight Fighter (LWF) requirement. The intent was to demonstrate what modern technology could achieve to obtain the maximum in maneuverability for air-to-air superiority. Northrop submitted a design based on the P530 Cobra powered by two General Electric J101 engines. It was selected in April 1972, along with the General Dynamics entry, for a 12-month flight evaluation of two prototypes to be built in accordance with each contractor's interpretation of the Request for Proposal specifications. The Northrop aircraft was designated the YF-17.

F-5E's IN "BATTLE DRESS" being assembled at Palmdale facility, 1974. These aircraft were equipped with electronic equipment and other optional features according to customer's requirements. Customer in this instance was Saudi Arabia.

223

F-5E's *(FROM SAME ALLOTMENT SHOWN IN PRECEDING PHOTOGRAPH) being refueled in flight above Saudi Arabian desert, 1975 (above). Probe-and-drogue method is used; F-5 pilot guides the probe on the right hand side of his aircraft into drogue receptacle of KC-130 tanker (below).*

In time the LWF program transitioned into the Air Combat Fighter (ACF) program which called for a commitment to production not only for USAF but also possibly for a consortium of European countries (Belgium, The Netherlands, Norway, Denmark) seeking a replacement for the obsolete F-104's. Simultaneously, Northrop joined with McDonnell Douglas to submit a carrier-based version of the YF-17 in answer to a request from the Navy for a Navy Air Combat Fighter (NACF) mission. The YF-17 was not selected in the air combat fighters' competition; however, in 1975 the McDonnell Douglas (St. Louis)-Northrop F-18 (redesignated from YF-17) won the NACF competition.

F-5F "TIGER II" INTRODUCED MID-1975. Fully capable as both trainer and fighter, it is faster and more maneuverable than the earlier "B" model.

WALT FELLERS, Chief Designer, received the Aircraft Design Award for 1975 from the American Institute of Aeronautics and Astronautics (AIAA). He was cited for ''outstanding achievement over the past 30 years in the design and development of fighter aircraft.''

PRESIDENT TOM JONES congratulates Chief Test Pilot Hank Chouteau following first flight of YF-17 (Prototype No. 1), June 9, 1974.

''FAMILY OF AIRCRAFT'' displayed during rollout ceremonies for YF-17 (foreground), April 4, 1974. In background are an F-5E (camouflage paint), an F-5B (extreme left), a T-38 (rear), and an F-5A. The F-5F was still in a test stage at the time this photo was taken.

United States Patent Office

Des. 187,405
Patented Mar. 8, 1960

187,405

AIRPLANE

Welko E. Gasich, Pacific Palisades, George L. Gluyas, Garden Grove, Arthur M. Ogness, Rolling Hills, and Leon F. Begin, Jr., Pasadena, Calif., assignors to Northrop Corporation, a corporation of California

Application February 24, 1959, Serial No. 54,718

GENEALOGICAL LINES. Today's F-5E Tiger II, superimposed on the actual patent of the N-156F Freedom Fighter, dramatically shows the retention of sound aerodynamic lines. (See Chapter 4 for issuance of N-156F patent in 1960 to Welko Gasich et al.)

M2-F2/F3, HL-10 LIFTING BODIES

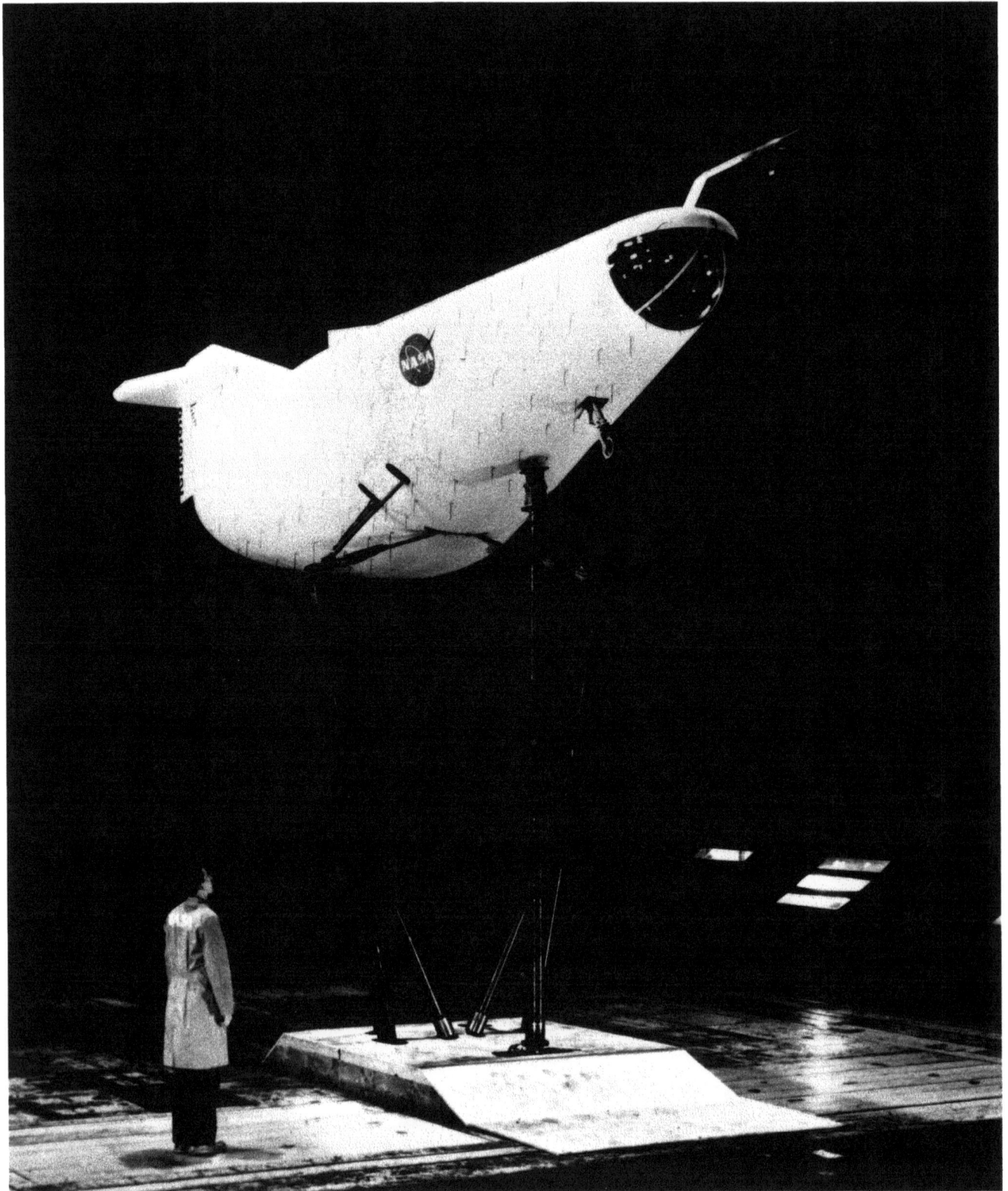

M2 CONFIGURATION was created by NASA at Ames Research Center, California, where Dr. Alfred J. Eggers first conceived the idea of lifting reentry bodies in 1957. Here, the experimental plywood glider M2-F1 – forerunner of the Northrop-built M2-F2 – is tested in full-scale wind tunnel at Ames. (Photo courtesy of NASA)

The first flight of a specially designed National Aeronautics and Space Administration (NASA) plywood lifting body in 1963 marked a distinct breakthrough in the field of manned maneuverable reentry from space. It came after a long series of laboratory tests by NASA and its predecessor agency, the National Advisory Comittee for Aeronautics (NACA). Those early flights of the 1,200-pound wooden M2-F1 glider from Edwards Air Force Base proved the feasibility of maneuvering and landing a free-flight lifting body. In all, more than 500 gliding flights were completed between 1963 and 1964 using automobile or airplane tow to launch altitude.

The advantages of a spacecraft that could reenter the earth's atmosphere without burning up, and still maintain maneuverability to put down at selected landing sites, were self-evident. NASA's laboratory tests had shown that a "half cone" lifting body experienced markedly reduced heat loads at hypersonic reentry speeds, compared to a winged design. A lifting body was able to take advantage equally of aircraft and ballistic missile technologies. The half-cone lifting body was envisioned as a space station shuttle, or a Mars return vehicle.

Convinced of the need for a more thorough examination of lifting body flight at representative mission weights and wing loadings, and at higher altitudes and speeds, NASA asked industry to bid on the design and

fabrication of two new research vehicles. They would be based on NASA-developed lifting body configurations, and would incorporate all the lessons learned with the M2-F1 glider.

Although the aerodynamic shapes of the new lifting bodies were designed for hypersonic speeds, the structures were not built to withstand the corresponding heat loads because of time and budget limitations. Instead, the test bodies were intended only to explore the earth landing phase.

The new all-metal lifting bodies were designated M2-F2 (Manned, Modification 2, Fuselage No. 2) and HL-10 (Horizontal Landing, 10th concept). The "M" series had been developed at NASA Ames Research Center, California, and the HL-10 at NASA Langley Research Center, Virginia. Competing with four other bidders, Northrop was awarded a contract to produce both vehicles in mid-1964.

The goal of the new program was to cover the performance spectrum for the "half-cone family," rather than to design any final operational configuration. Objectives were to evaluate handling characteristics, particularly in landing and transonic and supersonic flight, to investigate pilot-vehicle compatibility, and to correlate flight and wind tunnel data.

EXPERIMENTAL M2-F1 under tow for glider flight.

229

M2-F2 UNDER CONSTRUCTION. The NASA Ames-configured lifting body was built under a modest budget, with minimum paperwork and short lines of communications. Rollout was June 15, 1965.

HL-10 FABRICATED IN SAME PROJECT AREA where engineering, tooling, manufacturing, planning, material coordination, and assembly were all adjacent or nearby. Rollout was January 18, 1966.

MILTON THOMPSON, NASA Chief Lifting Body Research Pilot, getting "feel" of HL-10 at time of its rollout. Six months later he flew the first unpowered flight in the M2-F2, dropped from a B-52, to a successful landing on Rogers Dry Lake.

SHAPE OF NASA LANGLEY-CONFIGURED HL-10 differed from that of Ames-designed M2-F2. The former was cambered flat bottom, round on top, delta shaped, canopy flush with basic body lines: the latter, flat on top, round bottom, with a projecting bubble canopy.

The M2-F2, like the M2-F1 plywood glider, was a round bottom, flat top, half-cone design, while the HL-10 was a flat bottom, round top, half-cone design. Both vehicles were designed for supersonic flight loads, and for underwing drop from a B-52 test airplane in the manner of the X-15 research aircraft. A Northrop-built adapter allowed either the M2-F2 or the HL-10 to be suspended from the X-15 pylon on the B-52 wing. They were to be dropped at an altitude of 45,000 feet, at a speed of Mach 0.8, and were to glide to conventional aircraft landings. Provisions were included for later installation of an 8,000-pound-thrust rocket engine to enable flight testing up to an altitude of 85,000-90,000 feet at supersonic speeds. Both the M2-F2 and HL-10, however, were initially equipped with small hydrogen peroxide rockets solely for the purpose of extending the landing approach if necessary.

In view of the demands of the Apollo space project, the NASA budget for the lifting body program was very limited. Therefore the Northrop program was conducted with a minimum of paper work and personnel. NASA program manager John McTigue and Northrop program manager Ralph Hakes, who had earlier distinguished himself as a leading designer of the ballistic nose for the Snark missile, agreed on a practical working arrangement called JAMP (Joint Action Management Plan). The plan featured: use of off-the-shelf hardware; shortened chain-of-command with on-the-spot decisions by key personnel; nucleus of specialists to staff the project; use of only those specifications necessary for the actual environment; team members indoctrinated with the goals; and project location in one integrated area, combining engineering, manufacturing, and materiel. Warren Klauer was the engineering manager; Rex Thornhill, the manufacturing manager.

The Air Force became interested in the lifting body program during the construction phase. As a result, a joint flight program was formulated between the Air Force Flight Test Center and the NASA Flight Research Center at Edwards AFB.

The completed M2-F2 was rolled out at the Hawthorne plant in June 1965. It was then shipped to the Flight Research Center where test instrumentation was installed. Following instrumentation, the M2-F2 was transported to the NASA Ames Research Center at Moffett Field for testing in the full-scale wind tunnel during July and August 1965. Upon return to Edwards, it was prepared for flight test.

AS SEEN FROM THE REAR. Two fins of the M2-F2 (top) had rudders on their outer aft faces; they could be flared outward together to act as speed brakes. Control flaps on the upper and lower surfaces of the squared-off tail served as ailerons, elevators, and trim surfaces. The HL-10 (bottom) had a split rudder on its center fin. A pair of elevons on the boattail and flaps on the upper portion of each elevon provided added stability at transonic and supersonic speeds.

NASA's chief lifting body research pilot, Milton O. Thompson, piloted the first flight of the M2-F2 as a glider on July 12, 1966. The M2-F2 was dropped from the B-52 at an altitude of 45,000 feet, following which it flew a straightahead glide, a 90-degree turn, a practice "landing flare-out" at 25,000 feet, and then a "deadstick" landing on Rogers Dry Lake.

A typical M2-F2 flight from 45,000 feet required four minutes from launch to touchdown. In the thin air at drop altitude, the glide angle was very steep with sink rate of about 250 feet per second, the vehicle slowing to a more comfortable five-to-ten feet per second at the 1,200-foot "landing flare" level. Air speed dropped from 350 mph to 250 mph during the flare maneuver and as low as 190 mph on actual touchdown. Test pilot Thompson said that the most tiring part of the air-launched flights was "the 45 minutes I sat in the M2-F2 at the end of the pylon waiting for the B-52 to reach launch altitude."

After rollout in early 1966, the three-finned HL-10 was tested in the full-scale wind tunnel at NASA Ames and returned to Edwards to prepare for flight tests. After being equipped with the XLR11 rocket engine at Edwards, the HL-10 made its first flight on December 22, 1966. This was an unpowered glide from the B-52, similar to the M2-F2 flights made during the previous July. NASA test pilot Bruce Peterson flew the vehicle.

By May 1967, sixteen subsonic flights had been made with the M2-F2; the XLR11 rocket engine had been installed but not operated in flight. All were free-fall unpowered glides. Varying amounts of water ballast in the rocket fuel tanks permitted tests over a wide range of body weights. The sixteenth flight encountered a mishap. It had been programmed to evaluate the effects of reduction in automatic damping for roll and yaw. During the landing flare, NASA test pilot Bruce Peterson experienced lateral oscillations which were difficult to control. Drifting off the normal flight path and on a converging course with an observing helicopter, the M2-F2 touched down before the landing gear was fully extended. In the ensuing ground somersaults, Peterson suffered severe injuries but later recovered to resume his flying duties.

The popular television program "The Six Million Dollar Man" was based in part on Bruce Peterson's accident at Edwards. The actual filmed sequence of the M2-F2 crash is shown each time at the beginning of the program. The film was taken from the TV tracking tape used to monitor all the lifting body flights.

SPECIAL ADAPTERS allowed airdrops of M2-F2 (top) and HL-10 (bottom) from a B-52 at 45,000 feet. Typical unpowered flight time was approximately four minutes. The lifting bodies assumed a glide angle of 3/1 and descended at a rate of 250 feet per second. Under powered flight (XLR11 rocket engine), the vehicles could reach over 85,000 feet and supersonic speeds.

M2-F2 LIFTING BODY, deriving atmospheric support or "lift" from the shape of the body rather than extended wings. Lifting bodies like this and the HL-10 were envisioned as returning astronauts from space missions, penetrating the earth's atmosphere and "gliding" to a horizontal landing.

NASA PILOT BRUCE PETERSON brought HL-10 to first unpowered landing December 22, 1966. The lifting body is shown immediately before touchdown at Edwards and just prior to landing gear extension.

In late 1967, the M2-F2 was returned to Hawthorne, where it was completely disassembled and ultimately restored to flight status under the direction of Fred Erb, Northrop project manager. Redesignated M2-F3, the lifting body was fitted with an additional central vertical fin to improve yaw control.

Following a series of gliding flights at Edwards, the HL-10 made its first rocket-powered flight from the B-52 Stratofortress on November 13, 1968. John A. Manke, NASA research pilot, was in the cockpit.

On June 2, 1970, the three-finned M2-F3 made its first unpowered flight after release from the B-52 over Edwards. NASA's William H. Dana was the test pilot. This key event was followed by the first powered flight on November 25, 1970, achieving Mach 0.8 at 53,000 feet after Dana ignited three of the four XLR11 rocket engine chambers. Later in the program, the M2-F3 reached a maximum altitude of nearly 90,000 feet and a speed of Mach 1.7. By the end of the program, the M2-F3 had logged 27 flights. The basic M2 airframe recorded a total of 43 flights.

By the end of 1971, a total of 37 flights had been completed by the HL-10: 12 unpowered, 25 powered. During the powered flights, the HL-10 atained an altitude of over 90,000 feet and a speed of Mach 1.9.

All activity on the M2-F3/HL-10 programs came to an end in 1973. Two years later, the rocket-powered M2-F3 was sent to the Smithsonian Institution's National Air and Space Museum in Washington, D.C., where it was placed on display.

Externally, the M2-F2/3 and HL-10 had dissimilar aerodynamic lines; internally, they were alike, with identical systems and accessories. Both vehicles had a riveted aluminum alloy, semimonocoque forebody. The aft structure was basically an aluminum box with side fairings. Two full-depth keels extended from the cabin to the base of each vehicle. The box allowed for the provision of nonstructural equipment access doors on the outside and acted also as an isolation bay for the rocket fuel.

THREE LIFTING BODIES at the NASA facility, Flight Research Center, Edwards AFB. In the foreground, HL-10; alongside, M2-F2; third in line, the plywood glider M2-F1. (Photo courtesy NASA)

Most of the system components were "off-the-shelf": for example, a retractable tricycle landing gear which included a modified North American T-39 nose unit; Northrop F-5 main legs with T-38 wheels and brakes; and a modified version of the F-106 ejection seat in the pressurized cockpit.

The M2-F2/F3 was controlled in pitch by a flap on the aft lower surface and by two flaps on the aft upper surface which were used for pitch trim. These surfaces were also used for roll control. Flaps on the aft outer face of each of two vertical fins served for yaw control. These surfaces could also be flared simultaneously to behave as speed brakes. Each flight control surface was moved by dual hydraulic system actuators (3,000 psi).

Stability augmentation was provided in all three axes.

The flight control surfaces of the HL-10 consisted of a rudder on the central fin that was split vertically for use as a speed brake, and two very thick blunt-edged elevons, extending the full depth of the vehicle's boat-tail. Each of the outer fin trailing edges had two surfaces which could be flared for transonic stability. Each elevon also had a movable flap on the upper surface which could be raised for transonic stability. All the surfaces used for transonic stability were powered by irreversible electric actuators. The rudder speed brakes and elevons were moved by dual 3,000-psi hydraulic system actuators. Stability augmentation was provided in all three axes.

M2-F3 RESTRUCTURED AND RECONFIGURED in 1969 from the original M2-F2 damaged in a landing accident on Rogers Dry Lake. The new vehicle contained a center fin to serve as a stabilizer and give greater directional control. Desert crew watch flyby.

M2-F2

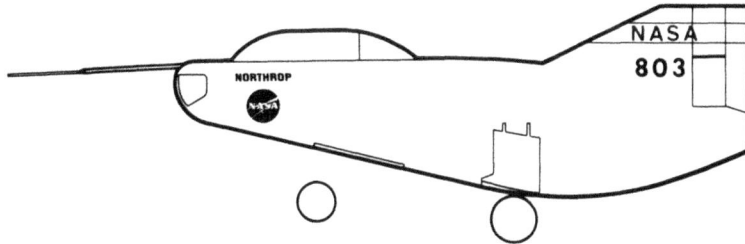

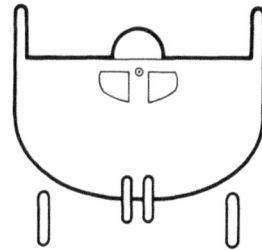

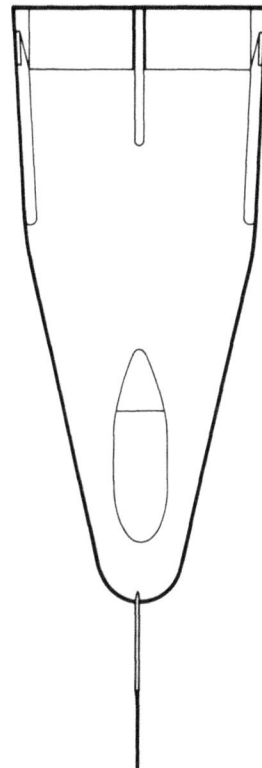

SPECIFICATIONS

WIDTH ....9 FT., 7 IN.

OVERALL LENGTH ....22 FT., 2 IN.

OVERALL HEIGHT ....9 FT., 8 IN.

PLANFORM AREA ....160 SQ. FT.

LAUNCH WEIGHT ....9,400 LB

SPEED — MAXIMUM ....MACH 1.7

SERVICE CEILING ....90,000 FT.

POWER — (1) THIOKOL XLRII ROCKET ENGINE, 8,000-LB
       THRUST

HL-10

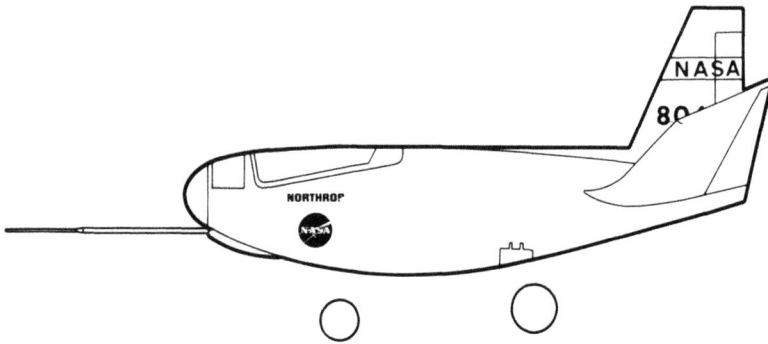

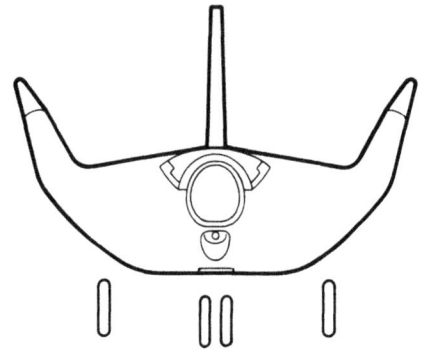

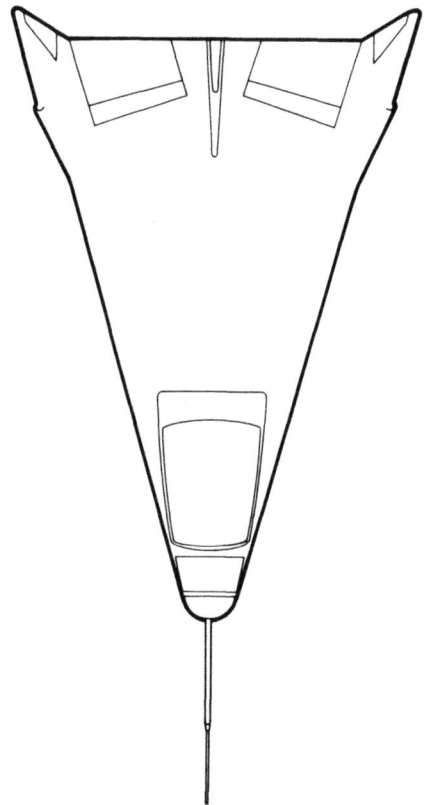

SPECIFICATIONS

WIDTH . . . . .15 FT., 1 IN.

OVERALL LENGTH . . . . .22 FT., 2 IN.

OVERALL HEIGHT . . . . .11 FT., 5 IN.

PLANFORM AREA . . . . .162 SQ. FT.

LAUNCH WEIGHT . . . . .9,400 LB

SPEED-MAXIMUM . . . . .MACH 1.9

SERVICE CEILING . . . . .90,000 FT.

POWER — (1) THIOKOL XLRII ROCKET ENGINE, 8,000-LB
       THRUST

F-5E/F TIGER II

By the early Sixties, F-5A tactical fighters were deployed in a defensive role in Military Assistance Program (MAP) countries facing the periphery of the Soviet bloc and Red China. Many of the Soviet bloc countries were then equipped with early model MIG-21's supplied by the USSR. But by the late Sixties, reports were circulating about an improved MIG-21 and a new fighter, the Sukhoi 7, entering service. Recognizing the potential threat, U.S. military planners began to establish requirements for an advanced, higher performance MAP defense fighter.

Anticipating the need for an upgraded version of the F-5A to fill this role, Northrop designers were investigating the new higher-thrust General Electric J85-21 engine. The -21 engine was able to produce 23 percent more thrust than the existing -13 and showed a higher

thrust-to-weight ratio. In April 1968, the Air Force issued G.E. a contract to flight-test the new engines in a modified F-5B serving as a test bed. Northrop served as subcontractor to G.E. The modified F-5B, redesignated YF-5B-21, was also fitted with the plenum chamber takeoff doors developed for Canada and The Netherlands, and the two-position nose gear developed for Canada.

Performance projections for the F-5 with the new engines were so favorable that in January 1969, even before the test bed airplane had flown, the Air Force issued a Contract Change Notice to alter the F-5A production configuration to accept the advanced power plant. Delivery of the first production aircraft, designated F-5-21, was scheduled for late 1970.

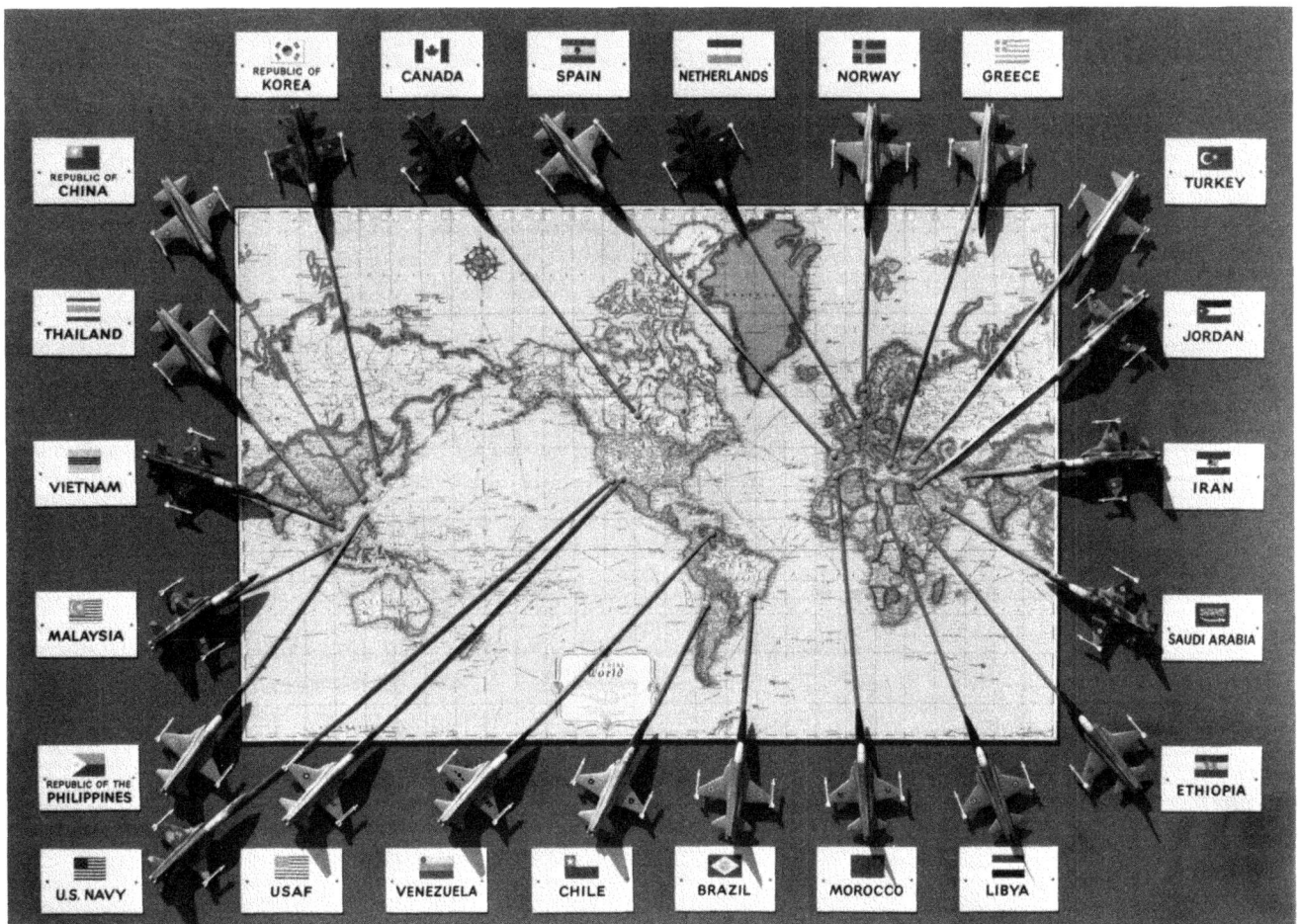

F-5 WORLDWIDE DEPLOYMENT. Twenty-two countries, including the United States, were flying the F-5 at the end of 1975. Under a mutual participation agreement, Switzerland joined "the family" in early 1976.

239

GENERAL ELECTRIC TEST PILOT John Fritz first flew test bed airplane YF-5B-21 in March 1969. Upgrading of the J85-13 engine to the 5,000-pound thrust J85-21 opened up a new generation of tactical aircraft. An F-5B was modified in 1968 under Air Force contract to carry two -21 power plants in an intensive flight test program. The F-5-21 designation eventually became the F-5E Tiger II.

In addition to the greater-thrust engines and the two-position nose gear, the F-5-21 was further enhanced with a larger wing leading-edge extension (LEX) for better lift, a multimode maneuvering flap system first used on the Netherlands NF-5A and NF-5B, and other specialty features which had been individually tailored for countries operating the earlier F-5's.

The test bed YF-5B-21 made its flight on March 28, 1969, at Edwards Air Force Base. John Fritz, a General Electric pilot, was at the controls. While design work proceeded on the production version of the F-5-21, the engine test bed airplane was flown repeatedly by Fritz. Eventually a 130-hour flight test program was completed leaving little doubt about the impressive performance provided by the new engines.

In the fall of 1969, a decision was reached to select competitively the most appropriate airplane for the new International Fighter Aircraft (IFA) role. As a result, work on the F-5-21 Contract Change Notice was halted. In the succeeding year, IFA proposals were prepared and submitted by Lockheed, LTV, McDonnell Douglas, and Northrop. After numerous evaluations and reviews, the Air Force announced on November 20, 1970, that the F-5-21 had once again been chosen to upgrade the air forces in a number of nations.

Design work on the IFA was immediately accelerated. Several aerodynamic features and electronic equipment not found on earlier F-5's were incorporated: stretching and widening of the fuselage because of the larger engines and inlet ducts; increased wing area; a modified and enlarged tapered area (LEX) from the inboard leading edge of the wings to the fuselage; increased internal fuel capacity, primarily the result of the stretched fuselage; integrated fire control radar system; and lead-computing gun sight.

JOHN K. NORTHROP AND THOMAS V. JONES, flanked by Lt. General James T. Stewart, Commander of Aeronautical Systems Division (in the cockpit), and Grant Hansen, Assistant Secretary of the Air Force for R&D (far right), at the rollout ceremony of the F-5E, June 23, 1972.

In January 1971, the Air Force changed the model designation of the F-5-21 to the F-5E. Later, in the fall of 1971, the F-5E was officially named "Tiger II," a close kin to the F-5A Skoshi Tiger which had successfully campaigned in Vietnam six years earlier.

The first F-5E Tiger II made its initial flight on August 11, 1972, at Edwards AFB. It was four months ahead of schedule. Northrop's Chief Test Pilot Hank Chouteau was the pilot. He claimed, "The minute you release the brakes you get the feeling that the airplane thinks it's airborne."

The Tactical Air Command (TAC), with assistance from the Air Training Command (ATC), was assigned responsibility for training pilots and technicians from user countries. Ten early production aircraft went to TAC before deliveries to foreign governments started at the end of 1973.

A Full-Scale Development (FSD) program for a two-place version of the F-5E was initiated in April 1973. A derivative of the F-5E, the F-5F retained the combat capability and weapon delivery accuracy of the single-place fighter but was also able to serve as an advanced trainer. Major differences were the stretched forward fuselage and the mounting of a single 20mm cannon in place of the two cannon in the F-5E.

The first of the two F-5F's ordered under the FSD program flew at Edwards AFB on September 25, 1974. Dick Thomas was the test pilot. The initial production F-5F first flew in April 1976.

USN

UNITED STATES NAVY added F-5E's (above) to its "Top Gun" aggressor squadron at the Navy Fighter Weapons School, Miramar Naval Air Station, California (below). Agile F-5E's assumed "enemy" role in simulated combat. Oceana NAS, Virginia, is also programmed to receive the Tiger II.

USAF

UNITED STATES AIR FORCE retained the F-5E (above) and the F-5F in its Tactical Air Command to train pilots of user nations and to act as aggressor aircraft in air combat maneuvering training squadrons in the U.S. (below).

JOINT TEST FORCE of USAF and Northrop pilots carried out an extensive test and evaluation of the F-5E and F-5F at Edwards. Here the first F-5F is readied for flight in 1974, eighteen months after initiation of the program to produce a two-place version of the F-5E.

By early 1975, countries ordering the F-5E and F-5F extended to Brazil, Chile, Iran, Jordan, South Korea, Malaysia, Republic of China (coproduction), and Saudi Arabia. Seventy-one F-5E's originally scheduled for delivery to the South Vietnamese air force were diverted to USAF inventory. They were to be used by the Tactical Air Command (TAC) as aggressor aircraft in air combat maneuvering training squadrons. The Navy also purchased five F-5E models for the "Top Gun" aggressor squadron at the Navy Fighter Weapons School. In all, more than 800 F-5E and F-5F aircraft had been ordered by the U.S. and nine foreign countries by January 1976.

The F-5E and F-5F airframes had basically the same structure as the earlier models. The fuselage was of all-metal, semimonocoque structure with stressed skin, consisting primarily of riveted aluminum. Some steel and titanium were used in the aft fuselage. Adhesive-bonded honeycomb construction and chemically milled skins also were used.

The carrythrough wing was constructed in one piece from tip to tip to provide structural continuity and eliminate splices in heavily loaded members. The continuous skins from tip to tip were extensively chemically milled. The wing was a multispar, all-aluminum structure except for steel ribs supporting the landing gear and wingtip stores. The all-movable horizontal stabilizer consisted of chemically-milled skins and aluminum honeycomb core. The spar and carrythrough torque tube were of steel.

The fuel system was contained within the fuselage as an independent supply for each engine with a pilot-controlled crossfeed. Rubber-impregnated nylon fabric fuel cells were located behind the cockpit; they extended from the cockpit bulkhead back to the leading edge of the vertical stabilizer. In the event of fuel pump failure, sufficient fuel would flow by gravity to maintain military power up to 10,000 feet altitude. These cells contained explosion-suppressant foam. Their capacity was 671 gallons usable. Additional fuel could be carried in a 275-gallon pylon tank under the center fuselage, as well as in underwing pylon tanks. External tanks were pressurized to supply the two separate fuselage systems as fuel was consumed. Single-point refueling of internal and external tanks was accomplished through a pressure fitting on the fuselage underside.

ROYAL SAUDI ARABIAN AIR FORCE F-5E's. Under a series of Foreign Military Sales (FMS) government-to-government agreements, Saudi Arabia had not only purchased tactical aircraft from Northrop but was also receiving support, services, and training under a program called "Peace Hawk."

The hydraulically retractable tricycle landing gear was equipped with a two-position nose strut. Nosewheel steering was controlled by movement of the rudder pedals. An emergency type of arresting hook was installed in the lower aft fuselage for barrier-type cable engagement.

Hydraulic power was provided by two completely independent 3,000-psi systems. These were the primary flight control system and the utility hydraulic system. The former furnished power solely for the operation of ailerons, rudder, and all-movable horizontal stabilizer. The latter, in addition to supplying backup power to the primary flight control surfaces, also powered the landing gear system, speed brakes, gun bay purge doors, gun gas deflectors, and stability augmentation system.

The primary flight control system incorporated a system of springs and bobweights to provide the pilot with an "artificial feel." Conventional control stick and rudder pedals were used. A two-axis pitch-and-yaw stability augmentation also was provided.

A unique automatic maneuvering flap system consisted of wing leading-edge and trailing-edge flaps with five flap modes. This electrically-driven system provided additional lift for takeoff and landing, additional load factor capability for maneuvering, and reduced drag for sustained turning maneuvers.

Engine compressor bleed air pressurized and conditioned the cockpit, defogged the windshield and canopy, inflated the canopy seals and pilot's anti-G

ORDNANCE AND EXTERNAL FUEL CAPABILITY. The F-5E and F-5F are configured to carry a wide variety of air-to-ground and air-to-air munitions and auxiliary fuel supplies. Modern combat tactics and the Tiger II's high maneuverability have shifted their defensive role more and more from ground support to aerial interception.

suit, cooled equipment, and pressurized the hydraulic reservoir. Each cockpit had its own manually operated canopy closure. The two canopies of the F-5F were automatically jettisoned if the pilots elected to operate their rocket-powered ejection seats.

Ease of maintenance was helped by 124 quick-open doors and access panels which provided fast access to "one-deep" components. Shoulder-level and eye-level serviceability, combined with easily removed components, quick-disconnect fittings and coupling, resulted in quick turnaround time. During periods of accelerated operations, only fuel and ordnance were required after each flight; all other inspection or replenishment normally was accomplished on a once-daily basis.

The two General Electric J85-21 engines were mounted side by side in the aft fuselage. Installed on built-in overhead tracks with simple mounting, the small and lightweight afterburning engines could be inserted or removed with ease. An integrated power package, including gearbox, alternating current generator, and hydraulic pump, was mounted on the airframe forward of each engine. By disconnecting the engine drive shaft from the power package, each engine could be removed without disturbing the electrical or hydraulic system.

The F-5E was equipped with two nose-mountd 20mm cannon; the F-5F with a single 20mm cannon. Both the single-place and two-place versions had seven external store stations, accommodating a full spectrum of ordnance and/or fuel for extended missions. Both models were equipped with a fire control system, which consisted of fire control radar and lead-computing optical sight system (LCOSS). Sidewinder missiles could be mounted on the wingtips, and many other combinations of external stores could be carried. In the photo-reconnaissance version of the F-5E, four 70mm cameras were mounted in the special nose which was interchangeable with the radar nose (both F-5E and F-5F) in the field.

F-5E EQUIPPED WITH TWO M-39 20MM GUNS and 560 rounds of ammunition, sufficient for 11 seconds of continuous firing. Guns, however, are normally fired in very short bursts. Ammunition for each gun is contained in an ammo box in the gun compartment. The ammunition rounds are linked together and fed through a flexible feedchute, shown here.

LOOKING TO FUTURE and 3,000th aircraft in the F-5/T-38 family of fighters and trainers. (Left to right) Dr. Thomas O. Paine, newly elected president of Northrop and chief operating officer, Thomas V. Jones, chairman of the board and chief executive officer, and Welko Gasich, Aircraft Division general manager, were on hand in early April 1976 when work began on "the 3,000th."

F-5E

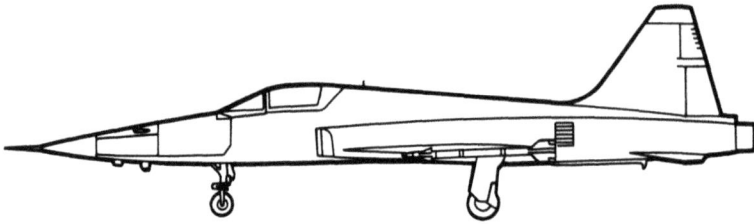

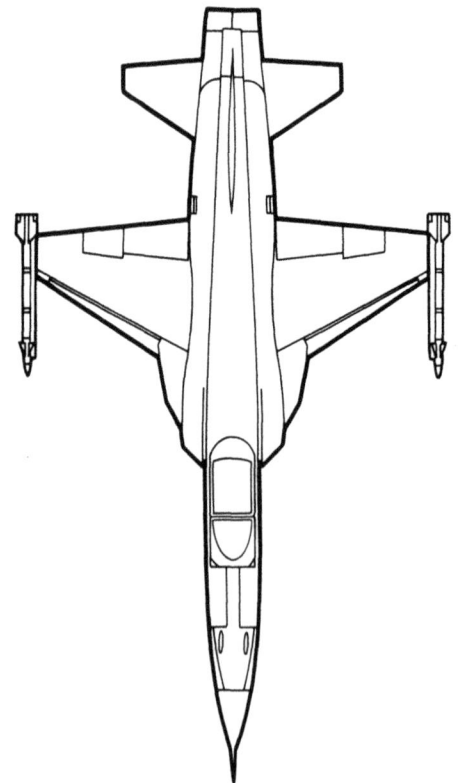

SPECIFICATIONS

WING SPAN . . . . .26 FT., 8 IN.

OVERALL LENGTH . . . . .48 FT., 2 IN.

OVERALL HEIGHT . . . . .13 FT., 4 IN.

WING AREA . . . . .186.2 SQ. FT.

CLEAN TAKEOFF WEIGHT . . . . .15,450 LB

MAX. TAKEOFF WEIGHT .24,680 LB

SPEED-MAXIMUM . . . . .MACH 1.6

SPEED-CRUISING . . . . .MACH 0.84

RANGE . . . . .1,880 MILES

SERVICE CEILING . . . . .52,500 FT.

POWER — (2) G.E. J85-21 TURBOJET, 5,000-LB THRUST

ARMAMENT — (2) 20MM CANNON
           (7) STORES STATIONS FOR 7,000-LB
           ORDNANCE INCLUDING (2)
           SIDEWINDER MISSILES

F-5F

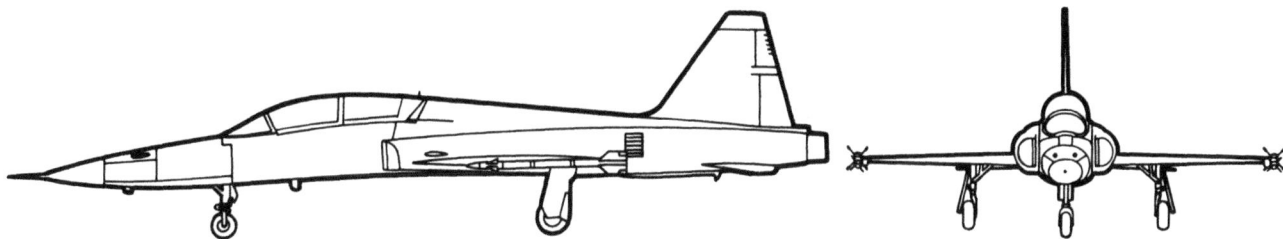

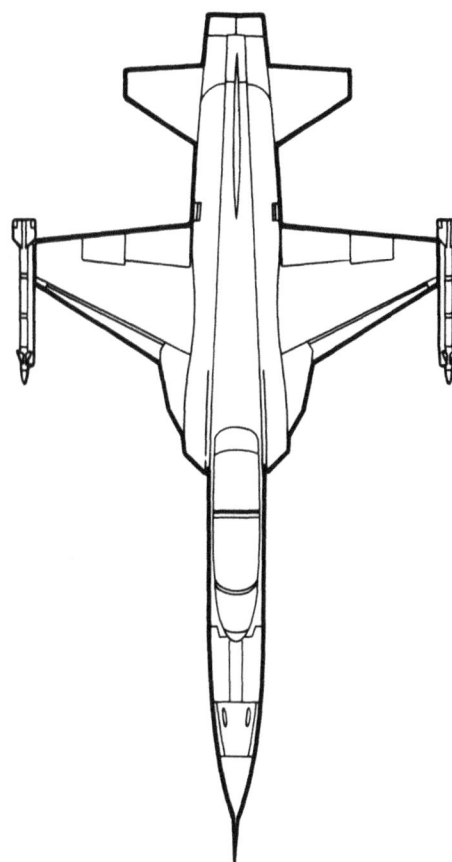

SPECIFICATIONS

WING SPAN . . . . .26 FT., 8 IN.

OVERALL LENGTH . . . . .51 FT., 8 IN.

OVERALL HEIGHT . . . . .13 FT., 2 IN.

WING AREA . . . . .186.2 SQ. FT.

CLEAN TAKEOFF WEIGHT . . . . .16,000 LB

MAXIMUM TAKEOFF WEIGHT . . . . .25,220 LB

SPEED — MAXIMUM . . . . .MACH 1.53

SPEED — CRUISING . . . . .MACH 0.84

RANGE . . . . .1,771 MILES

SERVICE CEILING . . . . .51,300 FT.

POWER — (2) GE J85-21, TURBOJET, 5,000-LB THRUST

ARMAMENT — (1) 20MM CANNON; (7) STORES STATIONS
FOR 7,000-LB ORDNANCE INCLUDING (2)
SIDEWINDER MISSILES

A-X/A-9A CLOSE AIR SUPPORT AIRCRAFT

Conceived in 1967 as a result of Air Force experience with close air support of ground troops primarily in Southeast Asia, the A-X was a "total weapons system" planned specifically and exclusively for that mission.

Following an initial four-month proposal phase as one of 12 competing aircraft companies, Northrop emerged in May 1967 as one of four finalists to prepare requirements studies for the new airplane. In announcing the contract awards, the Department of Defense (DOD) stated, "Contractors are expected to explore various design concepts for the A-X which would be relatively inexpensive, rugged and highly survivable."

By May 1970, the DOD had approved the Air Force plan for development of actual flying hardware. It was also disclosed that for the first time in many years, the Air Force was considering the development of an aircraft by means of building competitive prototypes, the ultimate winner of the production contract to be chosen in a flyoff.

The Air Force announced the choice of Northrop and Fairchild Industries in December 1970 as the two competitors under the new program. Also confirmed was the expectation that the A-X was to be developed in accordance with the "fly before buy" concept in an effort to reduce overall costs through a step-by-step progression and hardware flight demonstration. Each company contracted to build two prototype aircraft for the flyoff evaluation. The projected production unit price for the complete aircraft, including avionics, was $1.2 million target and $1.4 million ceiling (1970 dollars) based on a buy of 600 aircraft.

FLIGHT TEST DIRECTOR LEW NELSON made the first flight of A-9A Prototype No. 1 from the Air Force Flight Test Center at Edwards AFB, May 30, 1972. He conducted a 58-minute flight evaluation of the aircraft's handling characteristics, operating systems, and the two Lycoming YF102 turbofan engines.

AIRFRAME was of simple, rugged construction with redundant critical structural members, so that the aircraft could sustain damage and still return safely. Heavy armor (thick aluminum in the prototypes, titanium in the planned production version) around the cockpit protected the pilot from enemy fire.

The preliminary design and proposal effort was led by Walt Fellers, Manager of Advanced Systems. Prototype aircraft development was directed by Dave Deering. Warren Klauer was engineering manager, and Earl Nickles was manufacturing manager.

Preliminary design features centered on a rugged, twin-engine, single-place aircraft with short takeoff and landing capabilities and excellent maneuverability. It had to carry varied payloads, be capable of long loiter time over target areas, and have high survivability against enemy ground fire. Northrop's A-X design was assigned the designation A-9A in early 1971.

The A-9A prototypes were of all-metal riveted aluminum alloy, semimonocoque with stressed skin construction. Extensive use was made of honeycomb structure and chemically-milled skins. They were high-wing, single-place aircraft powered by two AVCO Lycoming YF102-LD-100 turbofan engines, developed under subcontract to Northrop, in accordance with specialized requirements. George Gluyas was the engine program manager for Northrop. Each engine developed 7,500 pounds of thrust. The engines were mounted in nacelles on either side of the fuselage just below the wing trailing edge. The pilot sat in a protective "bathtub" of aluminum armor (titanium was the metal planned for the production version). A bubble canopy gave the pilot a 360-degree over-the-nose visibility to reduce chances of a surprise attack and provide optimum target observation.

The A-9A also featured foam-filled fuel tanks in the wings well away from ignition sources. Redundant flight control systems afforded additional safeguard against battle damage. If one of the primary hydraulic systems became inoperable, the other would continue to function. A third manual backup system added a final measure of safety in the event both hydraulic systems failed.

Maintenance was "designed into" the aircraft. All field service functions could be performed at ground level. Easily replaced engines were chest-high on either side of the fuselage. Engine removal and installation was timed in less than 60 minutes.

FIVE HARDPOINTS on each side of the wing permitted the A-9A to carry up to a maximum of 16,000 pounds of mixed bomb loads.

HORIZONTAL STABILIZER was positioned midway in the vertical stabilizer to keep it out of the downwash from the wing and engine exhaust.

TOUCHDOWN CONFIGURATION OF A-9A. Operation of lift dumpers occurred automatically on touchdown with compression of landing gear struts when the throttles were below 85% rpm position, and the split aileron-speed brake control was set at 10 degrees or greater.

USING DOUBLE EJECTION RACKS, eighteen MK-82 bombs, weighing 500-pounds each, could be carried by A-9A in flight. (Bomb release in photo insert right.)

UNUSUALLY LARGE rudder and vertical stabilizer provided a high degree of directional stability, necessary in an aircraft designed to dive, strafe and bomb, and protect ground troops in a low-level support role.

The 58-foot wing had ten hardpoints for external carriage of mixed ordnance. Long Fowler-type flaps extended over half the wing span on either side of the fuselage. Large ailerons on the outboard third of the wing were split into upper and lower sections, serving both as speed brakes and ailerons — long a Northrop design feature. Flap-width "lift dumpers" on the upper wing trailing edge helped to kill lift in short-field landings.

The rudder and vertical stabilizer were unusually large, affording a high degree of directional stability. Stability was also enhanced by a pitch-and-yaw-axis stability augmenter. In addition, the large, movable rudder surface was an essential element in the Northrop-designed "side force control" system. The latter made use of the rudder and asymmetric application of the split-aileron speed brakes to provide sideward forces to the aircraft without need for banking.

Ability to displace the aircraft sidewards without banking and S-turning eliminated the resultant yawing and pitching reactions that could delay or upset target lineup. Studies showed that in a 45-degree bombing run, the A-9A could achieve up to twice the tracking accuracy with "side force control" than without it.

The production version of the A-9A called for a 30mm Gatling-type cannon then under development. The cannon was to be mounted in the belly, its barrel extending from a slot in the fuselage beneath the cockpit to a point just ahead of the off-center nose gear. The cannon was mounted along the longitudinal centerline of the fuselage to eliminate recoil effects about the yaw axis. Consequently, the nose landing gear was displaced one foot to the left of the centerline. For the flight and evaluation tests, both prototypes were equipped with a single 20mm gun.

The company placed heavy emphasis on cost controls throughout the A-9A program, sacrificing performance advantages in some areas for lower development and production costs. The Air Force encouraged this approach, holding the A-X competitors to the premise that low cost was preferable to performance in excess of stated requirements. As a result, considerable use of off-the-shelf hardware and equipment served to "hold the expenditure line." Producibility studies led to the adoption of several interchangeable left-side and right-side components such as the engines, main landing gear, flaps, speed brakes, ailerons, and spoilers.

Following a rollout of the A-9A at Hawthorne in March 1972 for employee preview, the Prototype No. 1 was prepared for shipment to Edwards Air Force Base for flight test. In its first flight on May 30, 1972, Northrop test pilot Lew Nelson flew for 58 minutes. He described the test as "routine" and "as planned."

Following development flight tests of both prototypes by the company, they were turned over to the Air Force for flight evaluation in the fall of 1972. A joint USAF test team flew them extensively in gunnery and bombing tests over a period of two months and an accrual of 123 flying hours. While the A-9A was assessed to be an excellent aircraft, it did not win the production contract. Nevertheless the A-9A did validate the company's belief that a close air support fighter could be built for $1.4 million flyaway price in 1970 dollars. Both prototypes were eventually transferred to NASA for its own aerodynamic test programs.

LYCOMING YF102 TURBOFAN had been selected by Northrop for the A-X program in 1970. Like the A-9A, the engine was a prototype. In seven months of flight usage in the two A-9A's, a creditable performance was recorded. Six engines participated in 238 flights, accumulated 652 flight hours, made 110 air starts.

INSTRUMENT PANEL shows five square indicators on each side just below the windshield. These are indicator-selector switches to the ten bomb-carrying pylon stations. Pilot can release salvo by pressing button on top of control stick. Control stick also contains trim button, nosewheel steering button, and gun trigger.

DURING TASK 1 TESTING at altitude, the A-9A was flown down to stall speeds on one engine. "The A-9A looks like a big aircraft but flies like a fighter," claimed Lew Nelson, Flight Test Director.

A-9A

SPECIFICATIONS

WING SPAN . . . . .58 FT.

OVERALL LENGTH . . . . .53 FT., 6 IN.

OVERALL HEIGHT . . . . .16 FT., 11 IN.

WING AREA . . . . .580 SQ. FT.

CLEAN TAKEOFF WEIGHT . . . . .26,000 LB

MAXIMUM TAKEOFF WEIGHT . . . . .42,000 LB

SPEED — MAXIMUM . . . . .449 MPH

SPEED — CRUISING . . . . .322 MPH

RANGE . . . . .3,622 MILES

SERVICE CEILING . . . . .40,000 FT.

POWER — (2) LYCOMING YF102-LD-100, TURBOFAN,
7,500-LB THRUST

ARMAMENT — (1) 20MM GATLING-TYPE GUN; 16,000 LB
ORDNANCE

P530 COBRA

Like the N-102 Fang which preceded it by more than 12 years and led the way to the N-156/T-38/F-5 family, the company-funded P530 ushered in the new era of YF-17/F-18 air superiority fighters. Also like the N-102, the P530 never progressed beyond the mockup stage, although its effects were to be far-reaching.

Weighing less than one-half contemporary first-line, twin-engine fighters, the P530 Cobra gave promise of nearly twice the range, maneuverability, and acceleration at a cost-competitive price that might appeal to an international market.

The origins of the P530 reached back to 1965, when operations analyses were conducted to define the requirements for an advanced F-5 lightweight, multirole tactical fighter, designated the N-300. The N-300 possessed certain F-5 configuration characteristics: a wing of F-5 planform, a stretched F-5 fuselage, and a propulsion system of two General Electric J1A1 engines. After a year of testing and analysis, the configuration was changed to a high wing location for maximum ordnance flexibility as well as maneuvering performance improvement.

By 1967, a new designation — P530 — had superseded N-300. Walt Fellers, then Manager of Advanced Systems, had the responsibility for seeing the P530 through an emerging series of design refinements. Lee Begin, active in the N-156 design program, headed the project office. John Patierno led the aero-propulsion effort, and Jerry Huben handled configuration integration.

COBRA WOODEN MOCKUP, completed in December 1972. Wing leading-edge extension was aerodynamically curved, giving it a "hooded" or "cobra" look. Longitudinal slots on either side of the fuselage served to control airflow to engine intakes.

257

NINE ORDNANCE POSITIONS on P530 (two on wingtips, six underwing, one below fuselage) afforded wide flexibility of stores for air-to-air combat or air-to-ground support.

In March 1968, the proposed power plant was the J1A2 engine, raising the thrust from 8,000 to 10,000 pounds. The aerodynamically curved, wing leading-edge extensions (LEX) and their longitudinal slots had been increased in size for greater lift and airflow control. Canted twin vertical tails replaced the single vertical to provide the desired lateral directional stability at high angles of attack. A more sophisticated avionics suite was added. Later that year, the twin-tailed configuration with a modified radar was documented in a major report to the Aeronautical Systems Division (ASD) of the Air Force for validation of both aircraft and program approach, based on production of 1,000 aircraft. The ASD reply essentially confirmed performance predictions and cost estimates.

In 1969, a more refined LEX shape was defined to increase lift and improve the vortex bursting character, thereby enhancing the stability and control characteristics at high angles of attack. The cockpit was moved forward for better pilot visibility and for improved avionics and gun system installations.

In 1970, the P530 was in its fourth design iteration. The engine under consideration was the J1A5 with a thrust of 13,000 pounds. The fixed cone inlet was replaced with a two-dimensional fixed ramp inlet.

The continual design optimization of the P530 had always been focused on air superiority in order to provide the balance of energy and maneuverability needed to achieve maximum multirole capability. Since the inception of the program, company engineers had concentrated on the tactical analyses of air-to-air combat and on the identification of those factors which "drove" design optimization. Thousands of hours of wind tunnel testing verified each step along the way.

The basic aircraft design was patented in 1970; those sharing patent honors were Walt Fellers, Lee Begin, John Patierno, Jerry Huben, Adam Roth, Hans Grellman, and Vern White.

MODERN AVIONICS EQUIPMENT characterized P530. Instrument panel shows Head-Up Display (HUD) in upper center part of panel; Radar Display (RD) below HUD; Projected Map Display (PMD) to right of RD; Radar Warning (RW) immediately above PMD. These were but a few of the many aids that helped pilot navigate, position, detect, and fire weapons.

In many respects the P530 program represented a unique concept wherein a military program had been designed to international industrial and economic requirements as well as to military requirements. The Mach 2-class P530 was conceived as an ideal offering to overseas countries from several standpoints: a multipurpose weapon capability, a low-cost initial outlay, large-scale industrial participation, and technology exchange.

The advanced technology features of the P530 were not confined merely to its shape and engines, but extended to electronics, armament, and materials. Advanced radar enabled pilots for the first time to detect airborne targets at low as well as high altitudes. Nine external weapon stations gave it a wide range of armament carriage in close support and air superiority mission roles. Finally, to lower cost and reduce weight, Northrop drew on its experience in graphite-epoxy composites, not only in the laboratory but also on F-5 reinforced structural components in actual usage, to apply the new materials to the P530.

In 1970, the U.S. Department of Defense and the Air Force had returned to the early concept of "prototyping." Among the first projects selected for prototyping was a specialized Lightweight Fighter (LWF). A request for proposal (RFP) was issued in the fall of 1971 calling for an aircraft highly specialized in the day fighter role, with particular emphasis on light weight and low cost. It was now evident that all of Northrop's work on the P530, especially the latest version and the full-scale mockup, was applicable to the LWF.

The P530 design was therefore refined in accordance with the RFP requirements, and the company submitted its proposal to the Air Force in 1972 along with four major U.S. competitors. In April 1972, the Air Force announced that Northrop and General Dynamics had each won a contract to produce two prototypes. The Northrop design was designated YF-17.

Further refinement of the P530 Cobra for the European market continued until 1974, when the P530 project was merged with the YF-17 project.

Structurally, the tricycle-geared P530 was to be primarily of riveted aluminum alloy semimonocoque construction. Steel and titanium were used in high temperature areas and for space-limited highly loaded components. Graphite-epoxy laminates and aluminum honeycomb were also used for certain doors and secondary structures.

Four bladder-type fuel tanks were located in the fuselage behind the cockpit, and single-point pressure refueling was provided. Polyurethane reticulated foam was used inside all fuel tanks to prevent vapor explosions.

The thin, dry wing was of multispar construction with thick, machined aluminum skins. It consisted of left-hand and right-hand panels attached to the fuselage with shear bolts. Aluminum honeycomb was applied extensively in panels, leading- and trailing-edge flaps, and ailerons.

The all-movable horizontal tail was an aluminum bonded assembly with honeycomb core. The twin vertical stabilizers were of thick aluminum skin with multiple spars, and the rudders were aluminum-bonded assemblies with honeycomb cores.

Many of the P530 systems were very similar to those proven in the F-5 tactical fighter, underscoring a long tradition of redundant systems. Dual hydraulic systems were provided for the primary flight controls, including a variable-camber high-lift subsystem for maneuvering, takeoff, and landing. An electronic Control Augmentation System (CAS) was incorporated in parallel with the mechanical system. It added or subtracted control travel and rate, as shaped by the airplane electronic model, to produce desirable handling qualities over the entire flight envelope, regardless of airplane loading, speed, or altitude.

OIL FLOW VISUALIZATION of earlier P530 model in wing tunnel. Bathed in fluorescent oil, it illustrated use of wing leading-edge extension and slot. Over 5,000 wind tunnel hours helped evolve aerodynamic shape for most efficient performance.

As in the F-5, the twin turbojet engines were mounted side-by-side in the aft section of the fuselage, except that the P530 engines were removed by lowering vertically without removing the horizontal tail or boattail. A three-point mounting arrangement permitted quick engine removal or installation. The engines were isolated from one another and from the forward airframe compartments by titanium firewalls. An integrated engine starter and accessory drive system was mounted on the airframe forward of the engines. By disconnecting the engine drive shaft from the power package, each engine could be removed without disturbing the electrical, hydraulic, or gas turbine starter units.

The P530 was to be equipped with a single 20mm Gatling-type gun mounted in the upper forward fuselage. Alternate arrangements included two 30mm cannon, or two 20mm cannon. In addition, four missile launcher rails were installed for IR missile carriage: one on each wingtip and two on wing pylons. A total of seven external pylon stations supplemented the two wingtip stations for a variety of ordnance or fuel stores.

P530

SPECIFICATIONS

```
WING SPAN ................................................35 FT.
OVERALL LENGTH ..........................55 FT., 4 IN.
OVERALL HEIGHT ..........................14 FT., 2 IN.
WING AREA ...................................400 SQ. FT.
CLEAN TAKEOFF WEIGHT ....................23,000 LB
MAX. TAKEOFF WEIGHT .....................40,600 LB
SPEED-MAXIMUM ............................MACH 2.0
SPEED-CRUISING ............................MACH 0.85
RANGE (FERRY) ............................3,660 MILES
SERVICE CEILING ............................60,000 FT.
POWER — (2) G.E. 15/J1A5 TURBOJET, 13,000-LB THRUST
ARMAMENT — (1) 20MM GATLING GUN
            (4) IR MISSILES
            (7) PYLON STATIONS AND
            (2) WING TIP STATIONS FOR ORDNANCE
```

YF-17 LIGHTWEIGHT FIGHTER

Among the first projects to be selected by the U.S. Air Force for prototyping or "fly-before-buy" was a specialized lightweight fighter (LWF). The move was expected to promote creativity among the leading aircraft design teams, as well as exploit technical advancements with flying hardware.

A Request for Proposal (RFP) was issued by the Air Force in the fall of 1971. It called for an aircraft highly specialized in the visual, clear weather, day-fighter role for air superiority over the battlefield, with particular emphasis on light weight and low cost. The new fighter would have to sustain high rates of turn and increased supersonic maneuvering capabilities, while retaining the ability to accelerate readily. The LWF would incorporate no compromises which might detract from its ability to maneuver inside the "combat arena."

No performance requirements were stated above Mach 1.6. Its role was to be confined to air superiority by limiting external stores capability and electronic equipment to a bare minimum. The prototype program was intended to evaluate advanced technology and design concepts, to determine aircraft capabilities, and to establish potential operational utility.

Although no commitment to production was in the immediate offing, the Department of Defense was tentatively exploring the possibility of a new "high-low" fighter aircraft mix not only for the Air Force but also for the Navy. Thus, the LWF, or Air Combat Fighter as it later came to be known, might be considered as a supplement to the F-15 and the carrier-based F-14.

YF-17 PROTOTYPES NO. 1 AND NO. 2 were built in Plant 3 at Hawthorne during 1973-1974. Production breaks allowed for three major assemblies: forward, center and aft. In addition to aluminum, steel and titanium, graphite composites were employed for light weight and strength in secondary structures such as doors and panels, leading-edge extension, wing trailing edge, and other control surfaces.

AIRCRAFT SERVICING. The YF-17 was designed to enhance servicing and maintenance. Wing, fuselage, and pylon heights permitted convenient access from the ground to most systems and components.

Upon issuance of the RFP, it became readily evident that all of the P530 development work was applicable to the LWF. Following a refinement of the P530 design in accordance with the detailed RFP requirements, the company submitted its proposal to the Air Force in January 1972. The new design was designated "P600."

The P600 incorporated the GE 15J1A5 engine (later designated YJ101) with thrust increased to 14,400 pounds. In addition, the wing area was reduced to 350 square feet to improve supersonic performance.

At the conclusion of industry competition and proposal evaluation in April 1972, the Air Force announced Northrop and General Dynamics as winners, each to produce two flying prototypes. The Air Force designated the General Dynamics entry the YF-16, the Northrop entry the YF-17. The Northrop team leaders were Walt Fellers, program manager; Tom Rooney, engineering manager; and Rex Thornhill, manufacturing manager. When the engineering development phase was completed, Roy Jackson became program manager on through the flight test phase.

The YF-17 was a single-place, twin-engine fighter in the 20,000-pound weight class, featuring a high thrust-to-weight ratio and low wing loading for maximum maneuverability. Advanced propulsion technology was closely integrated with advances in aerodynamics, controls, and structures.

Featured among these design innovations were a hybrid wing with root leading-edge extension (LEX), differential area ruling, underwing inlet with wing slot for boundary layer bleed, and active control features such as automatically controlled wing leading-edge and wing trailing-edge variable camber. In addition, 900 pounds of lightweight graphite composite materials were used in secondary structures, and the cockpit was designed for high "G" maneuvering and optimal visibility.

From the synthesis of these and other advanced features emerged a fighter capable of penetrating a totally new spectrum of performance: sustained combat operation over an expanded arena starting from subsonic speeds through the middle supersonic regime.

263

HEAD-ON, LOOKING UP AND UNDER THE YF-17. *Basic wing planform, combined with the highly-swept leading edge root extension, is identified as a "hybrid" wing. Nose strakes and wing root slots add to the whole integrated aerodynamic concept.*

YF-17 COCKPIT ARRANGEMENT. *High-priority instruments were at the top of the panel for minimum eye movement during aerial engagement: armament controls on the left for ready access; angle of attack, accelerometer, and fuel on the right.*

264

BODY GEOMETRY *exemplified by topside and underside of YF-17 in flight. Differential area ruling – pronounced "pinching-in" of dorsal (above) and curvature of engine intakes (below) – optimally reduced drag for supersonic turning.*

AERIAL REFUELING. Prototype No. 2 YF-17 accepts boom from KC-97 tanker (Wisconsin Air National Guard) while Prototype No. 1 "stands by." Indicator lights on Head-Up Display frame tell pilot when boom is latched, ready, or disconnected. The pilot makes disconnect by button on control stick.

In April 1974, in full recognition of the escalating costs of heavy, multimission fighters, and of the mounting risk that insufficient quantities could be procured with available funds, the Secretary of Defense urged production of a low-cost air combat fighter (ACF). The LWF prototype program, followed by a development program for the ACF, provided the "best option" to meet this requirement.

YF-17 Prototype No. 1 rolled out of the Hawthorne plant that same month. It was trucked to Edwards Air Force Base for flight test preparation. First flight took place on June 9, 1974, with Chief Test Pilot Hank Chouteau in the cockpit. Following a 61-minute flight, Chouteau remarked, "When our designers said that in the YF-17 they were going to give the airplane back to the pilot, they meant it. It's a fighter pilot's fighter." Two days later, the YF-17 flew supersonically in level flight without afterburner — "a first" for any U.S.-built airplane.

First flight of Prototype No. 2 was on August 21, 1974. By mid-January 1975, an accelerated seven-month flight test program was completed. A total of 288 flights, or 330 hours of flight test time, had been recorded. Prototype No. 1 made 191 flights; Prototype No. 2 made 97 flights. The earlier aircraft was used for a majority of the test program elements, including flight controls development, flutter, airframe-propulsion compatibility, armament-propulsion compatibility, performance, and stability and control. The second aircraft was used for structural loads, stall/poststall, and handling qualities during tracking. Both aircraft were employed simultaneously to evaluate operational factors and subsystems development-evaluation, and to assess reliability-maintainability.

The information obtained during the flight test program clearly established the high-performance and low-cost characteristics of the YF-17. The Air Force decided that the YF-16 would be better suited for its specific operational requirements, notably the supplementing of its air-to-air fighter force and including considerations of its force structure mix and logistics commonality with other aircraft already in service. The YF-17, designed to a concept of mission versatility and therefore providing a high degree of air-to-ground as well as air-to-air capability, went on to win the Navy air combat fighter competition where multimission suitability was a greater consideration. The YF-17 design was selected by the Navy to be modified for carrier operations and was redesignated the F-18. The F-18 will replace the F-4 and A-7 in the U.S. Navy and Marine Corps.

Structurally, the YF-17 was of riveted semimonocoque stressed skin, employing high-strength aluminum alloys as its primary material. Steel and titanium were used in space-limited areas of high temperature or loading intensity. The fuselage consisted of stressed skin supported by frames, longerons,

and bulkheads. Graphite-epoxy composite material was used for engine bay doors, landing gear doors, and various equipment access doors and panels. The forward fuselage equipment section housed the ranging radar, air data computer, battery, and emergency power unit.

Internal fuel was contained in four bladder-type cells located in the fuselage behind the cockpit. A separate system for each tank gave a crossfeed capability. The fuel system had a receptacle for aerial refueling and a single-point ground refueling fitting.

The wing consisted of right and left panels attached to the fuselage with shear bolts. The thin dry wing was of thick skin, multispar construction, with fuselage attach ribs of welded and machined titanium. Various sections of the wing featured aluminum or Nomex (nylon/phenolic) honeycomb core with graphite-epoxy facesheets. These included sections of the LEX, wing trailing edge, trailing-edge flaps, and ailerons.

NAVY-MARKED YF-17 (PROTOTYPE NO. 1) was temporarily transferred to USN control in mid-1975 for use in a preliminary flight test program to support the Navy-Northrop-McDonnell Douglas F-18 development effort.

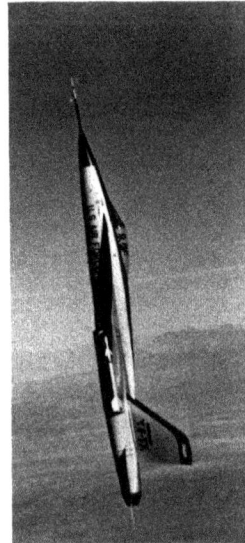

YF-17
FLIGHT
ASPECTS

YF-17/YJ101 ENGINE INSTALLATION

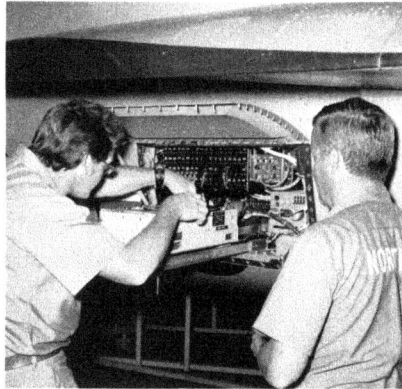

YF-17 AIRCRAFT SERVICING

The all-movable right and left horizontal stabilizers were all-aluminum bonded assemblies with full-depth honeycomb cores, and machine-tapered and sculptured skins having an aluminum integral leading-edge wedge, and a full-span machined aluminum channel spar. The vertical stabilizers were of thick skin, multispar construction with leading edges and rudders of aluminum honeycomb core, laminated graphite-epoxy spar, and graphite-epoxy facesheets.

Mechanical power was supplied by two independent 3,000-psi hydraulic systems. The left engine drove one system which provided one-half power for the flight controls and the leading-edge flap actuators, as well as all of the power for the tricycle landing gear, brakes, gun, and pitch control augmentation system. The right engine drove the second system which provided one-half of the power for the flight controls and the leading-edge flap actuators as well as all of the power for the trailing-edge flaps, nosewheel steering, and emergency main gear extension.

The primary flight controls consisted of ailerons, rudders, and the all-movable horizontal tail. Basic roll control derived from "fly-by wire" ailerons, supplemented by the differential motion of the horizontal tail. All primary control surfaces were powered by dual hydraulic cylinders for redundancy.

The two General Electric YJ101 engines were installed in the aft fuselage utilizing two thrust mounts and an aft steady rest for each engine. The engines were removed by lowering vertically from the engine bay without disconnecting any of the empennage control system. The "engine removal" access door and panels were attached with quick-release structural fasteners.

The accessory drive system consisted of two airframe-mounted, engine-driven gearboxes interconnected by a common starter gearbox. During engine removal, the gearboxes remained in the aircraft while the drive shaft was mechanically disconnected to avoid disturbing aircraft systems. The speedbrake was externally located above the engine installations, between the vertical tails, and was positioned by a single actuator in the upper fuselage.

BOMB SEPARATION TEST conducted with prototype No. 1 YF-17 at Edwards AFB.

Armament consisted of one palletized 20mm Gatling-type gun located in the forward fuselage, and two wing tip-mounted Sidewinder IR missiles. Additional ordnance stores could be carried on four under-wing pylons. Two 600-gallon drop tanks could be carried on the inboard wing pylons. A centerline pylon was provided to carry an empty 300-gallon drop tank to demonstrate aerodynamic compatibility.

YF-17

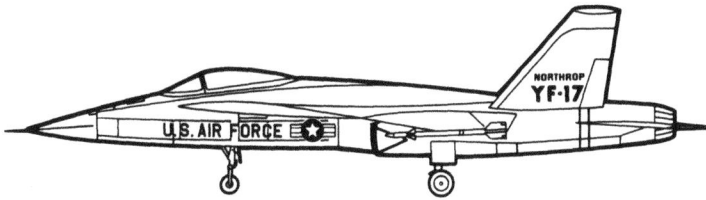

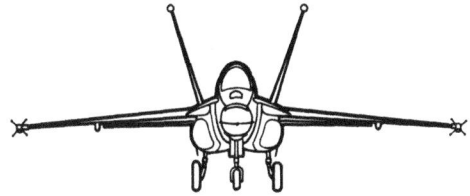

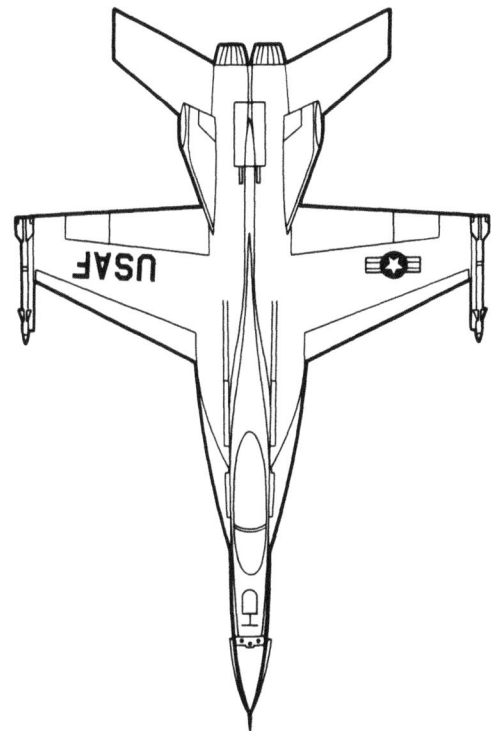

SPECIFICATIONS

WING SPAN ....35 FT.

OVERALL LENGTH ....55 FT., 6 IN.

OVERALL HEIGHT ....14 FT., 6 IN.

WING AREA ....350 SQ. FT.

CLEAN TAKEOFF WEIGHT ....23,000 LB

MAXIMUM TAKEOFF WEIGHT ....30,630 LB

SPEED — MAXIMUM ....MACH 1.95

SPEED — CRUISING ....MACH 0.85

RANGE (FERRY)..............................2,800 MILES

SERVICE CEILING ....60,000 FT.

POWER — (2) GE YJ101 TURBOJET, 15,000-LB THRUST
      CLASS

ARMAMENT — (1) 20MM GATLING GUN, (2) WING TIP IR
      MISSILES, (4) PYLON STATIONS FOR
      STORES

F-18 NAVY AIR COMBAT FIGHTER

In late 1973 and early 1974, the U.S. Navy was seriously weighing the possibility of starting development of a low-cost, lightweight, multimission strike fighter, identified as VFAX, as a replacement for its aging F-4, F-8, and A-7 carrier aircraft, and as a supplement to its new, more sophisticated F-14 fleet. Industry was requested to submit comments on the proposed VFAX study. Six companies — General Dynamics (both Convair and Fort Worth), Grumman, LTV, Rockwell International, McDonnell Douglas, and Northrop — all expressed an interest. At the time, Northrop and General Dynamics were engaged in their YF-17 and YF-16 Air Combat Fighter (ACF) prototype programs, respectively. For the sake of economy and nonduplication of effort, Congress in August 1975 terminated the VFAX concept and directed the Navy to consider a carrier-suitable version of the air combat fighters then under a flyoff evaluation by the Air Force. By way of differentiation from the ACF, the Navy portion of the program was designated NACF.

NORTHROP-McDONNELL DOUGLAS F-18 (EARLY MODEL) revealing lines similar to those of the Northrop YF-17. Under full-scale development, the multimission strike fighter will join the carrier fleet to supplement the F-14.

Two months later Northrop and McDonnell Douglas reached an agreement to jointly propose and develop the NACF, based on the existing YF-17 design. A Northrop internal information announcement, dated October 7, 1974, said in part:

". . . Northrop Corporation and McDonnell Douglas Corporation today announced that the two aerospace firms have entered into an agreement under which they will jointly develop and propose an air combat fighter for the U.S. Navy which is based on the YF-17 design . . . Under the teaming agreement, McDonnell Douglas will have prime contract responsibility for a carrier-suitable version of the YF-17 to meet the requirement of the proposed NACF. Northrop will have prime contract and design responsibility for YF-17 variants for use by NATO nations and other allies.

"Over the past 20 years, both companies have concentrated their fighter design efforts on the development of high-performance, twin-engined aircraft. Both companies also have extensive experience in the international marketplace. Northrop has produced and delivered more than 2,200 twin-engine tactical and trainer aircraft, which are in service with the USAF and more than 20 nations around the world. The company's latest combat aircraft are the F-5E International Fighter and its two-place campanion, the F-5F.

"McDonnell Douglas has produced more than 4,500 of the F-4 Phantom fighter, including the F-4B model, which has been in operational service with the U.S. Navy since 1961. Its newest combat aircraft is the F-15 air superiority fighter for the U.S. Air Force, which goes operational next month."

After months of careful evaluation and flight testing the respective aircraft, the Navy selected the NACF version of the YF-17 as the more suitable carrier-based strike aircraft. The new Navy aircraft-to-be was designated the F-18.

In May 1975, short-term contracts were awarded by the Navy to the Northrop-McDonnell Douglas team and to General Electric for continued engineering studies and refinement of the projected airframe and power plant. These contracts were intended to sustain the engineering effort pending Congressional approval for full-scale development of the F-18. The Navy long-range plan was to procure 11 Research and Development aircraft in Fiscal Year (FY) 1977, 15 production F-18's in FY 1979, building up to a rate of 108 aircraft annually by FY 1982.

Like the YF-17, the F-18 traced its origins to the operations analyses started in 1965 and leading to the P530 lightweight, multirole tactical fighter. Refined in accordance with the 1971 Air Force requirements for a Lightweight Fighter (LWF), later the Air Combat Fighter (ACF), the P530 design eventually evolved into the prototype YF-17.

Slightly larger and about 10,000 pounds heavier than the YF-17, the F-18 retained all fundamental aerodynamic lines of the ACF prototype. The wing area was increased 50 square feet to 400 square feet. The wing itself now carried fuel for increased range and featured folding outer panels for carrier storage. The fuselage was made wider and longer to provide greater internal fuel capacity, and the nose section was enlarged to accommodate the 28-inch radar antenna to meet Navy search range requirements. In addition, the airframe structure was strengthened to satisfy the increased loads generated by carrier launches and arrested landings.

Final Congressional endorsement for full-scale development of the NACF came in November 1975. In accordance with the team agreement with McDonnell Douglas, Northrop was responsible for developing and building the center and aft fuselage sections and vertical tails. McDonnell Douglas would build the rest of the airframe and be responsible for final assembly. Roy Jackson, Northrop F-18 program manager, and prior program manager of the YF-17 and ACF flight competition, provided the continuity of effort required to develop the F-18.

Cost estimates were predicated on a potential purchase of 800 aircraft. The F-18 was intended to replace both Navy and Marine Corps F-4 Phantoms for the primary missions of fighter escort and interdiction. Moreover, the F-18 was intended for eventual use in the attack role as replacement for the A-7 Corsair II in the mid-1980's. Programmed also was a two-place fighter-trainer version.

275

F-18 NAVY

F-18 MARINE CORPS

ADVANCED TACTICAL FIGHTER EVOLUTION					LWF PROPOSAL		
HIGH WING FORWARD INLETS N-300	LARGER LE EXTENSION UNDERWING INLETS P530	TWIN VERTICALS LARGER LE EXTENSION P530-2	CONTOURED LE EXT LARGER TAIL P530-2	REFINED FUSELAGE SHORTER INLETS P530-3	P600 TWIN ENG LWF P610 SINGLE ENG LWF	YF-17 PROTOTYPE	F-18 LAND-BASED VERSION
1966	1967	1968	1969	1970	1971-72	1973	1976

F-18 10-YEAR CONFIGURATION GENEALOGY. As graphically illustrated, the design configuration of today's Navy Air Combat Fighter and its land-based version trace their origins from the N-300 through the P530 series to the YF-17 prototypes. Continuing design refinements reflect a balance between the latest advances in technology, known mission requirements, and cost-weight considerations. (Note: The P530 of 1967 may be considered the first of the "Cobra" series, or P530-1; the P530-2 underwent a second iteration in 1969.)

FULL-SCALE MOCKUP of F-18 forward fuselage at the McDonnell Douglas facility, St. Louis. Functional mockup demonstrates reliability and maintainability features of Navy Air Combat Fighter. (Photo courtesy of McDonnell Douglas)

With certain exceptions, principally in avionics equipment provisions, the F-18 was similar to the YF-17, aerodynamically and structurally. High-strength aluminum alloys were the primary material, supplemented by extensive applications of graphite composites. A fly-by-wire flight controls system was provided with mechanical backup in the horizontal tail pitch and roll control system.

In the Spring of 1976, plans were formalized with the U.S. Navy and the Department of Defense for a land-based version of the F-18. It has been especially developed by Northrop to satisfy worldwide requirements for an advanced aircraft, operating efficiently from conventional runways on land, with both the performance versatility and economic features of the Navy F-18.

The land-based version of the F-18 incorporates the same design philosophy applied to the internationally successful F-5 series of fighters. Technological innovations permit it to be a multipurpose successor to aircraft such as the F-4, capable of performing as an interceptor, as a long-range interdiction aircraft, and in the close-support and air-to-air combat roles.

A key design criterion of the new fighter is the achievement of reliability much higher than the aircraft that it will replace. As a result of designed-in high reliability, reduced maintenance and manpower requirements follow. Built-in test capabilities, rapid fault isolation and location, and quick ground-level access are among its desirable maintenance features.

Northrop's land-based version is over 6,000 pounds lighter than the Navy and Marines F-18. Of this total, 3,500 pounds are the reduced fuel load alone. Elimination of the carrier operations requirement generated other "weight savers." These included a lightweight landing gear, the use of a non-folding wing, a lighter arresting gear, and a simplified avionics package. The reduced weight, coupled with the use of the same twin engines (General Electric F404, 16,000-pound thrust class) and the same aerodynamic lines, contributes to the aircraft's very high performance.

The principal external difference between the Navy F-18 and the land-based version is the elimination of the wing slots that are needed for carrier-deck landing approaches at high angles of attack. Both the land fighter and the Navy F-18 benefit from their 60 percent commonality of parts by weight and 85—90 percent commonality in high-use systems.

A wide range of weapons options are available on the land-based aircraft for both air and ground missions, with a total external stores capacity exceeding 13,000 pounds. Options include Sparrow and Sidewinder missiles.

F-18

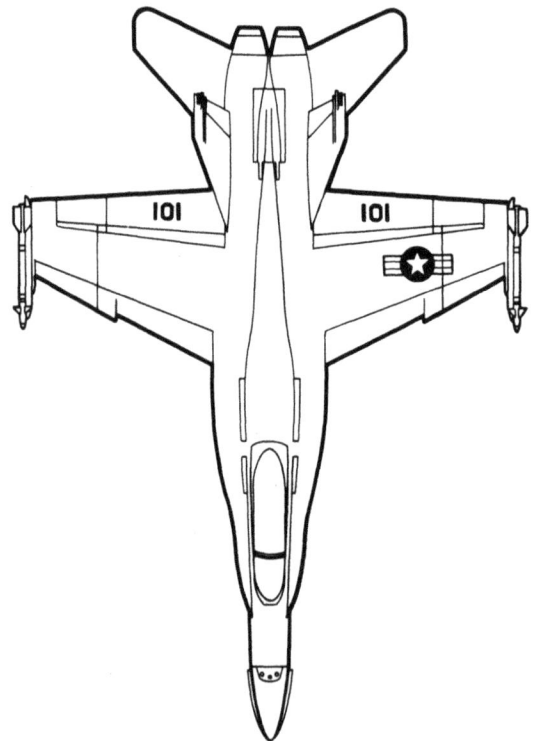

SPECIFICATIONS

WING SPAN (WITHOUT MISSILES) ....37 FT., 6 IN.

WIDTH, WINGS FOLDED ....27 FT., 6 IN.

OVERALL LENGTH ....56 FT.

OVERALL HEIGHT ....15 FT., 2 IN.

WING AREA ....400 SQ. FT.

CLEAN TAKEOFF WEIGHT ....32,520 LB.

MAXIMUM TAKEOFF WEIGHT ....44,000 LB.

SPEED—MAXIMUM ....MACH 1.8+

SPEED—CRUISING ....MACH 0.83

RANGE (FERRY) ....2,300+ MILES

SERVICE CEILING ....50,000+ FT.

POWER — (2) GE F404 TURBOJET, 16,000-LB THRUST CLASS

ARMAMENT — (1) 20MM GATLING GUN, (4) PYLON STA-
TIONS, (2) NACELLE FUSELAGE STA-
TIONS, AND (1) CENTERLINE STATION
FOR ORDNANCE

EPILOGUE

This must of necessity be an unfinished aeronautical history. Notwithstanding, an increasing need is foreseen for Northrop's ability to apply new technology creatively to meet customer's needs reliably and economically. The stringent monetary restraints that every nation faces, as it seeks to balance social, economic, and security requirements, will demand the selection of new programs only after careful assessment of the reputation of the manufacturer for technical performance, cost, and reliability. In so highly a competitive environment, Northrop has already developed a leading position. This position is the achievement of the thousands of experienced men and women of Northrop. Leaders in their fields, they are also skilled at working together productively. They are committed to providing defense systems of the highest quality for the national security of the United States and its friends allied for mutual security. Their dedication made possible the company's impressive past accomplishments and gives us confidence in a bright future.

INDEX